AUGUSTUS

THE GOLDEN AGE OF ROME

G. P. BAKER

Cooper Square Press

First Cooper Square Press edition 2000

Copyright © 1937 by George P. Baker

This Cooper Square Press paperback edition of *Augustus* is an unabridged republication of the edition first published in New York in 1937.

Published by Cooper Square Press
An Imprint of the Rowman & Littlefield Publishing Group
150 Fifth Avenue, Suite 911
New York, New York 10011

British Cataloguing-in-Publication Data Available
Library of Congress Cataloging-in-Publication Data

Baker, G. P. (George Philip), 1879–1951.
  Augustus : the Golden Age of Rome / G.P. Baker.
    p. cm.
  Originally published: New York : Dodd, Mead, & Company, 1937.
  Includes bibliographical references and index.
  ISBN 0-8154-1089-1 (pbk. : alk. paper)
    1. Augustus, Emperor of Rome, 63 B.C.–14A.D. 2. Rome— History— Augustus, 30
  B.C.–14 A.D. 3. Emperors— Rome— Biography. I. Title.

  DG279 .B3 2000
  937'.07'092— dc21
  [B]   00-03540

♾™ The paper used in this publication meets the minimum requirements of American National Standard for Information Sciences— Permanence of Paper for Printed Library Materials, ANSI/NISO Z39.48–1992.
Manufactured in the United States of America.

"Hic vir, hic est, tibi quem promitti saepius audis
Augustus Caesar, Divi genus, aurea condet
Saecula qui rursus Latio regnata per Arva
Saturno quondam; super et Garamantas et Indos
Proferet imperium."

Aeneid, VI. 791–795.

"This is the man, so often you hear promised you,
Augustus Caesar, scion of the god-like kindred,
Who shall begin the Golden Age, the Saturnian,
Over the land of Latium, spreading his sovereign power
Beyond Sahara and the banks of the Indus."

PREFACE

AUGUSTUS occupies a quite peculiar place in history altogether his own. His significance is made up of many elements. He was certainly an interesting person, considered
simply as a man standing for his portrait. Any artist, of any
kind, would like to search into the curious problems of his
face, his expression, his individuality, his twists and turns
of character, the grandness of his personality, the tale, the
romance and the tragedy of his life. The difficulty is that
instead of standing among sweet dim shades, like King
Arthur, where our poetry tells to the full, Augustus lived
in the full glare of a great blundering, blaring civilization,
and he suffers somewhat from the well-known unpaintabil-
ity of sunshine. In poetry we adumbrate the infinite: but
we use prose for anything we know a great deal about—
and we do know something of Augustus. . . . But this is
not all. Augustus embodied and represented the tremendous
currents which changed Rome from a small Italian city situ-
ated on the Tiber to the world-power which bestrode the
earth as no other colossus ever bestrode it. The emperors
and pontiffs of Rome all took their colour from Augustus.
He stands there, the first of the line, the head, the chief, the
well-spring, the great original, the key to the meaning of
Constantine the Great and Innocent the Third. From every
point of view, we begin our study of Rome with the study
of Augustus—and we are liable to end with him too. . . .
Julius would have faded out of history if his grand-nephew
had not taken over his work and made it good. . . . Augustus walks into the Gospels as if he belonged there. Even the
birth of Jesus Christ is mixed up in a story of all the world

going to the census of Caesar Augustus, so that the inn was full: and it has always been a tradition in the Christian church that if it happened at that particular juncture, it was because of something peculiarly apposite about the reign of Augustus. Some spirit of order, concord and universality did descend upon the world at that time. Something more than hitherto divine did dawn upon mankind in the days of Augustus—and it was a conception of peace, reconciliation and mediation which we see in Horace and Virgil as well as in the New Testament. Christians themselves have found a certain common ground of agreement and admiration in the Augustans—from the Spanish Jesuit who so well edited Virgil to the English Quaker who fondly quoted Horace and found in the latter a not altogether alien philosophy of life. . . . Augustus, therefore, dominates secular history as no other single person does. . . . And he was "a mirror in which the world beheld its own face."

Augustus received from his predecessors and developed to a high pitch a political philosophy that is likely to be disturbing to the average modern person. It does not praise the wisdom of the average citizen, nor exalt the genius of the common people. It respects them without enthusiasm. It was based upon the thesis—a terribly true one—that if you give the ordinary man what he wants, he will let you attend to the rest of the world yourself. It is a lesson that both the Right and the Left in our own days have still to learn. . . . Give the baby his bottle, and you may settle down in comfort to your work. Neither the Right nor the Left like to hear this maxim.

But the truth is, that the beneficient and effective government of the world is, and always has been, conducted by quite a few people, and in most ages mankind at large has been quite content that it should be so. The political ideal is that there shall be no politics. To create a world in which strife is calmed,[1] men reconciled, and useful work happily and satisfactorily done—this is the grand aim of government: and in proportion as we approach it we behold a world in which there are no general elections or national conventions, and one in which no man cares about any of these things, nor can be persuaded to attend them. Man is only a political animal when he is desperately unhappy and is pursued by the devils of want and uncertainty. Feed the brute; give him certainty; give him peace and contentment, and the ugly drama of politics will dissolve like a morning mist, displaying the happy world of work behind it. . . . This is what Augustus has to teach us.

He created a world which lasted, until undesigned and unwanted war broke it up, for two hundred and fifty years —and those years remained for mankind permanently a sort of dream of the Golden Age. From the ideal point of view it had many defects; but only a few cared much about the ideal, as long as the real was in existence, and hard, selfish, self-centred, worldly men, as well as saints and sages, deeply regretted and long mourned over the disappearance of that lovely world which fell so far short of perfection. The very name of Rome had magic to them.

This secret—to the best of the writer's ability—is described and set forth in this book. It is perhaps worth the while of politicians, whose labours often enough are ungratefully received by their fellow-men, to cast a glance at the career of one whose work was so warmly and so permanently admired. They may not be enthusiastic—but let them read.

G. P. B.

Elmer, Sussex.

1937.

[1] We know, of course, that on a historic occasion All was Quiet in Warsaw: but no one ever pretended that this was the Golden Age.

CONTENTS

ILLUSTRATIONS

MAPS

The author has to thank Mr. Harold Mattingly for very kind help in choosing the portraits here reproduced from Roman coins.

AUGUSTUS

CHAPTER I

THE HEIR OF GAIUS JULIUS CAESAR

I

Caesar had said: "Well—the Ides of March are come!" The soothsayer, Spurinna, answered: "But not over!"

THAT was the morning of the fifteenth of March in the year 44 B. C. A few days later, a weary and dusty courier, after riding post haste along the great white roads from Rome, through Beneventum and Venusia and Tarentum to Brundusium—embarking on a tossing and storm-threatened Adriatic, and gaining the port of Apollonia on the rocky Macedonian coast—handed his mail-bag to the young Gaius Octavius, who, staying at Apollonia, was trying to occupy himself according to programme with philosophic study. It had been a disturbing time, full of the things that the Romans regarded as signs of coming trouble. The sun had been darkened in heaven; violent and terrifying explosions had shaken the huge volcano of Aetna, and her underground furnaces had blazed and poured forth molten fires; the Eridanus (the river which we now call the Po) had overflowed its banks and carried away the very cattle-sheds with the cattle inside them; there were earth-shakings in the Alps, and the auguries were strange and adverse.[1] . . . It is easy to conjure up the picture which that young man presented as he took the letters and glanced at the courier. Much could always be learned by the look of the courier. Gaius Octa-

[1] The omens and signs at the assassination of Julius Caesar were not merely popular superstition; Virgil, a contemporary, reports them in Georgics I, 461–497.

vius would never have become Caesar Augustus had he not been the kind of man who can scent trouble with preternatural acuteness. Perhaps he guessed, before he began to read, what was to follow.

He was of medium height, something between dark and fair, slender, and so delicate of build and feature as to give the impression almost of femininity. It was the spirit that looked through his features that removed any sense of femininity. There was a hard, clear quality about him. He impressed men in something of the way in which a diamond does, which they feel is very fragile, and must be kept in a velvet case, though they know it quite well to be the hardest of all substances. Gaius Octavius had such a fragility, such a brightness and such a hardness.

At this time he was eighteen and a half years old, having been born ("just before sunrise" Suetonius says) on the twenty-third of September in the year in which Cicero was consul, in which the conspiracy of Catiline took place, and in which Pompeius Magnus captured Jerusalem and stood in the Holy of Holies: that is to say, the year we call 63 B. C. It was in any case a remarkable year, but not until much later did any one realize that it had gained added distinction from the birth of the child of Gaius Octavius and Atia, the niece of Julius Caesar. In after years, long tales were told concerning the omens, prodigies and miraculous prognostications that accompanied the child's entrance into the world, but we may safely guess that, at the time, his future fame would vastly have surprised the affectionate relatives and the polite but indifferent neighbours. . . . Gaius Octavius, his father, was a prosperous citizen of Velitræ, one of the very ancient and famous Latin cities which once had been rivals and equals of Rome itself, but now were quiet provincial towns. The family had never been particularly eminent. The child's grandfather had been content with the purely

Birth of Octavius

local honours of his native city, where he lived to a vener-
able age with credit, but without special distinction. The
proud father, however, had been more ambitious, had
passed through the lower Roman magistracies, had become
a praetor, and had achieved entrance into the charmed circle
of the Roman senate. He had, in fact, become a member of
the Aristocracy, and had even risen to the honour of being
pointed out by Cicero as a model to be copied by aspiring
youth. But just as he was about to put his fortune to the
test by entering for the supreme dignity of the consulship,
which would have made him an Aristocrat indeed, he died,
and the child, at the age of four, was left an orphan, though
very far from an indigent one.

Although the child had thus a quiet and undistinguished
ancestry on the father's side, the case was somewhat differ-   Ancestry
ent on the mother's. Atia lived to bring her son up, and to
see him started on his great career. Her mother had been
the sister of Gaius Julius Caesar, the dictator, the conqueror
of Gaul and author of the Commentaries, while her father
had been of a family of Aricia, connected with the family
of Pompeius Magnus.² There was some uncertainty concerning exactly where the future Augustus was born. The
senate officially accepted the statement that he had been
born on the Palatine Hill at Rome ³—while at Velitrae a little
room like a store room in his grandfather's house was long
pointed out as his nursery, and the place where he was
born. It was regarded as sacred, and not to be entered without preliminary purification. One rash person who defied

---

² Suetonius seems to be mistaken in thinking that M. Atius Balbus had
a particularly distinguished ancestry. The Atilius Bulbus who was consul in 245 B.C. and 235 B.C. does not seem to have been his ancestor.
Antony (see Suetonius, Divus Augustus, IV, 2) had heard a rumour that
Balbus was the son of a perfumer and baker at Aricia. There certainly
was a story to this effect, and it may have been true.

³ Suetonius, Divus Augustus, V.

the consequences and tried to sleep in this room was found next morning thrown out, and only half alive before the door, with his bedclothes around him.

Altogether, we may take it that the child Octavius came of a plain, undistinguished but prosperous social class, and that his only appreciable connection with the great world was through his grand-uncle, the famous Gaius Julius Caesar. It was as if he had been born a simple bourgeois, but related to the Bonapartes.

II

The contemporary world

Born when he was, the child Octavius grew up in a world not devoid of stirring news and the report of great deeds. He was an infant when Pompeius Magnus had just completed his marvellous conquest of Asia, reaching the Caucasus and the remote mountains that border upon the Caspian Sea, bringing the frontiers of Rome into contact with those of the Parthians. As the child grew to boyhood, his grand-uncle Julius was bridging the Rhine, fighting sea-battles in the English Channel, and invading Britain. It was a world in which extraordinary men did extraordinary things. While the conventional institutions of the state limped painfully and imperfectly along, the great individual everywhere triumphed in competence and audacity. . . . And just at the time when Pompeius and Caesar were giving the world actions to wonder at, Cicero was creating a Latin prose which would express the wonderment and admiration and the thought which such deeds suggested. . . . We, looking back, may see in that age the sunset

The new age

glories of the Roman republic. Young Gaius Octavius, looking forward, can only have seen in it the splendid dawn of a new and more heroic age of greater men and larger

THE YOUNG MARCUS ANTONIUS
with a beard, in mourning for the
death of G. Julius Caesar
(*From a coin in the British Museum*)

MARCUS BRUTUS
(*From a coin in the British Museum*)

minds. When and where had a world ever before existed, so united, so firmly based, so universally subject to law, so generally administered for the good of mankind? Never!

Such dreams and fancies were perhaps heightened by his personal contact with Caesar, his grand-uncle, a cordial, friendly, talkative man, capable of putting into better perspective the impressions of a boy. . . . The young Octavius heard direct from the lips of Julius the narratives which we read in books; he handled and read the very first versions of those Commentaries which have now become so famous and so commonplace. . . . Julius was by no means a silent and reticent person. Carefully as he might judge his audience, shrewdly as he might adapt his words to those who heard him, he was eager to talk and zealous to persuade others of the views he himself held. We need not doubt that on his visits to his niece Atia and her husband he talked freely and at length of all he had done and seen—defended and explained his own actions, criticised those of others, and indulged in table-talk of a kind for which a modern historian would rate no price too high.[4]

From all that happened afterwards it is obvious that the child took more than common interest in these conversations, and that the grand-uncle appreciated the interest and intelligence of the boy, and took pains to form his mind and direct his thoughts along the right channels: for as time went on, and Gaius Julius rose into that tremendous dominance which marked the later years of his life, the dictator turned more and more to the boy as his possible heir and successor, who would carry on the torch he had lit, and utilize the power he had accumulated. Caesar

[4] Julius left Rome for Gaul in the spring of 58 B. C., when the child Octavius was four and a half years old. He did not see Rome again, nor could Octavius have seen him, until 49 B. C., when the boy was fourteen. Close touch dates from that year, and culminates in 45 B. C., when Octavius, aged eighteen, was in Spain with Julius.

III

If there were faults and defects in the boy's vision of that glorious dawn of the world, Julius was the right man to point them out. His memory went back to what must then have seemed the very beginning of things; the civil wars of Marius and Sulla, the return of Sulla from the east, his Italian campaigns and his dictatorship. Julius—himself a nephew of Marius—had gone through the great proscription; he had seen Sulla face to face and had successfully defied that Metternich of the ancient world. Julius, indeed, had been one of the men who, through an age of fierce reaction and bitter persecution had preserved the tradition of the *populares*, the party of Gaius Marius and of the Gracchi, the party which defended the supremacy of the popular Assembly against the dominance of the oligarchic senate. His hard work and genius for intrigue had been one of the main forces which revived the *populares*, gave them a fresh programme and ideal, and organized them so that they could make their numbers felt. Julius was not in the least likely to suffer under any illusions respecting the ideal happiness and beauty of the world he lived in. None knew better than he the savagery of the civil strife that had raged between the parties of Sulla and Marius, the widespread anarchy and discontent that had darkened the history of those times; he knew the wicked misgovernment under which the provinces had groaned, and he had certainly heard with his own ears the details that were bandied about in court during the trial of Verres, the governor of Sicily, when Cicero was in charge of the prosecution. He, Julius, more than any other man, had engineered those coalitions by which first Pompeius and then himself had been given exceptional personal powers in order to carry out great

The
Civil Wars

projects of conquest and settlement which the senate had been unable, and sometimes unwilling, to attempt. He, Julius, had held the ring at home while Pompeius began the work of clearing up the disastrous ruin in the east created by fifty years of oligarchic rule. Pompeius, with his special powers, had driven piracy off the seas, cast down King Mithradates of Pontus, put Tigranes of Armenia into his proper place, reorganized the east, and turned that chaos of warring powers and misdirected activity into a settled and peaceful, if sore and uncertain, land, which was at any rate beginning the task of recovery. It was Julius who had superintended the political manoeuvres which had compelled the senate to ratify the acts of Pompeius and had given his work legal confirmation. That Pompeius had not done everything that needed to be done was common knowledge. The Parthian menace in the farther East still disturbed the peaceful traffic of Asia. When old Marcus Crassus, the millionaire banker, had tried his hand at the task of subduing it, the frightful disaster of Carrhae had damaged Roman prestige and set back the work of recovery. . . . Egypt, too, was still an independent power, ruled by the descendants of Ptolemy Lagos, Alexander the Great's general—disturbing the peace of the east with its ambition, its enormous wealth, its utter inefficiency, its hopeless corruption. Long ago it would have been absorbed into the Roman system had it not been for the mutual jealousies and suspicions at Rome. Egypt had been far too great a prize to be put into the control of any one man. Egypt would continue to be a potential danger to the rest of the world until her resources came into the possession of a ruler who could be trusted to use them intelligently. . . . All these problems and defects, together with many others, vexed the welfare of the east and pressed for remedy.

Julius had calculated with a shrewd eye to his own in-

Pompeius
Magnus

terests when he helped Pompeius to accomplish his tasks in
the East; for Pompeius had repaid his help by securing to
Julius the command in Gaul, and so enabling him to undertake the conquest of Gaul, to carry the frontiers of
Rome up to the Rhine, to clear away for ever the constant
threat of a Gallic invasion that for centuries had seemed to
impend over Italy and to turn Gaul itself into a peaceful
and settled country, more interested in developing its own
wealth than in seizing its neighbours'. The death of Crassus
at Carrhae had destroyed the Committee of Three which
had enabled these gigantic tasks to be carried out, and afterwards Cicero had got hold of Pompeius and talked him
over to the senatorial side. But Julius, by that time, had been
too strong to be shaken. Then had followed the great political crisis—the breach between the senate and Pompeius on
the one hand, and the Assembly and Caesar on the other.
Determined to destroy the man whom they feared above
all others, the senate challenged a new civil war. At the
battle of Pharsalus, Caesar had destroyed Pompeius, overthrown the senatorial oligarchy, and made himself the most
powerful man in the Roman world. That had been four
years ago, when Gaius Octavius had been some fourteen
years old.

What a man to visit, amid the soldiers of his headquarters,
the invincible legions of the Gallic war!—what a man to
receive, when he came to visit his niece and her husband! [5]

[5] Atia had married again, and her second husband (who proved a
good stepfather to the boy) was a far more important person than
G. Octavius: namely L. Marcius Philippus, of an old senatorial family,
whose father, great-grandfather, and great-great-great-grandfather were
consuls, and appear in the lists; and who himself was twice consul. The
difference—a very considerable one—represents the advance in social importance achieved by Julius. In 64 B.C. Julius had been a bankrupt politician, and an Octavius had been good enough for his niece; in 58 B.C.
Julius had begun the conquest of Gaul, and his niece could aspire to a
Philippus with a long list of consular ancestors. It also meant an advance
in the social status of Atia's son.

Conquest
of Gaul

THE ROMAN WORLD

in the First Century B.C.

. . . Julius was always gracious, always affable to rich or to poor: always eager to secure a convert, obtain a vote, or win a recruit. He was always ready to charm: and he must have charmed his young grand-nephew. What a wealth of anecdote and reminiscence he could pour out! What stories of Cilician pirates, Spanish tribesmen, moustachio'd Gauls and woad-stained Britons! What romance—as when at Alexandria the carpet was unpacked, and revealed the pink and smiling Cleopatra! . . . What hair's-breadth escapes— as when he dived in Alexandria harbour, while the water around him boiled with the impact of arrows, and he swam under water to safety! . . . But the charming was not all upon one side. Julius was on the look-out, not merely for converts, votes or recruits, but for a successor. It is evident that his grand-nephew impressed him. He invited young Octavius and some friends to be with him in Spain. When the lad of eighteen, blown out of his course by a storm, sick, shipwrecked, more or less destitute, led his band of companions through the lines of a ferocious and watchful enemy, and brought them in safety to his uncle's camp, Julius was delighted! This was the kind of thing he appreciated!—this was moral courage and power of leadership, the rare and precious gifts that he was looking for, the sense of responsibility, the ability to master physical weakness. . . . He continued to watch carefully over young Octavius and to ensure that he should receive an education calculated to make the best of these gifts. Julius could command the best teachers of the day—and it is certain that Octavius received good teaching, which developed his intellectual curiosity and refined his intellectual tastes, so that all his life he remained interested in things of the mind—though he never was able to speak Greek very fluently.

It is certain, at any rate, that he was put in possession of the expressive arts which enable a man to formulate his

Charm of Julius

Octavius approved

thoughts clearly to himself and communicate them to his
fellows. The use of clear, simple, exact language is one of
the most essential requirements of a statesman—in his own
interests, if not in that of others. Julius, as all the world
knows, used a prose style that has remained a model in these
respects, and young Octavius followed him in the taste for
simplicity. He never achieved quite so classic a style, but
it was terse and clear, suited to convey thoughts with
promptitude and clarity. It was a business-man's prose,
suitable for transactions, official documents, letters and the
like. The fact that he trod in the steps of Julius in this matter of language is almost equivalent to saying that he followed him in his methods of thinking—for as language is,
so is thought. His lack of fluency in speaking Greek implied, perhaps, just that he had a determinedly Latin mind.
He read Greek perfectly well.[6]

**Education
of Octavius**

IV

Part, of course, of the gift of Julius lay in his supreme
confidence in himself. Many men—then as now—thought
him foolish when he elected, in the midst of a civil war, to
spend a winter in Egypt with Cleopatra. Men think—and
thought then—that he ought to have been more prudent,
more nervous, more careful and fussy, more assiduous in
calculating his chances: in short, that he ought to have had
much more doubt about his ability to win through. But he
did not entertain all the doubts about himself that they
think he ought to have felt. With entire sureness in his own
powers, he dallied the months away; and in good time he
took his departure—for Zela, as it chanced, of which he

[6] Suetonius, *Divus Augustus*, LXXXIX. His teachers were Apollodorus
of Pergamon, and afterwards Areus and his sons Dionysius and Nicanor.
In LXXXIV to LXXXVIII Suetonius refers at length to these things
and to the peculiarities of Augustus in matters of style and diction.

wrote "I came, I saw, I conquered": and that phrase has always remained his own verdict upon himself. He was fully justified in his policy. He had needed a holiday, and he had taken one.

Julius did not leave behind him any very particular maxims upon this head: but his grand-nephew did. Suetonius [7] reports the principles on which the latter worked. "A thing **Principles** is done quick enough if it is done well": and "Hasten slowly," "Safety before dash," and "Do not fish with a golden hook"—that is to say, do not risk valuable things for a trifling return. It was a maxim of Augustus never to fight unless the estimated profits would be greater than the probable losses. All this is a very cool, a very self-confident wisdom, and is evidently the basis on which Julius also commonly worked. . . . But Julius, at times, had the gambler's spirit, when he deliberately elected to hazard his fortunes: and this he never managed to impart to his grand-nephew.

Why, we may wonder? This leads us to a certain lack of vitality, a lack of abundance about the youth which we have already noticed. The Roman character had been built upon a robust physical constitution, erring rather upon the side of coarseness. Upon this perhaps exuberant excess had been based the iron will and grim stoicism that to the end remained typical of born Romans. The Romans were never "amenable." This was the secret of their political freedom. **Fragility** They never had been amenable. They had always possessed a restless and rebellious temper, they had been men who would fight to the death against things they disliked—their own deaths, if not the other man's. The story of Scaevola's right hand may be legendary, but it represents a real truth. When they agreed together it was of necessity a voluntary, a rational agreement. Their decision of character was founded upon an abounding vitality, a gross amplitude of

[7] Suetonius, *Divus Augustus*, XXV.

nerve and courage. . . . Julius had never shared this robustness, and in many of his ways and habits showed his consciousness of the difficulties which are felt by men of softer clay. He never showed this sympathy more than when he penetrated past the superficial fragility of the boy Octavius to the real strength behind it.

In order to achieve some sorts of success, a man needs a sensitiveness and a responsiveness to subtle suggestions which are impossible to the robust man. This delicacy of constitution and fineness of apprehension young Gaius Octavius possessed. His biographer [8] has described his handsome and graceful appearance, his bright eyes, small teeth, fair hair and slightly aquiline nose; and some of his surviving portraits convey to us with unusual force the idea of a man who was more than usually subject to fatigue. In later years he developed a weakness of the left leg and hip, and even at times limped a little: and throughout his life he was subject to those slight ailments and seasonal afflictions which beset some types of nervous organization. He needed warmer clothing in winter and more protection from the heat in summer than was absolutely normal with his fellow-countrymen: and he always had occasion for just that sort of attention to health in minor matters which town dwellers in our own age find in vegetarian diets and Swedish exercises. . . . Julius could not teach such a man quite the dare-devil recklessness which he himself sometimes felt the impulse to show. The future Augustus could never afford to be a reckless man. In this restraint, put upon him by his natural constitution before he was born and without his will, was destined to lie one of the sources of his power.

This handsomeness, this fragility and sensitiveness, this imperative necessity of prudence and restraint, seemed to

Physical delicacy

---

[8] Suetonius, *Divus Augustus*, LXXIX–LXXXIII. See also the definite details about Julius given in Plutarch.

be an integral part of the character whose chief, outstanding power was an extraordinary clarity of vision. Some men look before they leap—some do not trouble to look—some do not even see when they do look: some cannot be bothered to draw the natural deductions when they have both looked and seen. Some men are too busy talking to be able to hear: and there are, for most men, too many distractions and interruptions, sometimes from external sources, sometimes out of the depth of their own characters, for them ever to be able to regard anything steadily and see it whole. But beyond most normal men, the future Augustus had the gift of looking attentively at things, and seeing them undistorted by passion or prejudice. What artists call the Innocence of the Eye was his. He could see; and he could judge upon the evidence of that very clear sight, and could form opinions of probability far beyond the power of most men of his age, or of any other age. To us, looking back, he seems to have possessed some extraordinary genius; but his contemporaries, who gradually came to look upon him as very extraordinary indeed, have made it quite clear to us that there was nothing extraordinary about him except this calm judgment working upon an astonishing clearness of perception. He was an instrument which registered accurately to the finest shade of a degree. Like other instruments of the kind, he had not many original remarks of his own to make. . . . His contemporaries found it simpler to explain him as of a certain divine nature.

The supreme virtue

v

It was impossible to guess what the future might hold. Julius, in this year 44 B. C., was at the height of his power and prestige. Young Octavius, at Apollonia, was spending a little useful time in study while waiting for his grand-uncle

to get away from Rome and reach Macedonia on the road
to the east. They would go thither in company, along the
track of Lucullus, Pompeius and Crassus, though with
armies far finer and better trained than these had ever had.
. . . Then the Conquest of Parthia would follow upon the
famous Conquest of Gaul, and the *De Bello Gallico* and the
De Bello Civili would be followed by a *De Bello Parthico*.
They would travel in the track of Alexander the Great,
and perhaps reach India, as he did—and the marvellous
deeds of Alexander would be excelled by the marvellous
deeds of Julius, who would then have conquered the whole
world from Britain to India, and brought all alike under
one government. . . . By the time all these things were
finished, young Octavius would be some years older. He
would be married, no doubt—to whom?—and would stand
at the right hand of his ageing grand-uncle; until at last, in
due time, that mighty head nodded, and that wonderful
hand fell—and Octavius would step into the vacant seat,
and . . . Such a train of thought could only end vaguely.
One could do no more than contemplate the possibilities.[9]

The difficulty about communications from a higher
sphere is their frequent ambiguity. It is not that we do not
receive them, but that we stand helplessly turning them
over and over when we do. Young Octavius, with his friend

[9] All this is probably what Octavius himself foresaw. We are not
obliged to agree with it. Cicero (*Letters to Atticus*, XV, 4) thought that
Julius would never have returned. It is just possible that the tactical
difficulties which had already proved too much for a competent soldier
like Crassus and were destined to be too much for Marcus Antonius,
would similarly have been too much for Julius, and that he would have
lost in Mesopotamia the laurels he gained in Gaul. The immortal military reputation of Julius may have owed a good deal to his early death,
which saved him from the results of meeting the Parthian mounted bow-
man and the Parthian mailed man-at-arms upon their own ground. It
is interesting to contemplate the possible reactions of a military defeat
of Julius in the east. The history of Gaius Octavius would certainly
have been very different!

Marcus Vipsanius Agrippa (who was at Apollonia with him), ventured into the study of the astrologer Theagenes. Agrippa—a pushful, determined youth—put down his money and gave the necessary information about the date and time of his birth: and Theagenes cast the horoscope—very thrilling—and then, with admiration and astonishment, read out the startling results: the marvellous future that lay waiting for Agrippa. . . . And then he turned to the shy youth who remained hiding behind Agrippa's broad, self-confident person. Would not he also have his horoscope cast? Octavius hastily declined, in case it should turn out to be much inferior to Agrippa's. . . . Theagenes pressed him, and after much persuasion obtained the data necessary. But when he had cast the horoscope he sprang to his feet and fell upon his knees in front of the boy.

The horoscope of Octavius

That, at any rate, is the story.

But even so, what could it mean? Did it refer to the wonderful future he could foresee, when he should stand at the right hand of his grand-uncle and perhaps help him with the preparation of his Commentaries on the Parthian War? Or was it something different?—something unlike anything he foresaw?

VI

The answer to that question lay in the communication brought him from Rome shortly after the fifteenth of March in the year 44 B. C. The message was that his grand-uncle, Gaius Julius Caesar, had been assassinated by Brutus and Cassius and their group of oligarchic zealots, and lay dead at Rome.

And all the dreams of the future had vanished with him.

CHAPTER II

CAESAR'S MANTLE

(At Rome)

I

SHAKESPEARE is responsible for convincing us that Caesar fell easily before the swords of his foes.

"Ingratitude, more strong than traitors' arms,
Quite vanquished him; then burst his mighty heart;
And, in his mantle muffling up his face,
Even at the base of Pompey's statue,
Which all the while ran blood, great Caesar fell."

The truth was very different. None of the great men of history who have fallen before the assassin made a more determined fight for life than Julius. Ringed round by armed men, he fought them with his bare hands and unaided strength. Not until he had received twenty-three wounds did he fall, "with rage and cries, like a wild beast." He would have escaped, had his friends been at hand to bring rescue. But at the critical moment blind panic fell upon the onlookers. Marcus Antonius—a brave man, and the descendant of brave men—fled with the rest. . . . Caesar had had no military guard. He did not like guards. Only the usual attendants of a high magistrate had surrounded him. All these deserted him and fled. Only three slaves remained, who, when all was over, and that "bleeding piece of earth" lay still upon the floor of the senate house, soberly entered, placed the body upon a litter, and unsteadily (since there was an odd number of them to man

16

it) carried it homeward to Caesar's house . . . one arm
(so they say) hanging loose over the edge.

He had been master of the world; but the strange thing **Caesar**
was that he still remained so. Any one who heard the story **remains**
would be struck by this truth. The foes of Caesar, who had **master**
retreated in due order to the Capitol; his friends, who had
at once put the troops under arms; the onlookers, who
had fled; all these without exception had no will or plan of
their own, and hardly knew what they intended to do, or
ought to do, or could do. Those (and in all crises they
are numerous) who only wished to see how the cat would
jump, could not guess the real trend of events, and some of
them fell into disastrous errors. In short, utter chaos and
confusion fell upon Rome.

Through this confusion a clear path was soon cleft by
the powerful will of the dead man, which, though he himself would never speak again, still continued to operate
with its old force. The purpose and direction of the dead
Caesar, the commands he had signed, the appointments he
had made, the schemes he had sketched out, the processes
he had set in motion, all produced their proper results.

By the afternoon, a few senators began to look out of **Confusion**
doors, and perceived that there was no immediate danger. **in Rome**
Cicero, among others, appeared at the Capitol. It was plain
enough that no strong mind, individual or collective, was
taking charge of events. The advice of Cicero was that
Brutus and Cassius, as praetors, should convoke the senate
in the Capitol and issue decrees to ensure public order and
the recognition of the legal government. . . . But the "legal government" was just what the murder gang were not!
The legal government, the executive, was constituted by
the consuls, who were Caesarians. This awkward fact was
the first, but it was a fatal, blow to the anti-Caesarian party.
Not being the legal government, they could not very well

ride the high horse and shake the finger of moral reproba-
tion at their opponents. They decided that their best course
was to approach the surviving consul, Marcus Antonius,
and see if they could not effect a peaceful settlement.

Cicero afterwards asserted that he opposed this decision,
and told them plainly that they were making a serious
mistake. It may have been so; the man who executed the
Catilinarian conspirators without trial was no doubt quite
capable of brushing aside the ancient forms of Roman government, and usurping by force an authority that his party
did not possess by constitutional law—and perhaps this
course, however cynical, would have been the most practically effective. But he was talking to men whose chief
objection to Caesar had been that he violated the letter of
the law—and they refused to violate it themselves. That
this logical consistency fatally tied their hands and ultimately destroyed them only illustrates how little virtue
there is in the letter apart from the spirit.

**Policy of
the con-
spirators**

Brutus and Cassius were not without good reasons for the
policy they preferred. For one thing, it was not so much a
matter of course then as we may now imagine it to be that
Marcus Antonius should prove to be a convinced and irrevocable partisan of Caesar. So far from that being the case,
it was well known in Rome that Caesar had endured no
nonsense from his lieutenant, and had more than once compelled him to toe the line of correctitude. This quiet hostility between them the conspirators had counted on when
they spared Antony's life. They believed that they were
sparing a man none too friendly towards Caesar, and one
who might serve their purposes. . . . Besides, did not the
Caesarians, Antonius and Lepidus, in addition to the strictly
legal right, possess also the practically effective force?
Lepidus had a whole legion under his control. . . . And
then, too, Dolabella, who was to have held the consulship

while Caesar carried on the Parthian War, and who was now the dead man's successor, had shown them a friendly face. . . . Finally—and not least—they wanted the whole subsequent proceedings to be arranged in and by the senate, of which they were members, and in which they had an overwhelming majority. They did not want Antonius to take the case to the Assembly, where the Caesarians had the majority. Hence there was substantial reason for the policy adopted by Brutus and Cassius.

So Cicero took no part in the negotiations that followed.

Antonius was a men of impulse, who leaped first and looked afterwards. At the awful moment of the murder of Caesar, he had bolted, and taken refuge in a house, from which he had stealthily and unobtrusively taken his way to his own. Here he shut himself in and prepared for defence. It was only by degrees that the truth dawned upon him, and he found that every one else also was in a state of panic. When he realized this striking fact, he emerged from his seclusion.

II

Tradition held that the family of Marcus Antonius was descended from Anton, the son of Hercules; and since Hercules was a Semitic hero, linked rather with the world of Tyre and Carthage than with that of Sparta and Athens, there may be some connection between this ancestry and the curious, sinister, hook-nosed, Assyrian cast of the face of Marcus Antonius, as we see it on his coins, smiling the deep ironic Assyrian smile, sensual and predatory. There was something Assyrian in his powerful frame, abundant strength, fondness for wine and women, his immense adequacy, royal carelessness, tremendous good-humour; his vaunting, his prodigality. . . . He was far from being a bad fellow. As Plutarch tells us, he was frank and trusting,

Reasons for their policy

Marcus Antonius

slow to see his own faults but quick to repent of them when
he did; ample in his reparations, extravagant in his generosity, ready to laugh at a joke at his own expense, free in
his words and flamboyant in everything—altogether a
richly coloured man, as luxuriant in his ways as any Sen-
nacherib or Esarhaddon. And with all this he was a man of
great and abundant artfulness. Once his sense of humour
was touched and his self-confidence was aroused again, he
bent a very curious and searching eye upon the gang of
incompetent amateur assassins in the Capitol. They had
made him run, for once in a way—now it was time that the
case should be reversed, and that he, Marcus Antonius,
should get a little amusement out of them.

So sudden had been Caesar's murder, that no one had
been prepared for the results. No one in Rome had any
clear right of succession to the dictator. His heir, Gaius
Octavius, was in Macedonia. If there was any legal government, it undoubtedly resided in the surviving consul—Antonius himself. He saw this perfectly, and he saw, too, that
the man who obtained possession of Caesar's papers would
be master of the situation. . . . When night fell, quiet did
not descend upon Rome. The consul issued his orders: the
streets were picketed, and watch-fires lit at the important
junctions and crossings. While the emissaries of the *optimates* descended from the Capitol to canvass the senators,
and to beat up an audience for the Assembly next day,
Antonius proceeded to the Temple of Ops, where Caesar's
treasury was, and seized it. It lay on the westerly part of
the Capitoline Hill, near the Tarpeian Rock, so that to
reach it he must have passed close to the conspirators.
Neither party interfered with the other. He also seized the
papers of Caesar, which contained not only his archives, the
record of work done and money spent, but also his plans
for the future, his drafts of projected legislation, in all stages

Succession
to Caesar

of progress towards perfection; his schemes and jottings. All these were removed to the house of Antonius. To judge by his actions on the next and subsequent days, Antonius at once set to work to gather an idea of the contents of these papers. They were destined to play a very great part in the drama that followed.

By his capture of Caesar's papers, Antonius captured the principal strategic point of the entire struggle. He obtained possession of the Caesarian machine, and knowledge of its purposes. It may have been at this point that he realized that the whole power of Caesar had fallen into his hands. Nothing prevented him from stepping into Caesar's place, if only he proceeded with the necessary intelligence and tact. *Caesar's papers*

In the mean time Lepidus, who was stationed on the Island of the Tiber with a legion of time-expired soldiers, transferred his men across the river to less restricted quarters in the Campus Martius, which lay below the Capitol outside the walls, just as the Forum lay below it inside the walls. Lepidus was not likely to act without the concurrence of Antony, whom he respected as consul and as the lieutenant of Caesar. But his men had been on their way, under his guidance, to Spain, there to take up the grants of land which the dictator had procured for them, when their proposed journey was rudely stopped by Caesar's death. They formed a very important and definite centre of organized opinion, for they were all very keen that their grants should not be (as they feared) cancelled—and they had very little confidence in Brutus and his friends.

III

Day dawned again—the day after Caesar's death: making it clear that the sun still rose and set, wind blew and water *March 16th 44 B. C.*

flowed, even though Caesar was dead. The day—the sixteenth of March—was passed in negotiation. The determin-
ing fact of the whole situation was that since no one really
knew the comparative strength of the parties, it was ur-
gently necessary for all of them to gain some inkling of
the truth. Before the day was over, Marcus Antonius at
least had grasped the essential facts and had realized what
he could do.

The conspirators were already confident of their hold
over the senate. Their task now was to gain over the Assembly if they could. An effort had been made during the
night to beat up a core of voters who could be relied upon
to set the tone of a meeting. Money had changed hands
freely. The dilemma of Brutus and Cassius was that they
expected these paid supporters to exhibit the Catonic tone
of the long-ago Assemblies when the voter was stern, wise
and incorruptible. The hired men knew rather more about
the real trend of public opinion than their hirers, and when
the meeting in the Forum began, they were a great deal too
wary to shout for the murderers of Caesar, or to shout
Public   against Caesar at all. Instead, they took the line of shouting
opinion   for general reconciliation—which would include, as a matter of course, an amnesty for the murderers. Unfortunately,
L. Cornelius Cinna, the praetor, chose this moment to intervene with great lack of tactfulness. Publicly casting
from him his official robe as the vile rag imposed upon him
by a Tyrant, he denounced Caesar and all his works and
lauded the glorious deed of the Tyrannicides. They should,
he thought, be rewarded as public benefactors. . . . At
this point the unpaid part of the Assembly began to get out
of hand, and to shout down the hired stalwarts.

L. Cornelius Dolabella was now put upon the platform
by the organizers of the meeting. Dolabella was the somewhat youthful man whom Caesar had nominated to take his

place as consul after he himself, Julius, had left Rome for the East and the Parthian war. By the demise of Caesar, the young Dolabella had automatically become consul with Marcus Antonius, and he had hastened to array himself in the appropriate robes, and to put in an appearance at the meeting. Believing himself to be siding with the stronger party, Dolabella made an anti-Caesarian speech in which he claimed to have been in the conspiracy all along, although unfortunately he had been unavoidably absent at the crit- Dolabella ical moment. . . . The hired men cheered this speech enthusiastically, while the Caesarians, knowing that Dolabella was one of their own men, were puzzled.

Brutus and Cassius, with delighted smiles, now appeared upon the stage to receive the plaudits of their fellow-countrymen. They were fervent in each other's praises, and implored the meeting to take as guide, as they had taken, the noble example of their remote ancestors who had expelled the Tarquins. They pointed out that Caesar was even worse than Tarquin the Proud, who had at any rate been a legal King; and they demanded the recall of all political exiles. Amid thunders of applause from the hired men, they then returned to the Capitol, rather gloomy over the undoubted fact that, despite the hired men's efforts, they had been totally unable to stampede the Assembly.

Antony had evidently noted the fact too. During the afternoon there was a perceptible change in the tone of both parties. Neutrals who had had no share in the conspiracy were persuaded to undertake the task of visiting Antonius and Lepidus, not in order to justify the slayers of Caesar—that would have been too dangerous—but in order to excuse them, to point out the purity of their motives, and to urge, in the interests of their native city, the necessity of peace and reconciliation. They mentioned the public welfare, the danger of civic strife, the beauties of concord and the virtues of forgiveness.

Marcus Antonius could lie like a diplomatist when the
spirit moved him; and no one could have received these
advances with more bland cordiality. He assured the deputation that he and his friends would do nothing from
merely personal motives, and after pointing out that he and
Lepidus were bound by their military oaths to protect and
avenge Caesar, and that a strict view of their duty would
compel them to punish the murderers without regard for
the consequences, he went on to declare that nevertheless
they were willing to meet them on equal terms in the senate, and to abide by whatsoever was agreed upon there.

This seemed very hopeful to the conspirators. They
never dreamed with what deadly effect Antonius was preparing to carry the war into the enemy's camp.

IV

On the seventeenth of March the senate met. The gathering of the august body was not entirely without event.
L. Cornelius Cinna turned up in the official robe which he
had so contemptuously cast off and repudiated the previous day. The reason for his recantation was that while on
his way to the meeting he had been noticed by some of the
Caesarian voters who had heard his speech. Attacked with
stones, Cinna took refuge in a house. The incensed electors
were just bringing up faggots to burn him out, when the
troops of Lepidus appeared upon the scene to restore order, and the sovereign electors scattered. Cinna was glad
to resume the protection of his official gown. The hired
men themselves felt that things were becoming ugly.

In the senate, however, the conspirators, as they rightly
anticipated, had an overwhelming majority of sympathisers,
and Cinna had nothing to fear in that comfortable environ-

ROME IN THE AGE
OF AUGUSTUS

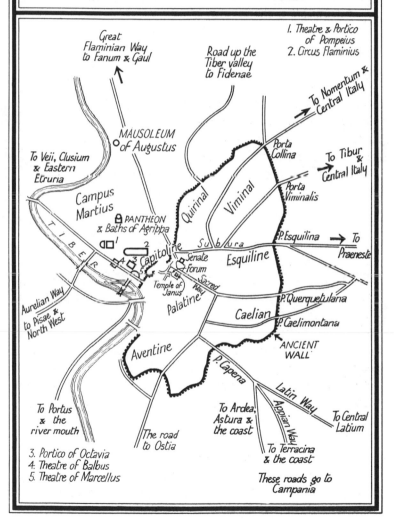

Great
Flaminian Way
to Fanum & Gaul

Road up the
Tiber valley
to Fidenae

1. Theatre & Portico
of Pompeius
2. Circus Flaminius

To Nomentum &
Central Italy

MAUSOLEUM
of Augustus

To Veii, Clusium
& Eastern
Etruria

Porta
Collina

To Tibur
&
Central Italy

Campus
Martius

Quirinal

Viminal

Porta
Viminalis

PANTHEON
& Baths of Agrippa

Sub ura

P. Esquilina

To
Praeneste

Capitoline

Senate
Forum

Esquiline

Temple of
Janus

Sacred
Way

Palatine

Aurelian Way

to Pisae &
North West

P. Querquetulana

Caelian

P. Caelimontana

Aventine

P. Capena

ANCIENT
WALL

Latin Way

To Portus
& the
river mouth

The road
to Ostia

To Ardea,
Astura &
the coast

Appian Way

To Central
Latium

To Terracina
& the coast

3. Portico of Octavia
4. Theatre of Balbus
5. Theatre of Marcellus

These roads go to
Campania

ment. The first motion was a proposal to invite the conspirators who were senators to take their places in the house under a special pledge for their safety. To this suggestion Marcus Antonius cordially assented. The conspirators, however, for some reason, shrank from putting in an appearance. Then, by way of testing the real opinion of the house, some members made openly anti-Caesarian speeches, declaring that Caesar was a tyrant, and his slayers tyrannicides—in which case, as all men know, killing is no murder. There were suggestions that the murderers should be rewarded. To this, other members objected, pointing out that the slayers of Caesar had acted from noble and enlightened motives of high idealism, not to be rewarded by filthy lucre. Some put forward the idea that instead of a reward, public thanks should be rendered to the murderers. Finally, there were some who thought it would be sufficient to pass an act of oblivion and indemnity.

The senate was in thorough confusion. There were those to whom the thought of murder was morally repugnant; **The senate** but they felt that perhaps they ought not to be too severe **uncertain** on sinners of such exalted idealism and high social degree. It was pointed out that to have it both ways was impossible, and that they must decide whether Caesar was a tyrant automatically self-outlawed and therefore rightfully slain, or whether he was a legally protected citizen and his slayers legally murderers. The house decided to vote on the issue—but the majority stipulated first that it should not be brought against them that they had on previous occasions voted for Caesar's measures, since they did it upon compulsion. . . . But at this point Antonius, who had been quietly waiting his opportunity, rose to make a few remarks which created an extraordinary sensation.

The consul pointed out that if they condemned Caesar as a tyrant, they nullified all his acts, which thereupon became void and of no effect. Most of these acts would continue to operate whether the senate liked them or not, so that they would not gain much by annulling them; but among those that could be effectively nullified were all the appoint- ments to office made under the direction of Julius. Most of those present (said Antonius) either had been appointed to one office or another by Julius, or were going to be in due course. However, if they really wanted to give up these appointments, he, as consul, was ready to put the motion for the condemnation of Caesar as a tyrant and usurper, with all the consequences that would automatically follow.

This bombshell brought the senate to its feet. With one voice the house declared itself against cancelling the ap- pointments. A good many of them had reasons which they were not anxious to avow. For example, Caesar had never troubled unduly about the laws limiting the age at which candidates might take office, and he had made a number of appointments of men who, if the matter of their qualifica- tions were reviewed, would almost certainly be disqualified as under age. Dolabella himself was one of these men, and a remarkable change came over him as he realized the posi- tion. So far now from claiming to be one of the conspira- tors, he made some unkind criticisms of the proposal to declare Caesar a tyrant, in which he referred to Caesar's slayers as murderers. . . . It was, of course, pointed out by zealous anti-Caesarians that such an annulment of the ap- pointments meant nothing worse than that they would all have to be re-elected in due form by the Assembly; but experienced members regarded with scepticism any like- lihood of the Assembly's ratifying some of the appoint- ments. While the house argued, Antonius and Lepidus arose, and for the time being left it arguing.

A crowd had been gathering for some time, and calls

Caesar's acts

for the consul had been insistent. When he appeared, some one called out: "What is going to happen to *you?*" An- Popular attitude tonius very coolly unfastened an inch or two of his tunic, and showed a chain mail shirt underneath. This caused a great uproar of scandalized amazement. There were cries for the punishment of Caesar's murderers, and cries for reconciliation, which were rather in the majority.

"Peace is what we are all trying for," said Antonius to the latter. "It would be easier to achieve it, if the case of Caesar did not illustrate how unreliable solemn pledges may be." And, turning to those who wanted vengeance, he said: "You, evidently, are particular about the oaths and pledges you have taken. I should be on your side if I were not the consul, who has to consider what is to the common good rather than what is right in the abstract. So, at any rate, these people inside," indicating the senate, "think: and no doubt Caesar thought so too when he, for the common good, pardoned and entered into friendly relations with the men who took the first opportunity of murdering him."

This was very subtle and very incendiary. Lepidus, addressing another meeting close by, took the same line. When the two, after some interval, returned to the senate, the crowd had taken a distinct move to the left under the Opinion hardens influence of such contentions. Dolabella was still addressing the Fathers when the consul resumed his seat. Antonius regarded him with amusement, and in due course rose to speak.

He now began to outline to the house the real reasons why most of Caesar's acts could not be nullified. They had been necessary acts of state, the revocation of which would be injurious to the Roman commonwealth, and many of them had been treaties or contracts not to be dissolved by unilateral action—and one good example of the latter type (he reminded his hearers) was represented by the very large number of ex-soldiers throughout Italy who were now waiting for the fulfilment of the promises of land-pensions made to them. Could they really take the risk of telling these men, who were still organized and were experienced fighting-men, that these promises were not to be carried out, because Caesar had been technically, in constitutional law, an usurper? They had seen, last night, the kind of thing that would happen—the kind of popular propaganda the ex-soldiers could make. Dare they, in the face of it, go through the whole ritual appropriate to the condemnation of a tyrant? He solemnly warned senators against the consequences of their prejudice against Caesar; and he ended by putting the formal motion to the house, that the acts and intentions of Caesar be ratified and that, as an act of grace, his murder be passed over without enquiry for the sake of the families and friends of the murderers.

Acts of Caesar confirmed

This motion was passed by an awed and subdued—and slightly confused—house, as the course most advantageous to the state. The partisans of the conspirators insisted upon emphasising that the motion was passed as a matter of expediency, not as being justified from the standpoint of abstract right. Antonius was not concerned to strive with them. He was willing to grant these refinements, as long as he obtained the main matter—the ratification of Caesar's acts.

The representatives of the ex-soldiers then asked for acts definitely confirming their rights to the land-pensions granted by Caesar. Antonius assented, put the necessary motions, and shepherded the house into passing them. The senate then rose, and it looked as if the proceedings of this crucial session were over.

V

Before the senators dispersed, however, a curious and threatening episode took place. A small crowd of senators surrounded Lucius Piso, the executor of Caesar's will, and informed him of their opinion that the will ought not to be made public, and that Caesar ought not to be given a public funeral, because of the danger of popular demonstrations. No man of the name of Piso was a likely subject for bullying, and Lucius was no exception to the rule. When the crowd of senators saw that he was unmoved by their arguments, they threatened to prosecute him for being in the possession of money which ought to have been paid into the public treasury—that is to say, they implied that Caesar's money had been illegally obtained at the expense of the state. . . . They made a singular error in fancying that Lucius Piso was likely to give way before threats. He at once demanded that the consuls should reconstitute the session.

This was done. When the house was once more sitting, Piso laid before it the story of this attempt to intimidate him. He observed that all these men who were so proud of having killed a tyrant were so many tyrants themselves, and that they went to the length of forbidding him to bury the Pontifex Maximus, threatening him against producing the will, and insinuating that the money had been stolen from the public purse. Evidently (said Piso) these people were eager to confirm those of Caesar's acts which touched themselves, but very unwilling to confirm those which touched him. He submitted the question of the funeral to the house for its decision—with the final remark that the question of the will was in his trust, which he would never betray unless somebody murdered him too.

Caesar's will

Public funeral authorised

These remarks, which perhaps did not err upon the side of excessive conciliatoriness, aroused resentment in some quarters; but in the upshot it became clear that the principles already laid down would have to be carried out completely—so it was agreed that Caesar should have a public funeral, and that the will should be publicly read. The house then really adjourned.

The resolution so made had the most momentous consequences. Atticus assured Cicero of his conviction that a public funeral of Caesar meant the fall of the oligarchy; but neither he nor Cicero had the power to prevent it. In the extraordinary mechanism by which the commands of the dead Caesar were now grinding out death and downfall to the murderers, the appointments to office which he had made compelled even his enemies to confirm his acts; and it was impossible to pick and choose between the acts —all alike had to be confirmed. But those who reflected over what would happen when Caesar's will was publicly read and Caesar's obsequies publicly celebrated must have shaken in their shoes. Trouble was on the way.

VI

Brutus and Cassius   Brutus and Cassius did their best to get their foot in first. As soon as they realized that an appeal to the people—the man in the street, the small man and proletarian—was now certain, they called a meeting on the Capitol. A good audience turned up, and Brutus addressed it.

He and his friends, he said, had nothing they needed to apologize for. They appealed to their fellow-countrymen because an attack had been made upon their good faith. It was said that no general settlement of a reliable nature could be made to which they were a party. Brutus had come to reply to these accusations in public.

The meeting then settled down to the task of hearing him do it.

Brutus admitted that he and his friends had been among those who, at Caesar's own request, granted him amnesty for all that he had done during the Civil War, sanctifying it by an oath. But no one had interpreted that oath as covering the future as well as the past, nor would even Caesar's friends have thought of taking an oath covering his future acts. If Caesar had never committed an illegal action subsequent to their taking the oath then without doubt they were all perjured. But the facts were very different. Caesar had committed many subsequent illegalities. He had never **Case of** restored the normal government of the state, but had made **Brutus** his own military government supreme. Intending to go away on a long expedition, he had taken the elections out of the hands of the people and had made all the appointments himself for a long time in advance. He had banished two tribunes, although these men were protected by usages of immemorial antiquity. His violation of their sacred right of immunity was a much more serious thing than the breach, by Brutus and his friends, of an oath which they had taken only under duress. Finally, Caesar had taken possession of the financial organization of the state and had issued no accounts.

What was all this talk about oaths?—Brutus demanded. Their forefathers had never needed any to safeguard their free institutions; while no oath will safeguard a tyrant. Those who slew Caesar were thinking of the good of the state, not of their own. Their enemies slandered them about the land pensions. If any were present who were entitled to such, he invited them to stand forward.

A good number promptly took him at his word. Satisfied that he was really addressing a gathering of the persons chiefly concerned, Brutus continued his speech.

He began by describing the old system of military colonization followed in ancient times by the Romans. Their
ancestors did not confiscate all the land even of conquered
communities, but took a certain proportion on which to
settle a military garrison. If there were not enough, they
bought the extra amount required. Thus colonies were
founded without injury or ill-feeling. But Sulla and Caesar
had introduced a different method. They had started the
practice of confiscating without compensation the land of
perfectly innocent persons, who had committed no crime
and were not public enemies, and of granting this land to
their soldiers.

Worse than this, they had settled the new colonists together in their military units; and the dispossessed, feeling
themselves to have been unjustly robbed, were always
watching for an opportunity to get their property back;
and the colonists, conscious of it, were always holding together ready to defend their possessions; and that was the
intention behind the plan—to bind the new colonists to the
tyrannical government through their consciousness of dependence upon it. They were made enemies of their fellow-
countrymen in order to bolster up a tyranny.

Brutus then proceeded to make a proposal. Very solemnly, in the name of himself and his companions, he undertook to guarantee the land-grants that had been made;
and he promised to remedy the fault he had pointed out by
compensating the former owners, so that the title of the
new ones should be secure and unquestioned, and they
should depend upon no government for its permanence.

This speech, with its proposal, was well received. The
soldiers perfectly appreciated the point made. No doubt
many of them reflected that nothing had ever prevented
the oligarchs from buying land for colonization in the past
—except determined hostility to popular needs. But all this

could be set aside in view of the positive and tangible advantages promised by Brutus. On these terms—if they were kept—reconciliation was possible.

The effect of Brutus's speech was at once seen when, next morning, the consuls convoked the assembly to consider the decisions of the Senate. Cicero supported the decree of amnesty and reconciliation, and the Assembly at once concurred. Brutus and his friends were invited to descend from the Capitol. When they hesitated, hostages were given them for their personal safety. On their appearance at last, they were enthusiastically received. The consuls wished to make a few remarks, but in this they were over-ruled. The meeting would tolerate nothing but hand-shaking, mutual congratulations, and general sentimentality. . . . A conclusion which somewhat alarmed the Caesarians. Was it possible that Brutus after all could stampede the Assembly? It looked like it! Concern of Antonius

It is very difficult to believe that either the conspirators or the Caesarians sincerely counted on the permanence of the reconciliation. Only the people—who in all ages are a sentimental crew—could possibly take it seriously. The struggle was only postponed. And now Marcus Antonius, having been somewhat disturbed by the success of Brutus with the Assembly, proceeded to play his great trump card —the funeral of Caesar, and the reading of Caesar's will.

VII

At the request of Piso, the will was opened and read at Antony's house. It was dated the fifteenth of the September preceding, and was therefore only six months old. In it Caesar named three heirs. The first was Gaius Octavius, his grand-nephew, to whom he left three-quarters of his estate. The remaining quarter was shared between his two other grand-nephews, Lucius Pinarius and Quintus Pedius. Finally it was provided that Gaius Octavius should take the name of Caesar, and should become legally Julius's son. A number of his assassins were named as guardians; and one of them, Decimus Brutus, was a residuary legatee. Caesar's splendid gardens near the Tiber were left to the public, and a sum of three hundred sesterces was bequeathed to every Roman citizen.

The will
is read

It was impossible for the citizens of Rome, when they heard of these bequests, to think evil of the man who had made them. Nearly all Romans, whatsoever their degree, shared a common tendency to be profoundly touched at the thought of being remembered in a will. Unreasonable although it may seem in the cold light of another age, a legacy was the quickest way to the heart of a Roman. The poorest, most insignificant Roman elector could entertain the thrilling thought that he—yes, he!—had been remembered by the greatest man of the age: and to the tune of three hundred sesterces! His feelings on the subject of Caesar underwent a sudden consolidation. He was conscious that he definitely disagreed with Brutus about Caesar's being a tyrant. More—he was conscious of genuine horror at the thought of Caesar's being murdered by men who had been mentioned in his will—one of them no less than a residuary legatee! A man must be evil to the core to assassinate some one who had left him money!

These feelings, at first vague and undirected, were still occupying the mind of the man in the street when the programme for Caesar's funeral was announced. The funeral oration was to be delivered in the Forum by Marcus Antonius. A procession would then be formed, and the body borne to the Campus Martius, where the funeral pyre would be ready. Sympathisers who wished to contribute to the pyre were expected to be so numerous that

Programme
of the
funeral

no regular queue would be formed to walk past the pyre, but each person would make his way thither by the most convenient route. The summit of the pyre was to be a model of the temple of Venus Genetrix, of whom Caesar had been a devotee. It would be a very magnificent funeral.

The intelligence which calculated all these things—some people thought it was that of Balbus, Caesar's secretary—calculated very surely. The Roman elector, warm with sympathy and indignation, crowded to the funeral in his thousands. He came ready to be moved to further sympathy and indignation.

VIII

We must remember that Marcus Antonius was of no obscure stock. His grandfather had been one of the greatest orators Rome ever produced—a man of whom even Cicero spoke with reverence. When Marcus Antonius faced the crowd in the Forum, across Caesar's bier, he did so with the composure and competence of an artist whose gifts were hereditary. He had been a loose-living fellow—but public speaking was in his blood. With necessity and passion to drive him he could rise to greatness: and he did.

In solemn procession Piso had brought the body into the Forum, through the wild crowds who filled the place. The bier was of ivory, with coverings of purple and gold. At its head hung the robe in which the dead man had been slain. With blast of trumpets and flashing of spears it was deposited on the rostra. There it stood while the lament was raised, the soldiers slowly clashing their swords and shields in measure. In due time there was silence; and then Antonius, standing there above the crowd, began the panegyric.

He began very quietly, even gloomily, reciting the

The Forum

names, titles, offices and dignities of the deceased citizen; giving in full the official decrees which had declared Caesar's person to be sacred and inviolable. After every quotation he added some little aside of his own. He read out the text of the oaths by which all were pledged to guard Caesar and to avenge him at need. Then, lifting up his hand to the Capitoline temple which rose high before him, he declared his own readiness to keep this oath—if it had not been that the decree of amnesty had been generally considered the most expedient course. . . . At this point the senators present became visibly uneasy; so he soothed them by remarking that they would all forget the past and think only of the present. Their present duty was to conduct the deceased to the abode of the blest.

The speaker then girded his garments around him and took his stand in front of the bier. Here he began a sort of rhythmic praise of the deceased, describing in rapid words, with vivid oratorical gestures, the famous deeds of Caesar, his marvellous victories, his incredible conquests, the miraculous successes and romantic adventures by which he had avenged upon the Gallic race the former burning of Rome. Increasing his pace, he reached a pitch of passion which began to sweep his hearers along on the stream of words; and then he dropped his voice down and down as he mourned and lamented the loss of his friend who had been so unjustly slain, and he proclaimed his willingness to give his life in exchange for Caesar's.

All this was the purest rhetoric—pure artistry, which did not appeal to reason at all, but appealed, with awful force and overwhelming compulsion, to the emotions and imagination of the packed crowd who heard him. This crowd was now tense and tearful with the thrill of Antony's agonized lament, and when he arose from his stooping posture, uncovered Caesar's body, and lifted on a spear-

The Pane-gyric

point the bloodstained toga, pierced with thrusts and red with blood, the tenseness and tearfulness began to reach the danger point. They groaned and wept: they chanted after him the praise of the great, the wonderful, the noble, the generous Caesar, and they told again, in versicle and response, the sad tale of his betrayal and death. And in the Emotion middle of this, Antonius suddenly began to dramatise the story—that is, to speak as if the actual Julius were speaking—and the dramatic Julius, so created, passed in review his murderers, recalled the benefits he had heaped upon them, and quoted the line from Pacuvius:

"Did I save these men that they might murder me?"

While the crowd was still groaning and weeping, a wax figure of Julius was raised for all to see, marked in red with the twenty-three wounds. Slowly the figure was turned around and about, so that all might see . . . and at this psychological moment the bier (contrary to the published programme) was taken out of the hands of the grave magistrates and ex-magistrates its bearers, carried into the midst of the Forum and the fire was set to it.

All that followed had so inevitable a logic about it that it may have been foreseen—certainly something like it had been foreseen by Atticus. The spectators crowded round to cast in their contributions. With tears, branches and incense were tossed into the leaping flame . . . women threw in their jewels, children their lucky charms. And then, of course, the musicians and choirmen tore off their wreaths and their processional robes, and rent them in twain and cast them into the consuming fire. . . . And the veterans heaped in their gilded processional spears and shields. . . . And excited spectators, carried away by the enthusiasm of the moment, caught up the benches and stools, now scattered about among the crowd, on which

Explosion   people had been standing, and threw them in. And others, rushing farther afield, tore down the rows of seats, and these were piled upon the roaring pyre. . . . By this time the crowd was out of hand. The senate house in which Caesar was slain was stormed by an enraged mob. Since it could not conveniently be carried to the Forum and cast upon the flames, it was set light to and burned. Others went to hunt out the murderers and to burn their houses; and while night fell the pyre and the senate house both roared to heaven, and in the half-deserted Forum isolated parties of foreigners were left to pay their respects to the dead Caesar according to the eccentric rites of their own distant countries—among whom was a party of Jews, come to mourn for a friend and benefactor of their race.

CHAPTER III

INDECISION

I

SOMETHING like a month elapsed while the tremendous explosion of popular feeling caused by the funeral of Caesar burned and smouldered and produced its natural results. The senate was appalled at the fury of the people and at first was inclined to charge Marcus Antonius with responsibility for vitiating the amnesty upon which they had been at such pains to agree. But Antonius soothed down these doubts and questionings. By arresting some of the more blatant rioters, and making a show of enforcing law and order against some of the less important disorderly persons who had very little power of hitting back, the consul persuaded the senate that he was heart and soul with it. The senate was easy to hoodwink. It nibbled at all the simplest and most obvious baits: it swallowed every hook presented to it. Not simple-mindedness alone was the cause of its errors. Deep within it was an only-too-well grounded fear of the future—a dread which paralysed its actions and froze its inspiration and made it rush upon the consequences it sought to avoid. It realized that the overwhelming majority of Roman citizens now sided with Caesar. It saw—and trembled to see—that it stood defenceless in a world of foes. It was only too anxious to believe Marcus Antonius to be its friend. When that arch-humbug, with wreathed smiles and sweet warblings, proposed the recall of Sextus Pompeius from Spain, his promotion to the supreme command of all Roman fleets, and the payment to

After-effects

Fears of the senate

him of a heavy indemnity, the delighted oligarchs were
happy to believe that this must foreshadow the return of
the exiles and the restoration of their old power. When
Antony represented to them how helpless he himself was
before the alleged revolutionary machinations of a small
stage-army which he himself had put up for the purpose of
impressing public opinion, the senate was rejoiced to give
him a body-guard. It was somewhat appalled at the bodyguard he proceeded to enrol. His "guard" consisted of
six thousand men, including all the centurions he could
persuade to join him—that is to say, in plain language,
Antony organized the cadres for a vast army of some hundred thousand men. Frightened at what they had done, the
oligarchs remonstrated. This, they pointed out, was excessive. . . . He promised to reduce his guard as soon as he
felt safe. . . . When that would be was left conveniently
vague.

While he was organizing this formidable military power,
he was at the same time busily engaged in gaining over to
his side all the important individuals whose alliance might
be useful to him, and whom fear, persuasion or bribery
could bring over. In this process he derived overwhelming
advantages from his possession of Caesar's papers—and of
Caesar's scribe, Faberius, who, being the actual writer of
the documents concerned, could alter, duplicate and substitute to any extent he wished. It was freely asserted by
Antony's opponents that he used this power as often as
he thought it profitable. The accumulation of a reserve
fund for coming emergencies was another task to which
Antonius devoted himself. For this purpose he did not
hesitate to adopt such measures as the restoration of King
Deiotarus to his dominions for a very large lump sum down,
and the sale of privileges and immunities to the rich towns
and provinces of the Roman dominion. The granting of

**Antony's
decisive
action**

HEAD OF AUGUSTUS AS A CHILD

from a Sculpture in the British Museum
No. 1876, xxvii c (30)

Reproduced by permission of the Trustees

these immunities not only furnished Antony's war-chest, but bound the recipients firmly to the Caesarian cause, since the grants, so heavily paid for, would certainly be revoked if the oligarchs recovered their power. . . . While Brutus and Cassius and their friends went about repeating high maxims of political philosophy, Antonius was hard at work building up the framework of an army and the financial reserves with which to back it—and he let no maxims, high or low, stand in the way of these objectives.

The purchase of Dolabella was one of the first purposes to which he devoted his new funds. It was in Dolabella's power to make himself very unpleasant; and if he went over to the enemy he could give them an air of legality and constitutionality which would not be without its effect on public opinion. In order to avoid this, Antony undertook to pay Dolabella's debts—an immense sum—and agreed with him that he should have the proconsular government of Syria. Dolabella—who was indifferent to philosophical maxims and political principles—heartily accepted these offers, and became a secure ally.

Purchase of Dolabella

Early in this process it became obvious to Brutus and Cassius that they were not safe in Rome, and were not protected by any large body of public support. Veteran soldiers, grimly and determinedly Caesarian in their political views, were pouring into the city to make their opinions felt; and many of these came to apply for employment under Antonius. A general exodus of the leading anti-Caesarians began. It was so spontaneous, and so little organized, that some of the leaders did not know where their colleagues were, nor what their plans might be. Cicero left the city at the end of the first week of April, some three weeks or so after the murder of Caesar, and began a quiet journey to his Campanian villa. When, on the tenth of the month, he passed through Lanuvium on the road

south, he had no idea that Brutus and Cassius were there.
. . . A curious but very general depression hung over the
anti-Caesarians, and Cicero became their spokesman, who
put the feeling into words. He had become conscious that
the assassination of Caesar, the supposed tyrant, instead of
resulting in the instant and glorious liberation of Rome
from all that was oppressing it, had had, as a matter of fact,
no result at all—except perhaps to saddle them with a worse
tyrant than Caesar: namely, Marcus Antonius. "We have
killed the tyrant but not the tyranny," he wrote.[1] Neither
he, nor any of the others, could understand the paralysis
that hung so heavy upon their hands. They had, as they
believed, a great and glorious cause—the liberty of mankind. And yet this glorious cause flagged. Nobody shouted
for it. Nobody was enthusiastic about it. Nobody—except
a few rich men—was warm for the noble Brutus and the
excellent Cassius. It was bewildering!

It was a week later, the seventeenth of April, when Cicero, having journeyed by the coast road through Astura,
Fundi, Formial and Sinuessa, at last reached Puteoli. He
had heard, during his journey, that Marcus Brutus had
gone to Lanuvium, where he had an estate, and that Trebonius, another of the conspirators, had gone to Asia. He
was to hear, before long, that Decimus Brutus had gone
north to Cisalpine Gaul to take up the military command
that was waiting for him there. He heard, no doubt, in
due time, that Tillius Cimber had gone to Bithynia. They
were all scattering, in fact, without a plan or a common objective, while Marcus Antonius and the Caesarians were
rapidly taking possession of Rome and organizing their
power upon a solid foundation. . . . How did it all come
about? . . . Cicero could hardly tell!

But, all unconsciously to himself, Cicero had walked

Cicero leaves Rome (April, 44 B. C.)

The murderers scatter

[1] *Letters to Atticus,* XIV, 14.

straight into the very centre of activity when he came to
Puteoli. He found that Hirtius and Pansa, the close personal
friends of Julius, and members of his personal staff, were
there; and so also was Lucius Cornelius Balbus, that dark
Phoenician man, the engineer and chief-of-staff to Julius.
What were they doing there? The answer almost at once
became certain. They had come to meet young Gaius Octavius at the house of his mother—the very next house ad-
joining Cicero's villa! . . . Cicero had wondered, during
his journey, where Octavius was, and what he was doing.
The unexpected answer was—he was coming to Puteoli!

II

On the eighteenth of April—the day after Cicero's arrival—Octavius reached Naples. With typical caution, he
had not landed at Brundusium, since he was not yet sure **Octavius**
of his reception; he had gone on south to Hydruntum, and **at Naples**
thence journeyed north along the heel of Italy until he
reached Lupiac. Here he tarried awhile until he had ascertained how matters stood. The Caesarian veterans were
swarming in Brundusium, full of zeal, full of anger at the
murder of Julius, full of eagerness to take the heir of Julius
under their wing. Satisfied on this head, Octavius went on
to Brundusium, where he made no mistake. His first great
reception might have turned any but a very cool head. He
was met by crowds of veterans, who cheered him and exhorted him to avenge the murder of Caesar. There could
be no doubt respecting the identity of the person whom
they regarded as the true successor of Julius. Octavius,
noting that they were ready and waiting for the summons,
made decorous, non-committal responses, and continued
his journey to Rome. But it is certain that he did not omit
to establish more intimate touch and closer understandings

with his followers at Brundusium than his public actions revealed, and that he left his agents there. As he crossed Samnium his entourage was increased by volunteers who determined to accompany him to Rome to protect him and to defend his claims.

Balbus has never been a very popular figure, whether with his contemporaries (as he himself admitted) or with subsequent historians; yet he was very probably one of those men, like Father Joseph, Richelieu's Confessor, whose importance has been vast, and whose influence has exceeded anything that their fellows supposed. Balbus met young Octavius at Naples—the old, experienced man, deeper in the counsels of Julius than any other, and the fragile, girl-faced youth who was Julius's heir. After accompanying Octavius to the villa of his step-father, L. Marcius Philippus, Balbus returned to Cicero to inform the latter of what had passed—or as much of it as he thought fit to divulge. Octavius, he told Cicero, had come merely to enter a claim to his grand-uncle's fortune. He probably hinted that in such an event there would be a serious collision between Octavius and Marcus Antonius—for Cicero included both thoughts in his next letter to his friend Atticus. Both were just what he hoped were true.

It was Balbus, too, who introduced the young Octavius in person to Cicero; and the young man was exactly fitted to make the right impression on the great orator. Quietness, modesty and refinement, and a profound respect for Marcus Tullius Cicero—these were the virtues that most quickly evoked Cicero's approval and admiration: and Octavius displayed all four. "He treats me with the greatest respect and friendship," wrote Cicero to Atticus. But then he set down his central thought, which really motivated his actions more than any other. "His own people refer to him as Caesar—but Philippus did not, so I did not. I declare that

Reception
of Octavius

it is not possible for him to be a good citizen, so many men Octavius and Cicero surround him who threaten death to our friends. They say that what has happened" (meaning the murder of Caesar) "is not to be endured. What do you judge will happen when this laddie gets to Rome, where our liberators cannot remain in safety? Renowned they will always be, and assuredly happy in the consciousness of what they have done: but we, as a party, unless I am mistaken, are fallen."

In short, it was impossible for Octavius—in Cicero's view—to be a really worthy citizen, seeing that his friends made lethal threats against their political enemies, who had murdered their beloved leader: but to murder Caesar—O! that was an act of the highest merit, and those who did the deed (twenty-two to one) would surely enjoy the beaming consciousness of moral rectitude and civic virtue. . . . To such strange inconsistencies men are sometimes led!

How are we to explain the extraordinary fact that Cicero whom we habitually—and with some reason—regard as one of the most enlightened men of his age, should praise political assassination? If there is any method of political activity which is utterly wrong in its conception, evil in its results, and a curse to the state that endures it, it is the habit of political violence, and a man who endorses the Cicero a "doctrinaire" murder of political opponents is as much the enemy of law, of order and of rational government as a man who commits it. How then does it come about that the author of such works as the *De Re Publica*, *De Officiis* and *De Finibus* should find himself glorifying the murder of such a man as Gaius Julius Caesar, and flattering and praising so dull, ignorant and incapable a person as Marcus Brutus? The question would remain an insoluble mystery were it not for the very books themselves which have given Cicero his reputation for enlightenment. It is in the pages of *De Re*

Publica that we may find the clue.

Marcus Tullius Cicero was a "doctrinaire"—that is to say, a man whose ideas of politics and government were entirely drawn from the former experience of other men in the past, and the literary criticism based upon it. There is no trace in any of his works that he ever thought of getting into touch with the living needs of the day, or, indeed, that he ever realized that the needs of his contemporaries had any claim to be considered. He thought entirely of ideas, never of human needs.[2] Here he differed fundamentally from Julius, who had taught the boy Octavius and planted his own principles in his heart. Julius, though he may have entertained general notions of the kind set forth by Cicero in *De Re Publica*, and such as had been stated generations before by Aristotle in his *Politica*—notions which were common form in that age—was guided first and foremost by expedience, and by the actual demand of the day. He may not have thought very highly of the voice of the people: but he listened intently to it. He would have violated every old traditional theory there was, at the demand of some oppressed, or even some merely annoyed part of the electorate. He lived in a world of men, not a world of ideas.

The result was that Cicero was constantly forming his policy upon the guidance of old and obsolete conditions of the body-politic, and was a good citizen of a long dead city, while Julius was cutting a pioneer-path through the jungle of human needs and requirements, which he perhaps did not understand, but whose call he obeyed. Hence the latter shaped, instinctively and by intuition, the institutions suitable for the great state that was to be. There was

Tradition of Julius

[2] If this seems to be contradicted by, e. g., *De Officiis*, II, xx, it should be noted that Cicero very clearly never did carry out the maxims there laid down.

no other way of shaping them. He no more foresaw what was to result from his work than Daniel Boone foresaw the Pacific Railroad or the Flatiron Building; but like Daniel Boone, he followed a trend, a pressure, a direction, whose current he felt. And here we see the eternal distinction between the intellectualist or doctrinaire, who sets out with ready-made theories, and the practical politician who follows a call from mankind at large. The call may be irrational and inexplicable—but only by following it can the new and unknown future be provided for. In politics, as in war, Julius proceeded upon a strange mingling of astute reasoning and even more astute hazard. The one thing he never was at any time was a systematic theorizer: and he had trained, in his grand-nephew, a successor to his power who was of all men the least doctrinaire or theoretical. Octavius listened, reflected—and very carefully adapted himself to the environment he chanced to be in.

Intuition in politics

III

The serious question which confronted him was the problem of what he was to do next—how he was to proceed in lodging his claim to be his uncle's heir. Even to be mentioned in the will of Julius was dangerous. To be his heir and adopted son was a very serious matter—especially in the peculiar circumstances of the time. Had Julius been able to shepherd his successor gradually into his new position, there would have been no such difficulty; but the trouble was that Octavius had been left alone and almost unprotected in a world in which nearly every one had a strong reason for opposing him and preventing his success. The oligarchs, it is needless to say, regarded him with hostility. But Antonius, who himself had every intention of becoming Caesar's heir and successor, had no less reason

Policy of Octavian

for hostility. If the two parties joined together to exclude Octavius, then excluded he would be, and his life would not be much longer than his career. Only one resort was left to Octavius. He must prevent this coalition, and persuade one of the parties—it did not matter which—to help him to crush the other. He could then deal with the survivor as circumstances might direct. There was no other course.

Skill in playing such a game as this was of supreme importance. Useful as the huge fortune of Julius might be, splendid as might be that wonderful engine of power, the Caesarian military and political influence, yet these things would avail nothing without the natural ability to use them well. Great as were the objects to be achieved, it would be safer to drop them and retire into peace and privacy unless the boy were quite clear about his competence to employ these great weapons. Did he dare? Had he such confidence in himself? He had very evidently told Balbus that he had, for the dark man was clear on the point that Octavius would press his claim. But his mother and his step-father had at first taken a very different view. Atia in particular implored her son not to enter into competition with so dangerous an antagonist as Marcus Antonius—and Philippus (a strong, sensible man) added his entreaties. It was the **His self-confidence** young man's first experience of the difficulties that affection could place in his way. But even at eighteen he was assured of his own power to take part in the strife of great parties. He said that it would be base and infamous to think himself unworthy of a heritage of which Julius had thought him worthy. He acted, indeed, with a modesty and grace that were very appealing to his elders, even when they were apprehensive about the safety of his conclusions. Every one —Cicero himself, as well as Atia and Philippus—felt as much. His mother and his step-father finally decided to trust his judgment even though they felt an inward doubt whether it was possible for him to make good against force so infinitely greater (as it seemed) than any that he himself possessed. His more practical advisers—Balbus, Hirtius and Pansa—needed to be a little surer of this before they could venture to be whole-hearted in his support.

Cicero looked upon the episode with interest, but with a sort of puzzlement. He could not square his liking for the boy with his sense that, politically, he ought not to like him. Cicero was still labouring through a sea of doubt and self-questioning. He still insisted on believing that a great and wonderful deed had been done on the Ides of March and that Rome had been freed from tyranny. He still looked to Brutus and Cassius to lead the forces of freedom. . . . The time was to come when he ceased at last to look to them—and when he, an old man, a civilian and a scholar, thought it his duty to step into the breach in their stead to lead the forlorn hope. And when that day came, it was to prove of very great importance that he had once met and liked young Octavius, and that Octavius had flattered the old man with the deference and charm of a young one.

Importance of his meeting with Cicero

IV

The death of Caesar, occurring abruptly without all those measures of prevision and preparation which pass on authority from one man to another with the agreement and consent of all concerned, had produced a state of chaos from which even the Caesarian party only slowly emerged. The self-appointed task of Marcus Antonius was to lull the oligarchs into inactivity while he himself gathered together the dropped threads of Caesar's power, tested them, made sure they were sound, and proceeded to use them.

The fact that the veteran soldiers of Caesar were settled

on Italian farms made everything much easier than it would otherwise have been. Italy was solid for Caesar and his successor—though there was destined soon to be some uncertainty respecting the identity of this successor. The oligarchs began to see that if they were to survive, they too must organize their power where Pompeius Magnus had organized it—in the provinces. Not all of them were as helpless as Cicero: though most of them shared his sense that their party was doomed. On the same day that Octavian arrived at Naples, Cicero heard the news that Nebonius had gone to Asia. Eight days later, Decimus Brutus left for Cisalpine Gaul. They went—none too soon —to raise for their own party the money and the men that Marcus Antonius was already collecting at Rome. Brutus and Cassius, the active heads of the party, were tied by the heel. They were the praetors for the year, and were forbidden by law to be absent more than ten days from the city. They obtained—somewhat to their humiliation—permission from the consuls and senate to retire from Rome, where they certainly were in personal danger: but they could not, without rather too open a breach with custom and convention, follow Trebonius. They were held, if not in Rome, at any rate in Italy, until their office expired on the last day of December ensuing—a time some seven months distant. Marcus Antonius could not bring back Trebonius and Decimus Brutus—but he could do something to side-track the purposes of the latter: and he proceeded with vigour to do it. Octavius can barely have left Puteoli on the road to Rome when Cicero received the notice that there would be a meeting of the senate on the first of June, to reconsider the distribution of the provinces. He saw what it meant, and resolved—not too resolutely: but still he resolved—to be there.

Marcus Antonius was not in Rome when Octavius, with

his growing train of vigorous Caesarian partisans, marched into the city. Antonius was making a tour of southern Italy —he was, indeed, at Miseuum, across the bay from Puteoli, a day or two before May 11th—to renew contact with the Caesarian veterans. In any case Octavius was introduced to the Roman electors by Gaius Antonius, the consul's brother. Once his identity was publicly established and his person formally made known, he proceeded to assert his legal rights. He lodged his claim to become Gaius Julius Caesar Octavianus, in place of the simple Gaius Octavius he had been before. And as Octavian he was henceforth known.[3]

As soon as Marcus Antonius returned, Octavian called upon him. The interview was a very peculiar one. Octavian remarked upon the way in which Antonius had taken matters into his own hands, and had compromised with the murderers of Caesar. From this course the young man dis- sociated himself. Finally, he reminded Antonius of the immense sums belonging to Caesar which were in his hands, and he requested their payment to him, so that he could carry out the provisions of his adopted father's will.

Marcus Antonius was a good deal surprised—almost a little incredulous—at his tone. He answered, rather sharply, that even if the young man before him were heir to Caesar's property, he was not heir to Caesar's political power. He, Antonius, as consul, was not called upon to account for his actions to him. He had acted in the interests of the state, not in the interests of Caesar's heir. But he pointed out that if he had not effected the compromise referred to, Caesar's acts would have been invalidated, and Caesar himself declared a tyrant—with the result that his will would have

[3] Writing to Atticus soon after May 18th Cicero calls the young man "Octavius." Writing at the end of June, he refers to him as "Octavian." (*Letters to Atticus*, XV, 2, 12.)

been annulled and his property confiscated, and Octavian would have got nothing. As for the money—they would have to look into Caesar's accounts and ascertain how much of it was public money and how much private property. He extended very little hope that Octavius would obtain much of it.

This was pretty crushing, and the young man took his leave with the conviction that he would have to fight Antonius. His first step was to try to sell his expectations; and at the same time he laid before the people an account of what had passed between himself and Antony. Caesar's personal friends and devoted admirers of all classes rallied round him, and the electors, who were entitled to three hundred sesterces each under Caesar's testamentary dispositions, heard with indignation the light way in which Antony treated their prospects of obtaining them. Octavian assured them that he proposed to carry out the dispositions without fail—a very popular declaration—and he began by preparing for the celebration of Caesar's Victory Games, which had not been celebrated, but which he now determined to celebrate.

Support for Octavian

To be on the wrong side of a consul, and that consul Marcus Antonius, was a serious matter, as Octavian soon found out. One of the tribunes of the people had recently died, and Octavian determined to become a candidate for the vacant post, which he felt would give him more standing. Antony thought so too, for he promptly saw to it that this plan should fail. When Octavian tried to exhibit in public the golden chair that had been voted to Caesar, the tribunes, at Antony's instigation, removed it and threatened him. Antony also inspired a number of legal actions respecting the title of Julius to certain items of property; and when Octavian fought these, he found that most of them came before the consul's court, where Antony himself, or Dolabella, would be sitting—or before Lucius Antonius, who acted as praetor in the absence of Brutus. Needless to say, Octavian invariably lost these cases, with serious results to Caesar's property, although in many cases he could produce the attested deeds of sale. This went on until his cousins, Quintus Pedius and Lucius Pinarius, who shared one quarter of the property with him, complained to Antony. **Difficulties of Octavian** The latter made a half-hearted apology for his conduct, and undertook that Pedius and Pinarius should get their due shares without fail. They accepted this, for prudential reasons, and withdrew. Even Antony's own trusted officers seriously expostulated with their leader over his treatment of Octavian—and Antony had to make an elaborate justification of his action.

But Octavian, surrounded by his stout henchmen of the Caesarian inner circle, held his ground and persisted in his programme. The Games were duly held, although, to finance them, Octavian had to sell everything he possessed, all the property of his step-father Philippus, and the shares of Quintus Pedius and Lucius Pinarius, which were willingly put at his disposal. The family, in fact, rallied round him to a man. The games—held at the end of July—were popular. . . . The money not only paid for them, but also furnished a fund for yet another purpose. . . . A little earlier, during the first week of July, had fallen the date of the Apollinarian Games, which were annually held by the City Praetor, who this year chanced to be Marcus Brutus. As Brutus was at Lanuvium, and thought it wiser not to risk a visit to Rome, he gave the games by deputy, hoping to hear that his own name would be loudly cheered by the assembled citizens. His hope might conceivably have **The Games** come much nearer realization had not Octavian planned to make the distribution of Caesar's money at the same time. The earnest citizens who lined up on this great occasion to receive their three hundred sesterces may have enjoyed the Apollinarian Games, but their loudest cheers were reserved for Caesar, and for that fine young man, his grand-nephew and heir. While the hired claque at the Apollinarian Games was shouting for Brutus and Cassius, a mob of Caesarians stormed the barriers and broke up the proceedings.

v

The failure of the Apollinarian Games was the final blow to Brutus and Cassius. Everything had gone wrong for them. Cicero, journeying up again from Puteoli, had after all not dared to be present during the meetings of the Senate early in June, at which the provincial governorships were to have been re-arranged. Hirtius had given him a friendly warning; Varro had written to caution him that the Caesarian veterans were threatening a reign of terror against their opponents—and Cicero had felt discretion to be the better part of valour. But even with the senate packed and the veterans breathing fire and slaughter Antonius thought it safer to apply to the Assembly for what he wanted. The Assembly—irregularly, for the proper notice had not been given, and illegally, in the teeth of a law passed by Julius himself—extended the proconsular commands of the two consuls from two years to five, and then proceeded to bestow upon Marcus Antonius the right to exchange Macedonia, which the senate had apportioned to him, for the governorship of the Gauls, but at the same time allowing **Ma-noeuvres** him to keep the Macedonian legions under his command. . . . The object of this was not only to strengthen the military power of Marcus Antonius, but to supersede Decimus Brutus, who had taken possession of Cisalpine Gaul. . . . Brutus and Cassius also were put down for provinces: but it was not yet determined what they should have, and

they were temporarily put in charge of the corn-supply—
Brutus in Asia and Cassius in Sicily. This appointment gave
them the right to leave Italy, and it would also part them,
and diminish their resources and their dignity, if they accepted it. They at once asked Cicero to come to Antium,
and a serious conference was held at that place. None of
them had any very clear idea concerning what they ought
to do; but Cicero thought matters over during his journey
to Antium, and concluded that they would best safeguard
the principles they held by safeguarding the persons who
held them.

They formed a remarkable meeting at Antium, where,
perhaps, was assembled the real inner circle of the anti-
Caesarian conspiracy: Cicero, the doctrinaire political philosopher: Marcus Brutus, slow, solid and heavy: Servilia,
Brutus's mother, famous as the one-time mistress of Julius
and the sister of Cato: Tertulla, Cassius's wife: Porcia, the
wife of Brutus; and Favonius, who attained a peculiar immortality as "Cato's ape"—they represented the very quin-
tessence of that obstinate opposition which had fought
Julius living and Julius dead, and was to go on fighting his
spirit for many a year to come. Cicero, as the senior person
present, was expounding his views when the lean and hungry Cassius arrived with his keen eyes and decisive temper
—a man who only missed being a great man of action because he had no creative originality. Cicero repeated for
the benefit of Cassius all that he had just said—that he
thought they should consult their own safety and accept
the posts to which they had been appointed.

Cassius flashed into fire at this, and cried out that he
never would go to Sicily! Why should he accept a post
only offered him as an insult?

"Well, then," said Cicero, "what are you going to do?"

"I shall go to Athaia," returned Cassius, furiously. This

Meeting at Antium

was significant, because Cassius had no authority to go to Athaia. But they were all of them beginning to see that they were helpless unless they broke the limits of the law and struck out vigorously in self-defence. Yet if they did, what became of the principles they were pledged to uphold?

Cassius

"What about you, Brutus?" asked Cicero.

"I will go back to Rome if you want me to," [4] answered Brutus in his heavy way; but his words were a tacit rebuke to Cassius.

"I don't want you to," returned Cicero. "It would not be safe."

"If it were safe," said Brutus, "would you want me to?"

"Very much so," answered Cicero. "I would not have you go away at all, if it were safe to stay."

Some lengthy conversation followed, in which Cassius inveigled bitterly against Decimus Brutus because of the opportunities he had thrown away; and Cicero silently thought of the opportunity thrown away when Marcus Antonius was not slain at the same time as Julius. Cicero contended that it was no use talking—though he agreed with the remarks of Cassius. He had just begun a little dissertation of his own upon the theme of how much better they might have managed the senate, when Servilia brought him to a full stop by saying: "In fact, we ought to have taken over the state and run it ourselves. Is that what we intended to do?"

Servilia and Cicero

It was not; and Cicero recognized the difficulty. He was always slipping into Caesarism himself!

Finally Cassius began to veer towards the notion of going to Sicily, and Brutus quite decided that he would go to Asia. Servilia undertook, since they disliked the reference

[4] Go back to Rome—i. e., to hold the Apollinarian Games. This meeting was on June 26th, ten days before the Games were due to begin.

to the corn supply, to get it deleted from their commissions
—by what means, she did not divulge. Cicero went away
somewhat depressed.[5] Very evidently they were tied in a
knot. The only means by which they could effectively resist Caesarism were as illegal as Caesarism itself! "No plan!
No reason! No system!" he exclaimed to Atticus. Since he
had none himself, he could hardly blame the lack in
others!

But if they were going, he too would go. He determined
to travel in the east, and to return next year, when Hirtius
and Pansa were consuls; and with this aim, and a permit
from Dolabella, he set off.

Cicero drifted as far as Sicily: but adverse winds discouraged him. Detained at Lencopetra, at the southern
issue of the straits of Messina, he heard news that gave him
pause. There was prospect of a peaceable settlement between Marcus Antonius and Brutus and Cassius: and his
own presence in Rome was wanted. . . . Cicero did not Cicero dis-
really wish to go abroad. He loved one day of Rome better couraged
than a cycle of anywhere else. The wind seemed to be a
predestined adversity, and this news seemed to be a call to
him. . . . He made his way back to Pompeii. On his way
he met Brutus, who explained what had really happened.
Servilia had been as good as her word. She had caused the
reference to the corn-supply to be deleted from their commissions; and instead, he had received the province of
Crete, and Cassius had received Cyrene. But they were not
going thither. Their quarrel with Antony was worse, not
better. Brutus was going to Macedonia, and Cassius to Syria.
. . . In a word, the constricting tie had been snapped. It
was war!

[5] This dialogue is given in detail because it is one of the best attested
in all ancient history. Cicero himself reported it in *Letters to Atticus*,
XV, 11.

Perhaps they were right. Perhaps there was no place among the rough and tumble of camp overseas for an elderly statesman and scholar. His place was Rome. Brutus thought so too. If he went thither to his death, why, so did they all go to their deaths, and all that mattered was to find the suitable place to die. . . . So he and Brutus parted: and they never met again.

VI

Cicero arrived in Rome on the thirty-first of August. A remarkable change had come over him. He no longer wondered what he ought to do. He was going to do something —he knew what it was—and whether he ought to do it, or ought not, no longer much mattered. It is true that he was not planning to face hostile legions—but to some people hostile audiences are even more frightening, and Marcus Tullius Cicero could face these. He meant, if possible, to overcome them and to prevail; but if not, he would perish, as other men before him had perished—Tiberius and Gaius Gracchus, for instance, to name two men whom every Roman knew of. As we can see from the name which he half-humorously gave the speeches he delivered this autumn— **Philippics** "Philippics"—he was thinking of the parallel between his present position and that of Demosthenes, the greatest of Greek orators, the withstander of Philip of Macedon. The likeness was real. If anything, the position of Cicero was the more dangerous of the two.

There was a meeting of the senate next day—the first of September—but since the chief item on the agenda was the consideration of divine honours to Caesar, Cicero did not attend it. The object of the proposal was to sift the sheep from the grass, and to compel waverers and trimmers to commit themselves—which, of course, Cicero perfectly appreciated. Marcus Antonius, resenting his pointed and conspicuous absence, girded and held forth. On the second of September, Antony himself was absent: and now Cicero **The senate** stepped upon the stage. It was his own stage—as much his own as the battlefield and the polling-booth had been Caesar's, or the counting-house that of Crassus. He might be a silly old man among the clash of swords—but he was not a silly old man on the platform. He knew his business.

That sitting of the senate was a famous date—for on it Cicero delivered the speech which we know as the "First Philippic." It was a declaration of war.

There is just this serious difference between fighting a man with weapons and fighting him with words, that the weapons may kill, and then there is no more of the foe: but words only wound, and they are liable to irritate and incense the enemy to greater effort. Cicero could use words that stung like the lash of a whip—and it is probable that some of his phrases had effects on those who heard him which we are no longer able to trace or comprehend. Latin is a dead language to us; but when Cicero spoke, it was as alive and kicking as the speech of Paris or New York. Cicero had a purpose in adopting the tone he did. What Antony would think of it he knew beforehand: the peo- **The "First** ple he was speaking to were the waverers, the trimmers and **Phillipic"** the doubters, who would go where the hardest push shoved them. These were his audience, as they had been Antony's the day before.

He told them why he had tried to go abroad, and why he had returned. He described his parting with Brutus, and the sorrow with which he, Cicero, the unworthy, had returned to a city where Brutus, the saviour of his country, dare not set foot. He had come today to say some things which needed to be put on record in case some regrettable "accident" should stop his mouth. He then proceeded to blast the proceedings of the day before by a thunderbolt of rhetoric, and told them that he would never have consented to contaminate the state with so detestable a region —he called it detestable—blending the honour due to the divine powers with those due to a dead man. . . . His peroration was an appeal to them all to consider whether dictatorship was the road to true glory, and whether the respect and love of one's equals was not a far better thing than any triumph over them, and any power to oppress them.

The senators heard and trembled; but of what may have gone on in the back of their minds as they listened, Marcus Antonius was a good judge. He was obviously enraged at this speech, but quite as obviously frightened. He gave notice of a meeting of the senate, not the next day, but on the nineteenth of the month; and in the meantime he retired to his country villa to prepare a speech in reply. That he should require seventeen days for this task is an interesting illustration of how high he rated the verbal bomb which Cicero had thrown.

Antony's reply

The nineteenth of September came, and the senate—which by an extraordinary irony met in the temple of Concord!—was crowded. Marcus Antonius came with a strong bodyguard, but Cicero was not there. He had meant to go, and be a martyr if necessary; but as in the similar case of St. Paul, his friends clung to him and begged him not to go. Antony's speech, therefore, had to be addressed to a senate which did not contain the man whom he most wanted to be present. There was going to be a point in his speech at which the Caesarians who heard him would want a little conversation with Cicero.

As we have already seen, Marcus Antonius was no contemptible orator. He made excellent play; and he got home with effect when he read a letter which Cicero had addressed to him only a few months back, containing warm praise of the goodness, nobility and patriotism of its recipient. He used this letter to show that Cicero was not a straight and upright man, but a crawling serpent; and then, by a natural transition, he went on to charge Cicero not only with complicity in the murder of Caesar, but with being the prime mover in the conspiracy, the secret head of the oligarchs, who had inspired stupid but courageous men to do the work while himself avoiding responsibility. . . . And from what we know of Cicero's position in the matter, through his own admission and statements, this charge, whether true or false, must have been very effective. . . . It was just at this point that, if Cicero had been present in person, the trouble would have begun. But Cicero was absent, and the charges of Antonius petered out—as far as that day was concerned—in words alone.

Counter-charges

Matters now came rapidly to a head. Cicero retired again to Puteoli, where he proceeded to compose the even more famous "Second Philippic." This was not a public speech, but a pamphlet privately circulated among Cicero's friends, and passed about to any one who seemed to be a suitable object of propaganda. It was a personal attack upon Marcus Antonius of a sort which has always been traditional among South Europeans, but rather rarer in the North. In return for the portrait of the secret assassin which Antony had drawn, Cicero drew the portrait of the drunken and lecherous swine, wallowing in the mire of self-indulgence, blood and hatred. It was a very powerful picture, read with bated breath and rounded eyes by the favoured few, who treasured it as a jewel of Latinity. It culminated in what was practically an invitation to some noble patriot to treat Antony as Caesar had been treated.

Whether the Second Philippic reached Octavian we do not know, but it is certain that a very curious episode befell

What was the truth? about this time. Certain men, arrested in the very house of Marcus Antonius, were alleged to have confessed that they, had been suborned by Octavian to assassinate the consul. The case was never made perfectly clear. The friends of Octavian asserted that Antony had invented it for political purposes. Cicero, in a letter, gleefully recounted the episode, with the comment that Antonius, though ready to make the accusation, did not venture to make the facts public.[6] As for Antony, he roundly declared that that serpent Cicero was once more at his baleful work of instigating political murder.

This proved to be, for all practical purposes, the point of explosion. Antony determined without further delay to take over the four legions, at this time stationed in Macedonia, which Caesar had intended for the Parthian war. With these legions he had made up his mind, as soon as his consulship had expired, to displace Decimus Brutus in the rule of Cisalpine Gaul, where he could keep a watch both upon Rome itself and upon the provinces to east and west. His plan was, in fact, very much that which was carried out by the later Roman emperors who fixed their capital at Milan. But when Antonius arrived at Brundusium a very disagreeable surprise awaited him. Though, as consul, he **Antony** had been successful in repressing the claims of Octavian, **at Brun-** the latter had got ahead of him in the matter of secret **dusium** propaganda among the Caesarian veterans. Three out of the four legions had arrived, and they refused to serve under Antony. There was a very angry scene. Marcus Antonius knew how to enforce discipline, but the punishment

[6] Cicero's testimony is in *Letters to Friends*, XII, 23: *Philippics*, III, 7–8. Suetonius in *Divus Augustus*, X, repeats the charge without comment; Plutarch refers to it as if it were a rumour. Dr. Rice Holmes (*Architect of the Roman Empire*, I, p. 27) seems inclined to believe the charge. Appian (*Civil Wars*, III, 39) is probably right in pointing out that Antony was still necessary to Octavian.

he inflicted on the recalcitrant legions only deepened their hostility, even if it silenced it. Antony returned to Rome, leaving the legions to join him at Tibur in due course.

It was a very angry man who came back to Rome. Ever since the first Philippic things had begun to go against him. He determined to take strong measures. He convoked the senate for the twenty-fourth of October, and denounced Octavian as a Spartacus, and Cicero as the inspirer of his disgraceful deeds. The senate never met on the twenty-fourth. On that day the astounding news reached him that the Martial legion, one of the Macedonian legions, had left Tibur and marched to Alba, where it declared for Octavian. He rushed to Tibur, where he did his best to conciliate the troop that remained loyal. On the twenty-eighth he was back in Rome—only to hear that another legion, the Fourth, had gone to Alba to declare for Octavian. He hur- War ried over the postponed meeting of the senate and hastily left the city. Civil war had begun.

CHAPTER IV

THE TREMENDOUS CAMPAIGN AGAINST MARCUS ANTONIUS

I

Overtures

MEANWHILE, much had happened elsewhere. On the first of November Cicero had received a letter from Octavian. The young man wanted a secret interview with him. The explanation of his presence in Campania was simple. As soon as Marcus Antonius had gone to Brundusium to meet the Macedonian legions, Octavian, fully informed by his secret service of all that was impending, set out to gather his own supporters. He had at this moment two legions of veteran Caesarians whom he had collected at Casilinum and Calatia, on the road from Brundusium to Rome. They were not organized, and they were not systematically armed, but they were experienced men. Cicero was much too prudent to agree to a secret meeting, which could not really be kept secret, and might fatally compromise him among his political friends. But the mere request was enough to explain everything. What should he do now?

"Octavian" was in reality a committee of certain Caesarian chiefs with whom Cicero had already been in friendly communication. It numbered five members, including Octavian himself, the legal representative of Caesar, Aulus Hirtius, C. Vibius Pansa and L. Cornelius Balbus.[1] Young

The prospects

as Octavian might be, the other three were men of mature age, established repute and wide experience, and their ad-

---

[1] *Letters to Atticus*, XIV, 21 and XV, 2: but Cicero only mentions Hirtius by name, and who the others were we are left to guess.

64

vice was probably as good as could anywhere be got. Hirtius and Pansa, moreover, were the consuls designate for the coming year. In two months' time, Marcus Antonius and Publius Cornelius Dolabella would cease to be the legal heads of the Roman state, and Hirtius and Pansa would step into their shoes.

Cicero was in a difficult position. The soldiers and men of action who belonged to his party had proved but broken reeds, and were dispersed in distant provinces. He himself, a civilian and a man of peace, was left to bear the brunt of a context which he could not carry on without allies. He saw that Octavian might be the predestined weapon with which the *optimates* could strike down the menace of Marcus Antonius. If they were to take Octavian under their wing, see that he obtained Caesar's legacy and succession, and enable him to overthrow Antonius, they might find it possible to suppress the boy afterwards and recover power themselves. At any rate, the opportunity was the best that presented itself; and if there were risks, these were no greater (and perhaps were rather less) than those involved in any other course. And (happiest thought of all, possibly, from Cicero's point of view!) instead of Brutus and Cassius running off with all the credit, he, Cicero, would be the great statesman who had engineered that master-stroke!

He did not jump to conclusions all at once. A month passed in consideration. It was very necessary for Octavian to obtain some sort of legal authority for the troops he was raising—and he must already have known that the two Macedonian legions would declare for him before many days were past. At present neither he nor his friends had the remotest right to possess any armed forces under their control. Hence he did not hesitate to make promises that certainly were bold, and possibly were incapable of fulfilment.

Nego-
tiations

. . . But it was not Octavian himself, but his agent, Oppius, who was actually responsible for making these promises. Cicero plainly told Oppius that a friendly attitude
towards himself, Cicero, was insufficient; Octavian must
include Brutus and Cassius in the alliance. Oppius said that
he would. Cicero replied that since they had until the first
of January to see what would happen, he would leave the
matter there.

But he had made up his mind, and the rapid course of
events confirmed it. Both he and Octavian needed one another, and neither of them looked too closely at the terms
of the verbal agreement between them. They could argue
about them afterwards. Octavian sent his volunteers home
to fetch their military equipments. He was raising more
men in Etruria. Early in December Cicero was at Arpinum.
His last written words to his friend Atticus were: "I am
coming." And on the ninth of December he entered Rome.

Cicero
goes to
Rome Dec.
44 B. C.

It was high time that he acted, for Antony had advanced
into Cisalpine Gaul. Moving northwest along the Great
Aemilian highway, he came to Mutina, which stands almost
in the centre of northern Italy, commanding the roads to
the crossings of the Padus at Placentia and Hostilia. Called
upon to give way to the nominee of the Assembly, Decimus
Brutus flatly refused, and produced the senate's commission. The siege of Mutina therefore was formed, and the
civil war began. Octavian sent word to Decimus Brutus to
hold out, as help was coming.

On the fifteenth of December the tribunes for the new
year took up office. Among them Casca, one of the assassins,
had been nominated, and Cicero was merely waiting to see
whether the undertakings made by Oppius would be implemented. All went off well. Casca was accepted without
demur by the Caesarians, who no doubt reflected that, after
all, the appointment was Caesar's own. The new tribunes,

in the absence of any superior magistrate, convoked the senate for the twentieth of December. The principal motion on the agenda was to consider the condition of the state. After preliminary business had been disposed of, Cicero rose, and delivered the speech known as the "Third Philippic." He pointed out the peril of the state, urged the need for prompt measures, referred to the patriotic action of Octavian in placing his resources at the disposal of the republic, and proposed a motion giving the new consuls full power of action as soon as they entered upon office on the first of January, and taking Octavian and his men under the authority of the state. So proposed, there was no question of the result. The motion was at once passed by the senate. Cicero immediately went down to the Forum, and there addressed the people, saying pretty much what he had said in the senate. There was no dissent; and in this manner a very strange result was produced—the Caesarians, by common agreement, returned to power and controlled the government, and yet Marcus Antonius, who a few months before had seemed without a rival, became a rebel and a fugitive pursued by the legal forces of the state.

"Third Philippic"

II

The siege of Mutina was not quite so famous as the Siege of Troy: but in magnitude, in desperation and in historical importance it was not undeserving of a Homer. Taking place in a more civilized and enlightened age it had, instead, a Cicero.

The first step of the coalition at Rome was to attempt to raise the siege. While there was substantial unity in the aim of repressing Antony, there were considerable divergencies in the tone and temper in which the various parties pursued this laudable aim. Prompt upon its meeting on the

first day of January, the opening of the official year, the
senate proceeded to consider the State of the Republic—
a motion which allowed a general debate or policy. The
new consuls, Hirtius and Pansa, gave their definite undertaking to suppress illegal rebellion and to ensure public
tranquillity. . . . They were expected to commit themselves against Antony to this extent. . . . When they
called upon the senior consular—who chanced to be Q.
Fufius Calenus, a Caesarian—to open the debate, the first
sign of trouble began. Calenus, though a Caesarian, was
an Antonian, and he took the definite line that before proceeding to hostilities with Antony, they should send him
a warning and give him the opportunity of coming to a
peaceable accommodation. This seemed to appeal to many
senators who were anxious for peace, for it was supported
by many subsequent speakers. It was passionately attacked
by Cicero, who denounced it as foolish, useless and dis-
honourable, and who urged the senate to use force to the
uttermost. Cicero spoke, not only as the leader of the *optimates*, the old oligarchic party, but also as the representative of Octavius and his policy. The two concurred in one
common object—the defeat of the armed power of Antony: and to this aim Cicero directed the whole of his
power. His "Fifth Philippic" contended at length for the
policy of Octavius.

    Cicero began by asserting the principles that a govern-
ment could not negotiate with rebels who bore arms in their
hands. He then went on to draw a lurid picture of the rav-
ening wolf who at that very moment was besieging an
Italian city he had no right to besiege with an army he had
no right to possess. He assembled all the new evidence he
had been able to find to prove the violence, the treachery,
the treason of this public enemy; the deliberate and malig-
nant wickedness of his intentions, the disregard for the laws

of God and man that he showed. To negotiate with a man like this was to go against all the tradition of the Roman republic. He would merely laugh at them; while it would check the zeal and damp the ardour of all the patriotic citizens who were now throwing themselves into the sacred cause of their fatherland. No; there should be no negotiation; instead, the whole republic should stop the works of peace and mobilize itself upon a war basis, until the danger was crushed. The Emergency Decree should be passed, and an offer of pardon made to all men of Antony's army who surrendered before the first day of February.

He then went on to propose definite measures for regularizing and linking up the forces against Antony: first, a definite establishment of the status of the faithful Decimus Brutus; second, a motion in honour of Lepidus, who was a waverer, but might be won over; third (and here he got to the serious part of these proposals), that Gaius Caesar, son of Gaius Caesar, be created a senator with the rank of a propraetor; last of all, he proposed that all the veteran troops who had supported the cause of the senate should receive allotments of land in Campania or elsewhere, and should be paid whatsoever sums of money Gaius Caesar (that is to say, Octavian) had promised them when they declared for his service.

For five days the struggle raged in a crowded house. The consuls were inclined to side with Calenus. It was pointed out that Marcus Antonius had legal right on his side, and that the act of the senate, granting Cisalpine Gaul to Decimus Brutus, had been superseded by the act of the Assembly, transferring it to Antony. Why, then, should Antony be condemned for enforcing a legally justifiable claim? It was unreasonable! The force of such contentions brought about a compromise, in which the influence of Cicero and his supporters was narrowly preponderant. Although the

Case for Antonius

form of sending an embassy was approved, it was not em-
powered to negotiate. It was authorized to deliver an ultimatum demanding the submission of Antonius to the lawful
government. On the other hand, Octavian was given his
pro-praetorian rank and an undertaking to make good the
promises he had made to his troops. . . . It was these last
that constituted the really important business—as Cicero
himself perfectly realized—for Antony was not in the least
likely to take the embassy seriously, and the whole struggle
now hinged on the military power with which Octavian
could confront him.

Views of Octavian

The young Octavian seems to have accepted the help of
Cicero and to have remained very little impressed by his
sincerity. He believed that Cicero and the *optimates* were
merely utilizing him as a convenient tool, to be cast aside
when he had served his purpose.[2] . . . And it would be
very difficult to show that he was mistaken.

III

Although, since the days of Julius, the proceedings of
the senate had been regularly made public, this five-days'
debate far outstripped the resources of the news-service
Julius had instituted, and a large number of Roman citizens
camped in the Forum while it was in progress. As soon as

Public interest

the vote had been taken, and the decisions were known,
Cicero hurried out into the Forum, where the tribune Ap-
puleius introduced him into the rostra. Here he explained
to the crowded assembly what had taken place, the arguments he had used, and the reasons he had for his policy.
The assembly listened attentively to his report, and evidently took a favourable view of what he had done. It was
almost impossible for a man of Cicero's temperament not to

[2] Appian, *Civil Wars*, III, 48, 64.

assume at once that this approval was given to his own views and policy. If he had been a little wiser, he might have suspected that it was given to his support of Octavian.

The embassy went to Mutina; and its fate was very much what Cicero had foreseen. It handed in the ultimatum without comment. Antony scowled, swore, fumed, and refused to let it communicate with Decimus Brutus. As for the ultimatum, he had not the least use for it. He was particularly outspoken on the subject of Cicero—a man (he observed) who, having been spared by Caesar, sided with Caesar's murderers; having detested Decimus Brutus, was **The** all for him: and who, having made a tremendous fuss about **embassy** **futile** the tyranny of Caesar, was now backing the magistrates nominated by Caesar against him, Antony, who had been given Gaul by the constitutional action of the Assembly. Finally he presented the embassy with his own conditions —which included the recall of Brutus and Cassius, the confirmation of the actions of himself and Dolabella during their consulship, and (for himself) the governorship of Transalpine Gaul for five years, with the right to maintain an army of six legions. . . . The senate replied by passing the Emergency Decree, declaring Antony a public enemy, and laying the same outlawry upon all the troops who followed him, unless they submitted to the legal government.

In the meantime, Octavian had pressed on his way, leaving the political front to be held by Cicero. Two days after Cicero had reported to the Assembly the legalization of Octavian and his army, they were at Spoletium on their march north. The consul, Aulus Hirtius, commanded the two legions which had come from Macedonia. Octavian took charge of the two legions of volunteer Caesarian veterans whom he had brought from Campania, together with a legion of green troops newly levied for the first time. As far as numbers were concerned, Antony had the advantage of possessing six legions to their five; but four of theirs, as against three of his, were of fully trained troops. Since Antony himself, by general consent, was much the best soldier, Hirtius and Octavian resolved to wait for Pansa before they fought a decisive battle. The second consul was engaged in raising new troops in central Italy, and as soon as he arrived they would have a definite preponderance in numbers. In the meantime, Hirtius and Octavian kept in close touch with Antony's besieging army; there were cavalry skirmishes almost every day, and the besiegers, if not themselves besieged, were at any rate kept under constant surveillance, and their every move was known.

Hirtius and Octavian

Hirtius, if not a brilliant, was a sound and reliable commander who could be trusted to do his work well. For long afterwards stories were told of the ingenious methods by which Hirtius kept up communication with the besieged garrison, and the various expedients by which he got messages through to Decimus Brutus. For some time he succeeded in sending letters written on lead tablets (which would not be injured by water, and which would sink to the bottom if thrown away) by means of divers. The engineers of Marcus Antonius, however, at last managed to stop this method by nets and traps: after which Hirtius resorted to the use of carrier pigeons. Decimus Brutus, when he first shut himself into Mutina, killed all his horses and oxen and settled down to hold out to the last. The garrison, though it successfully held the town, was a lean and hungry garrison by the time Pansa, on the nineteenth of March, set out from Rome with four legions of recruits.

The civil war was as much a war of the pen and the spoken word as of the sword and the soldier. While all these events were happening, the various parties were hard at work doing their best to convert their opponents or to

MARCUS ANTONIUS
the husband of Octavia
(*From a coin in the British Museum*)

OCTAVIA
when the wife of Antony
(*From the same coin*)

divide them from one another. We still possess among the letters of Cicero the correspondence that passed between him and Lepidus, Plancus and Asinius Pollia. The position of these three important members of the Caesarian party was obscure and ambiguous, and they did nothing to clear it up. If anything, they seemed to shrink back into the shadows, until they saw a little more clearly how the struggle between Marcus Antonius and young Octavian would go. To them (if not to Cicero) it was obvious that the Civil War in Italy was merely a struggle for the leadership of the party. . . . We have, too, embodied in Cicero's *Philippics*, a letter that Marcus Antonius wrote to Hirtius and Octavius. It is an excellent example of Antony's vigorous and aggressive style. It "told off" the two with great effect, reproached them with their friendship with murderers, and warned them that their policy was reviving the strength of the Pompeian party. . . . Hirtius and Octavius evidently read the letter with attention, and quite as evidently remained calm under the influence of its rhetoric. If anyone was to step off, they intended it to be Antony. With a perspicacity which we may attribute to Octavian rather than to Hirtius, the two recipients at once sent the missive on to Cicero, who perused it with great wrath, and read out parts of it to an assembly in the Forum, with comments of his own. . . . It is probable that Antony's artfulness wrought more results upon Cicero and the fellow-citizens than upon Hirtius and Octavian, and that the latter were perfectly satisfied that Cicero—and the fellow citizens —should be reminded of a few home truths which Hirtius and Octavian could not, with tactfulness, repeat on their own account.

Unable to move them by words, Antonius made up his mind to strike very suddenly just before Pansa could join his friends. Pansa's troops were green—and Antony realized

The Caesarian party chiefs

Antony's letter

that they were the weak spot in the army of relief: the weak spot to aim at.[3]

IV

But Hirtius also had learnt the art of war in the company of Julius, and, foreseeing the possibility of an attack upon Pansa just before he arrived, he despatched a trained legion, the Martial, with two praetorian cohorts, to meet the newcomers. They were approaching up the great Aemilian road when Antony, on the fourteenth of April, detached two trained legions (the 2nd and 35th), two praetorian cohorts,

Approach of Pansa

and a detachment of the highly trained volunteer veterans known as "Evocati." This very powerful force, with a strong body of cavalry, was intended to catch Pansa and his men just as they emerged from a difficult bit of road southeast of Forum Gallorum.[4] Here the road ran between two marshes, so that the available passage was constricted to a narrow front. Through this strait Pansa's army was bound to come; and at Forum Gallorum, just beyond its point of issue, the Antonians waited, well-concealed from observers on the road.

The surprise would probably have been perfectly successful had they been dealing, as they thought, with green troops; but the Martial legion was not so easily hoodwinked. Pansa made the march by night, and at daybreak the advanced parties noticed agitation in the reeds of the marshes, and an occasional gleam of armour; and then Antony's cavalry and light troops were espied. Seeing that

---

[3] The events of the siege of Mutina impressed all who witnessed them with the extraordinary difference between trained and untrained troops. See Mr. Strachan-Davidson, *Cicero*, pp. 412–416, quoting *Letters to Friends*, X, 30; X, 11; X, 24; XI, 14; *Philippics*, X, 7 and 9; XIII, 6, 13— to which may be added *Tusculan Disputations*, II, XVI, 37–38, and Appian, *Civil Wars*, III, 69.

[4] Castel Franco on the modern map.

they had no choice but to fight their way through, the Martial legion made a run forward and drove in the light troops. Almost at once the screen was broken, and the Martials found themselves confronting the legionary infantry who had been concealed in Forum Gallorum, with Antony's own praetorian cohort occupying the road. Lending word to the new levies, if they came up, to keep out of the struggle, as they would only get in the way, the Martials deployed on each hand, leaving Octavian's praetorian cohort to face that of Antony on the road. Then followed one of those battles which were fought only when Romans met Romans. The Antonians could not for a moment risk the damage to their reputation that would certainly follow if they allowed one legion to defeat their two; while the Martials went into the fight determined to gain the distinction of having beaten two legions with their one. At first the right wing of the Martials under Carfulenus drove the enemy before them, but had to retire again before the threat of the cavalry, which Antony ordered to come round to the rescue. The left wing of the Martials under Pansa fared less well. It was gradually forced back, Pansa himself was dangerously wounded by a javelin, and was carried off the field to Bononia. This retreat of the wing left the praetorian cohort of Octavius unprotected, and it was very badly mauled. The Martials retreated in good order towards the camp, which the quaestor Torquatus all this time had been toiling to prepare. The new levies took refuge in it, so the Martians, disdaining to show the white feather, took ground outside. They were exhausted and badly knocked about, but still full of fight.

The day was now somewhat late, and Antony decided to give the Martials a rest, while he had a try at the green troops. His attempt to storm the camp was not successful, and as he lost many men, he decided to withdraw. The

Forum Gallorum

Arrival of Hirtius

victorious army prepared to return home. As it marched back by the road, singing hymns of triumph, sudden and irretrievable disaster fell upon it. Hirtius had received word of the battle and had set out at once with two legions of his best troops. They arrived at this critical juncture, without any warning of their approach. The Antonians, in very loose order and wearied with their exertions, formed front and fought with great gallantry; but they had been taken by surprise by perfectly fresh troops, and their punishment was heavy. Night fell and forced an end to the battle. Hirtius was too prudent to risk a pursuit amid the marshes, and in the darkness Antony managed to get the remnants of his army away, together with many of his casualties. The cavalry packed the wounded men on their horses, or took them up behind them; and the walking cases were brought home in the dark, holding on to the tails. But in spite of all he could do, Antony left half his men in the marshes of Forum Gallorum, and his retreat to Mutina was that of a beaten general. Two eagles and sixty standards fell into the hands of Hirtius.

V

The battle of Forum Gallorum entirely changed the condition of affairs. Antony, no longer master of the situation, was now obliged to act upon the defensive. It was still possible for him to starve Mutina into surrender by a blockade, and if he could achieve this, he might even yet retrieve the prestige he had lost. Hirtius accordingly made up his mind to take the offensive and break the blockade by a pitched battle.

Battle of Mutina

Six days passed in the preparations necessary for this purpose. As the siege-works on the southeasterly side of Mutina were too strong, Hirtius decided to move right round the town to the northwesterly side, where they were much weaker. Antony still declined action, but followed with his cavalry. Hirtius was now adequately supplied with this arm, for he held off the Antonian cavalry with his own, while he kept on his march with the legionary troops. Realizing that he could not affect the movements of Hirtius with cavalry alone, Antony called out two legions. Hirtius instantly accepted battle.

Marcus Antonius was an experienced soldier, and if he was outmanoeuvred now, it is probable that no one else in his place, would have done much better. Hirtius threw the whole of his army upon the two legions. Antony's call upon his supports was made too late. They were unable to arrive in time, and Hirtius defeated his opponents piecemeal. Up to the very last stage of the battle Hirtius carried all before him. He drove Antony right back upon his fortified camp, stormed it, and burst in. A short distance from Antony's tent, Hirtius was struck down. But Octavian was at hand, and the reserves he led held on to the camp, and drove the Antonians out. According to the tradition, Octavian himself was the first person to pick up the body of Hirtius. That night, the twenty-first of April in the year 43, Marcus Antonius and the wreck of his army were in flight towards the Padus. Death of both consuls

Pansa died at Bononia the next day, seven days after he had received his wound at the battle of Forum Gallorum.

If the battle of Forum Gallorum had changed the situation, the battle of Mutina revolutionized it. The siege was raised, and Decimus Brutus was rescued. But the rescue of Decimus Brutus was a trifle compared with the momentous issues raised by the deaths of Hirtius and Pansa. The two consuls, the heads of the Roman state, were dead; and the armies they had commanded were now in the hands of a young man of nineteen, an honorary propraetor who had never held office, and whose sole claim to this remarkable eminence was that he was the heir of Caesar.

Few men ever rise to eminence without the help of fortune: and those who rise to the highest eminence of all usually owe it to a fortune as startling and rare as their success. We need not, therefore, be surprised to find the future Augustus a lucky man. Many men at the time, who knew him as nothing more than an uninspiring youth of nineteen, could not bring themselves to believe that the deaths of Hirtius and Pansa were natural. The luck seemed too good to be true. Why should they both have died at a moment so very noticeably convenient for Octavian? It **Suspicion** was whispered that Hirtius had been killed by his own sol- **aroused** diers—inspired by whom? The physician who attended Pansa was actually arrested upon suspicion of having hastened the consul's death by his treatment. . . . But when it came to the point, no one seemed to possess any convincing evidence of foul play; and two thousand years afterwards, the perspective of time reveals nothing to support the idea. Marcus Brutus intervened on behalf of the physician Glyco, whom he gave the highest moral character: and in fact, the whole idea that there was anything suspicious about the consuls' deaths rests solely upon the remarkable advantage so secured to Octavian, and of real evidence to support the suspicions there never existed one jot.

Perhaps even the supposed advantage to Octavian was a fancy in the minds of onlookers rather than a reality. At the age of nineteen it is impossible for any man to command armies and decide policies without the help of older men. When fifty years of labour and success had made the genius of Augustus unmistakeable, it was still unmistakeably not the sort of genius that enables very young men to do wondrous deeds of romantic prowess: it was always the sort of genius that gathers around itself other men of ability, and helps them to work together profitably for a common aim. The young Octavian needed the help of such men as Hirtius and Pansa; he could have trusted them with his interests, and relied upon their faithfulness to his cause. So far from their deaths being an advantage, he was robbed of two sound and capable advisers who were experts in an art at which he himself was never particularly good, and he was thrown into a prominence he can hardly have enjoyed. He was thrust into the forefront of things in a way far from being pleasant or convenient to himself. *Groundlessness of suspicion*

The remarkable thing is that he accepted the position so thrust upon him with calm adequacy. He still had advisers left, and the isolation in which he now stood attracted the interest of the stalwart Caesarian veterans he led. Their zeal in his cause was redoubled by a certain touch of paternal feeling towards him. The Caesarian chiefs in Gaul and Spain, who had been intently watching the context at Mutina, began to see their way a little clearer. They were not prepared to see Antony altogether cast down; but they realized that he was not destined to be the future leader of the party. The battles outside Mutina had at any rate established the power and importance of Octavian.

VI

Meanwhile, Marcus Antonius collected the remnant of his beaten army, and without hesitation took the road north westward across Italy. He still had one complete unbroken legion in fresh condition, and a very strong force of cavalry with which to protect the unarmed men whom he had gathered to their standards again after their defeat. With these he set out to get in touch with the Caesarian chiefs in Gaul and Spain. *Retreat of Antony*

It is difficult to say what might have happened to Antony's broken forces, had a man like Hirtius been still in command of the relieving army, and able and willing to pursue. But Hirtius was dead; and Decimus Brutus, after three months of starvation, and without cattle or horses, was in no condition to undertake such a task; and it became fairly clear that Octavian did not intend to undertake it. Octavian had other things to think of.

Octavian had fulfilled to the letter all the undertakings he had given. The most sanguine optimist could hardly have foreseen that within four months, he would have broken the military power of Antony, driven him a fugitive towards the frontiers of Gaul, and succeeded to the command of the relieving army at Mutina. Quite clearly, some re-arrangement of every one's views and attitude was called for. Had his success been pure chance? Had it been due to deep and unscrupulous treachery? Or was Octavian a man of supreme genius? . . . There was a fourth possibility—that Octavian was being carried forward like a straw upon the mighty current of the dead Caesar's will and plans. The importance of these questions lay in the likelihood that on the answers made to them depended the policy of the various parties; and on these policies the prospect of civil war, civil peace, the future of the state, the lives and deaths of thousands of men, the happiness or misery of many more thousands of their dependents.

The letters of Decimus Brutus to Cicero reveal to us the powerful under-currents which were now drawing Octavian away from his alliance with Cicero. Decimus wrote to explain his difficulties and the reasons why he could not overtake and hold Antony. He had plenty of troops; but they were exhausted, and in any case they were untrained men; and he lacked money and equipment. He wanted the Fourth and the Martial legions, which had been under

Position of
Octavian

Hirtius. Cicero wrote back deploring the delay, and explaining that the failure to complete the defeat of Antony had completely destroyed the hopes he had raised by his speeches. So great was the disappointment among the *optimates*, that Cicero's influence had received a check, and he was no longer confident of his power to sway the senate. The money that Decimus wanted would be forthcoming; but Cicero warned Decimus that every one who knew the mind of the troops had assured him that the two legions concerned—the Fourth and the Martial—would never consent to serve under him. His letter closed on a despondent note. He hoped the news was true that the Caesarian chiefs in Gaul and Spain did not intend to receive Antony; but he was ready to face the very serious fact that they might do so.

If Cicero envisaged the possibility of such an event, it is clear that he must have been anticipating the worst.

Decimus, who was in close touch with Octavian, warned Cicero that mischief was being made. Octavian had actually related to Decimus the very damaging story that had been repeated to him, to the effect that Cicero had remarked: "Laudandum adolescentem, ornandum, tollendum"—a very wicked pun, which hinted that Octavian was going to get what is nowadays known as an "Irishman's rise." Not only had Octavian heard this story—the identity of the man who carried it to him was known—but he evidently believed it. In his cold, restrained way, it was the only thing adverse to Cicero that he told Decimus: but it was obviously an index to many other unspoken thoughts.

Cicero's indiscretion

The truth was, that Cicero had been attempting an impossible task, and Octavian did not completely accept the sincerity of the man who had undertaken it. During these four months, news had reached him which had seriously affected his thoughts. While Cicero was arming him and his allies to strike down Marcus Antonius, Cicero had also been hard at work arming and encouraging Cassius and Marcus Brutus to establish their position in the east. Dolabella had been killed. Cassius was, with the approval of the senate, gathering a great army in Syria. Brutus had been equally successful in Macedonia. In the face of these facts

Divergence of interests Octavian, however young he might be, was not foolish enough to believe that he was being supported or loved for his own sake. It was obvious even to a lad of nineteen that he was being used as a catspaw, and that when he had overthrown Antony, he and his friends would stand very little chance before these great armies of Brutus and Cassius. His obvious course was to open negotiations with Antony.[5]

Throughout the early summer, letters were passing, not only between Plancus, Lepidus and Asinius Pollio and Cicero, but also between the Caesarian chiefs and Octavian. The latter pointed out to them the risk that they might be eaten up piecemeal, and suggested that while they should continue to present perfectly straight faces to the world at large, they should discuss among themselves the whole problem of their joint action. He pointed to the admirable unity of the rank and file of the Caesarians, who kept their organization intact even in civil life. . . . Besides writing to the leaders of the party, Octavian cultivated the friendship of both officers and men. Decius, one of Antony's officers, who was captured at Mutina and subsequently set free, ventured to ask in parting if he might give Antony any account of the feelings of Octavian. With a characteristic touch of the Delphian, Octavian replied that he had

[5] There is a story (Appian, *Civil Wars*, III, 75) that Pansa had an interview with Octavian before his death, and laid all these considerations before him. Historians have never quite accepted the genuineness of this interview, and there are certainly difficulties in the way of believing it: but all that Pansa is represented as saying was very obviously true.

given plenty of indications for the benefit of wise men, and fools would be better off if he repeated them.

The result of all this was a distinct but secret rapprochement among all the Caesarian leaders. Antony, making good his escape, reached the coast road beyond Genoa, and by easy marches attained Forum Julii (Frejus) at the mouth of the river Argentaeus. Here Lepidus met him, and the two joined forces. According to the despatch which Lepidus sent next day to the senate, his actions had been forced upon him by his army, which insisted upon his obeying the commands of compassion and humanity. He ended his letter with the significant remark that the senate would consult its own interests by showing a similar spirit.

Antony in safety

At Forum Julii Antony had an opportunity to retire, for the time being, into private life, and to consider the state of his soul and the prospects of the future.

VII

Before Octavian and Cicero broke away from one another and dissolved the strange alliance that had had such historic results, they had one more transaction together. Octavian had watched the retreat of Marcus Antonius, and the action of Lepidus, without in any way betraying his own intention. As long as he could be kept neutral, it was in Cicero's interest to keep him so; and for a long time Cicero half believed that he was succeeding in this object— with the result that he still kept up the attempt to succeed. But it is quite evident, from the trend of events, that no sooner was Octavian convinced that Lepidus and his colleagues both intended to save Antony and at the same time were disposed to recognize his own claims as Caesar's heir, than he saw the necessity of securing a more substantial rank than he yet possessed. He could not achieve what he

Octavian's plans

wanted, if he remained merely an honorary propraetor with four legions under his control, hesitating around Mutina. He had confronted Lepidus and Antony with a great accomplished fact, and they had bowed to the fact. He must confront them with another—and he thought they would bow to that too.

Now, the opening he needed lay before him glaring and unmistakeable. The moment it was known that Hirtius and Pansa were dead, the thoughts of all statesmen had turned to consider the great problem of their successors. Not only was the consulship necessary to him because it would enable him to claim the headship of the united Caesarian party, but it was necessary even to his personal safety. The senate, no longer afraid of Antony, was anxious to undermine his position and detach his troops from his control. Brutus and Cassius were being urged to bring their armies to Italy, and two legions were being hastily sent for from Africa, to defend Rome. Octavian, therefore, was obliged to grasp at office by one means, if he could not by another. Having reached the position he was in, he could not go back. He must go forward.

Octavian had now begun to realize the possibilities of the army he commanded, and the technique of its management. It differed fundamentally from the modern armies with which we are familiar, in that it had a vivid consciousness of its own corporate existence and of its collective interests and wishes, and was fully prepared to pursue these interests and wishes. Octavian first showed that he had mastered the peculiar art of gaining the support of the army when at this juncture he assembled his legions and addressed them.

The army

He described to them the hostility shown him by the senate, and the indignities imposed upon him; its anxiety to destroy the friends and allies of Caesar, and its continual attempts to transfer the legions of Caesarian veterans to the command of generals opposed to them in political opinions. The senate, he reminded them, was still under the control of the men who had murdered Caesar, and it wished for nothing so much as to divide the Caesarian veterans and to see them destroy one another. What confidence could he, Octavian, have in his own safety, or the men before him in the safety of their land-pensions, while the kinsmen and friends of the murderers dominated the senate? There was only one path of safety for him and them—and that was for him to secure the consulship. If he could do this, he would see to it that all the rewards due to them were paid in full, and he would also make sure that the murderers of Caesar were punished, and peace restored throughout the Roman dominions.

This was just the programme that appealed to the legionaries, and they accepted it with enthusiasm. The moment it was mooted, its realization became a point of honour with them. A deputation of centurions soon appeared at Rome to lay its request before the senate. The astonished senate answered that the proposed candidate was extremely young. As he was nineteen, and the legal age was forty-three, there was substance in this objection; but the deputation had been primed with arguments, and replied by quoting the case of Corvinus, and two Scipios, both of whom had held office before the legal time—and, of course, Pompeius and Dolabella. The senate was by no means convinced, and some of the senators went so far as to rebuke the deputation for its presumption in wrangling with the Fathers over such a subject. The spokesman Cornelius, a centurion, thereupon touched the hilt of his sword, and answered: "This shall do it, if you will not." The soldiers were in earnest. They had no intention of accepting more refusals from persons who could not make these refusals

The army accepts Octavian's programme

good. Still the senate could not make up its mind. Its only chance was to give way and seek to recover its authority afterwards: but it would not. It challenged a decision on the one particular ground on which it was certain to be beaten.

The deputation accordingly withdrew, and carried its report back to the camp, where it was heard with deep indignation. A general demand at once arose for a march upon Rome. The veterans—all of them, it is to be recollected, citizens and electors—said that they would conduct a special election and elect Octavianus on the sole qualification of being Caesar's son. Octavian, striking while the iron was hot, immediately issued the orders, and the whole army got ready for the road—eight legions, with their cavalry divisions and auxiliaries. Leaving the main body to follow at the regulation pace, Octavian set out on a rapid march with a picked corps, in order to reach Rome as soon as possible.

March on Rome

There was a panic in Rome when the news of his approach reached the city. Many people fled, and there was violent recrimination among the senators. A motion was hastily passed granting all the demands of the army, and giving a special permission for Octavian to stand for the consulship during his absence. No sooner had the message to this effect been sent off, than the two legions from Africa landed, and a great revulsion of feeling took place. The senate suddenly began to repent of its haste. The revered Fathers recollected their dignity and the majesty of Rome. Volunteers from the wealthier classes proceeded to picket the principal military positions of the city, and the decrees that had just been passed were revoked. An attempt was even made to discover the whereabouts of Octavian's mother, Atia, and his sister, Octavia, with the object of holding them as hostages. Fortunately, they could not be found.

The messengers carrying the first decree had met Octavian upon the road and were communicating to him the decision of the senate when the second set of messengers arrived to announce that the decisions had been revoked. The indignant Octavian, hearing with alarm that his mother *Entry into* and sister were in peril, pressed on his way. He sent on *Rome* horsemen to assure the general population of Rome that there was nothing for them, at any rate, to fear. When he reached Rome he was received with friendliness and even with enthusiasm. Large crowds cheered him and his troops; his mother and sister (who had sought refuge in the Temple of Vesta with the Vestal Virgins) met him and embraced him; and the newly arrived legions from Africa, instead of dying in defence of the senate, went over in a body to Octavian. There could be no doubt where he stood in popular estimation. The heir of Julius was the idol of the man in the street. The senate made one last attempt to raise the city in arms. Headed by Cicero, the Fathers met at night to witness the result of their call. As nobody rose, they gave in. . . . Octavian, somewhat amused, retired without the walls while the election of consuls duly took place. There could be very little doubt concerning the result.

VIII

On the nineteenth day of the month Sextilis, in the year *Octavian* 43, he was elected consul in company with his cousin, *consul* Quintus Pedius. So two grand-nephews of Julius Caesar presided over the Roman state. . . . And if Octavian had not been made consul in that month, we might be calling it

"Sextilis" still: for when, years afterwards, he had burst his chrysalis and became Augustus, he remembered that Sextilis had been a lucky month for him: so he renamed it "August," a name which we still keep.[6]

Thus, seventeen months after the death of Caesar, this boy of nineteen, who had left Apollonia with nothing but his ability and his expectations, had succeeded to the heritage of Julius, had swept Marcus Antonius out of his path, and had set himself down in the curule chair as one of the supreme magistrates of the Roman state. It was a remarkable feat to have performed. But it was the beginning, not the end of his career. He had aimed at and seized this dignity not as the consummation of all his hopes, but merely as something to bargain with. He had four months before him. On the last day of December his consulship would end. During that four months he had to come to an arrangement with the other Caesarian chiefs.

None of them—neither Octavian nor Antonius nor Lepidus nor Plancus nor Asinius Pollio—were despots who could impose their desires upon unwilling subjects. All of them were restricted and compelled by the public opinion of their troop—an opinion often very clear and very emphatic, and necessary to be obeyed. And in the present circumstances, however much the leaders might look upon one another with doubt and apprehension, the troops were perfectly plain about their expectation—nay, their demand —that the leaders, in the general interest of the party, should come to a definite agreement together. The rank and file had a most serious stake in the result. If the armies of Brutus and Cassius should be victorious, then goodbye for ever to the land-pensions—those little estates to which they hoped to return when their service was over. And they had no intention of losing these.

Next step

[6] Suetonius, *Divus Augustus,* XXVI and XXXI.

The consulship of Octavian was expected to be a step in the process of punishing the murderers of Caesar, confirming the land grants, and enforcing a general peace and security throughout the Roman dominion, in which the demobilized veteran might dwell pleasantly under his own vine and fig-tree.

Expectations of the army

CHAPTER V

THE COMMITTEE OF THREE

I

THE Romans were seldom satisfied with events unless they were accompanied by suitable signs and auguries. A few such signs were always welcomed, and their verification was not a matter that any one greatly troubled about. We need not be surprised nor unduly inquisitorial, therefore, when we are assured by the historians that when Octavian offered the first sacrifices during his inauguration as consul, twelve vultures were seen—the same number that appeared to Romulus when he laid the foundation of the city. There can have been few electors of the Caesarian party who did not think with pride of the obvious deduction.

His first step as consul was to cause his adoption by Caesar to be formally ratified by a curial act.[1] He obtained several practical advantages by following this course. For one thing the adoption was by this means confirmed and witnessed with a publicity and legality which left no more to be desired, and which put the whole matter permanently beyond any kind of question. For another, he ob-

Octavian consul: Aug. 19th, 43 B. C.

---

[1] This was the form of adoption technically known as *adrogatio*. As Octavian had no natural father alive, and Gaius Julius Caesar also was dead, Octavian could not be ceded by his natural father to his new father by the formality of the "Penny and Balance," which was originally a form of sale by one to the other. He was obliged to go to the supreme authority, the Assembly of the People considered as an assembly of the curies; and this Assembly legislated him into his new status by its sovereign power. There had evidently been some doubt or question about the validity of Octavian's adoption on the former occasion and he now had the matter conclusively settled.

tained exactly the same status in law as a real son of Caesar's body would have possessed, and therefore the same rights with respect to the other members of the family and the freedmen who were connected with it. One of the marked features of the private or domestic policy of Caesar had been the unusual number of his freedmen—slaves to whom he had granted liberty—and the wealth and influence to which many of these men had attained. Although free men, they were, by Roman law and custom, still bound to their former master in a number of ways which it is unnecessary to notice here in detail. By the method he took of ratifying his adoption, Octavian obtained the transfer to himself of all the rights Julius had possessed in these quarters.[2] It was a touch of worldly prudence and careful economy very typical of Octavian. . . . Marcus Antonius must have realized, when he heard of these legal transactions, that Octavian had registered a right to the name and heritage of Caesar which there was no possibility ever of revoking. *Adoption by Caesar confirmed*

Octavian next took in hand the question of punishing the murderers of Caesar. Informations were filed by various members of the Caesarian party, not only for actual participation in the murder, but for being accessory before the fact—and this last covered a number of persons who were absent from the city when the murder was committed.[3] A day was fixed for the trial of all these informations, and public proclamation was made of it. On the appointed day, Octavian, as consul, took his seat as president of the court. None of the accused persons ventured to put in an appear- *Prosecution of the assassins*

[2] To many readers of his Epistles, St. Paul no doubt seems rather pedantic in his metaphors about the adoption of sons—"wherefore thou art as more a servant but a son" (of God) "and if a son, then an heir." (Galatius, IV, 4.9.) But St. Paul had many current examples before him, in view of which his figure of speech had a force and cogency it now lacks: and this case of Octavian would have been one of them.

[3] If it were held to cover the case of Cicero, his defenders would have a good deal of trouble in rebutting the charge.

ance, and all were formally condemned in their absence.

This merely legalized an actual situation. The murderers of Caesar were at war with the Caesarian party, and had fled from the city and nothing new was begun nor anything existing worsened by these formal measures of condemnation. But there were great advantages to Octavian in being able to take formal and legal steps. It put him right with public opinion; it definitely put on record the truth that Caesar, an unarmed man, had been murdered in time of civil peace by men whom he trusted, and who were not justified by any lawful defence that they dared adduce in court. The friends of Julius—and much more his heir—were especially anxious to emphasise these facts. They did not

Reasons

admit that he was a tyrant or an usurper—an outlaw justly slain: they maintained that he was the victim of an illegal act, and that their own position was legal and justified by the laws of the state: and they appealed to the whole Roman world on this ground. They knew that on no other ground could they appeal to it. . . . And Octavian, having scored one point after another against Antonius, scored this last triumphant point: that he, Octavian, was the man who had legally and formally obtained the condemnation of the murderers of Caesar, while Antony remained the man who had compromised with them and had sought to gain personal advantages from condoning their act. This might be very unjust,[4] but he had elected to oppose Octavian and the point was fairly scored against him.

II

So completely, by all these acts, had Octavian proved himself the unmistakeable and undisputable head of the Caesarian party that the military chiefs in Gaul and Spain

[4] For Antony's very effective answer, see Ch. III.

were now ready to enter into a satisfactory agreement with him. While he possessed Rome, the consulship, and the adoption of Julius, they on their part possessed by far the greater proportion of the Caesarian army, and since they were in a position to bargain, an agreed settlement was indicated. Any hanging-back on either side was quickly corrected by the irresistible public opinion of the legionaries. This public opinion was the dominating fact of the situation. The absence of any such pressure among the *optimates* prevented the latter from achieving the same united front. Preparations were therefore made for a meeting, and Octavian took the road north to be ready for the conference when it was arranged. He left his kinsman and colleague, Quintus Pedius, in charge of the city. The Caesarian leaders

Quintus was a commonplace man with the simple beliefs and moralities of the ordinary unsophisticated human being. He was not in the confidence of Octavian, and, indeed, had no conception of what went on in that curious mind. He was exactly the right man to exert a little calming influence upon the senate, which began to grasp the idea—strange that it should be unfamiliar!—that its wisest course was to make a virtue of necessity; and senators began to contemplate the possibility of receiving Antony and Lepidus with politeness. Their change of heart came somewhat late in the day, and there was nothing to tell them—or Quintus Pedius—that it came too late. The decrees against Antony and Lepidus, declaring them to be public enemies, were repealed, and friendly messages sent them. As a friendly gesture this repeal came very opportunely for Octavian, and Antony and Lepidus accepted it in that sense.

The Caesarian legions were now pouring into Italy again by the roads from Gaul. Antony came with his seven, reorganized and refreshed; Plancus with five; Asinius Pollio with three; Lepidus with seven. As Octavian now had The armies eleven, the senatorial army under Decimus Brutus was hopelessly outnumbered, besides being inferior in training and equipment, and lacking in enthusiasm. Decimus made up his mind to retreat to Macedonia and join Marcus Brutus. It was a wild resolve and it came too late. Octavian, leaving three legions behind him in Rome, had already stationed himself at Ariminum, blocking the way south to Brundusium. Unable to take that route, Decimus attempted to go round the head of the Adriatic by way of Aquileia. His unhappy troops did not accompany him far. Very evidently they felt that his service was all kicks and no ha'pence. The new levies—six legions—were the first to break away, and to surrender to Octavian. Four legions of veterans were the next to leave him, with all their auxiliaries, and to join Antonius. Decimus himself did not succeed in getting across the mountains. He fell into the hands of a Celtic chief, who sent word to Antonius. All the ancient historians agree that Antony was not usually either cruel or vindictive. He had no especial personal feeling against Decimus, and was sorry to hear of his misfortunes. But Decimus had been condemned by a legal court for the murder of Gaius Julius Caesar, and the punishment for murder was death. Unwilling to see him, he directed that Decimus should be beheaded, and the head sent to him. Being satisfied as to the identity of the dead man, he ordered the head to be buried. Decimus Brutus was the second of the murderers of Caesar to meet his end.

With northern Italy now clear of all enemies, and completely in their hands, the Caesarian chiefs, advancing towards one another along the great Aemilian way, met **The conference** near Bononia, where the modern Bologna stands. The place and circumstances were very carefully prepared. Octavian, Antonius and Lepidus each advanced with five legions towards the banks of the river Rhenus, where a small island offered a suitable meeting place, visible from both banks, yet securely out of earshot. Lepidus went first and surveyed the island. As soon as he had certified that all was clear, the engineers of Antonius and Octavian threw their bridges across to the island, and the three principals met alone on this neutral ground, leaving the bridges guarded each by three hundred men especially told off by their commanders for the service. As a mark of good faith, each of the three submitted to be searched for concealed weapons. They then took their seats—Octavian, as consul, occupying the centre chair.

The conference lasted three days, and the decisions reached were of epoch-making importance. The three leaders agreed upon an arrangement by which the Caesarian party could present a united front to the common enemy, without either of them gaining any advantage over the others. Octavian was to marry Clodia, Antony's stepdaughter, as a sign of the harmony that was to prevail. In order to equalize their status, it was settled that Octavian should resign the consulship and turn it over to Ventidius for the remainder of his term; a new magistracy should then be created by law, a Triumvirate, or a Committee of Three for the Reorganization of the State,[5] which should possess consular power—and Octavian, Antonius and Lepidus should be the members of the Committee. It was, in fact, a triple Dictatorship, with the specific character that it was to be created by a statute law, and was to last for five years. The Committee was forthwith to nominate the ordinary magistrates for each of the years of this term. Italy was to be governed by these ordinary magistrates, but the rest of the Roman dominion, as far as it was under their

Triple Dictatorship

[5] "Rei publicae constituendae causa"—the technical term defining the dictatorships of Sulla and Caesar, and linking this triumvirate with them as a development of the same principles.

control, was to be apportioned between the members of the Committee. Lepidus was to have Spain and Southern Gaul—the "Provincia," Provence as it became in later ages; Antonius was to have the Gauls, Cisalpine and Transalpine, while Octavian had Africa, Sardinia and Sicily. The eastern provinces, not being in the possession of the Caesarian party, were not divided.

The purpose of this division was to give each of the three a separate revenue, so that disputes on this head should be avoided. And if we, reflecting over the taxable value of these areas in our own times, should at the first start to think that Antonius had much the better of the bargain, we must remember that the circumstances then were widely different. Africa was the granary of Rome; the power which controlled it had its hand upon the food supply of the metropolis; while Sicily was hardly less rich. Recently conquered Gaul was a much poorer country than these fat and ancient lands, where agriculture was pursued with a science and system unexcelled anywhere in the world at that time. As for Spain—a good deal of it, as well as of Sicily, was still in the hands of Sextus Pompeius, and would have to be fought for. Even if Gaul and Spain were better recruiting fields for soldiers, we must still think that Octavian had received the best share of the provinces.

Provinces allotted

It was further arranged that for the next consular year, beginning on the following first of January, Lepidus and Plancas should be consuls; Lepidus was to remain at Rome and take general charge of Italy, governing his own province of Spain by a deputy. He was to retain three legions, the other seven being divided, three to Octavian and four to Antonius.

The reward of the army had to be considered; and for this purpose eighteen cities of Italy were marked for confiscation and redivision. These included such places as

MARCUS ANTONIUS

(*From a coin in the British Museum*)

FULVIA

(*From a coin in the British Museum*)

Capua, Regium, Venusia, Beneventum, Nuceria, Ariminum and Vibo—some of the richest and most beautiful districts of the land.

These arrangements were reduced to writing and a **The army approves** formal document drawn up. Octavian, as consul, accepted the task of reading it out to the assembled troops, from whom it received an enthusiastic welcome. They had demanded peace and reconciliation among their leaders, and a united front for the common benefit—and here was the answer!

III

But there was a secret clause to the arrangement which Octavian did not read out. The Committee had resolved not only that the legal condemnation of the murderers of Caesar, already secured, should be implemented under their direction, but that the "reorganization of the state" would be facilitated by the absence of a certain number of persons who, at present, were obstacles in the way of peace and concord. A list of these persons was drawn up. It contained some peculiarities which, at a later date, received a good deal of criticism from the world at large. The first person to go down upon it, at Antony's demand, was Cicero. Rumour—it was no more—said that Octavian had held out for two days against this demand, but on the third day gave way.[6] It is not strictly necessary to believe this

---

[6] Suetonius, *Divus Augustus*, XXVII, represents Octavian as the hardest of the three triumvirs, apparently on the authority of Julius Saturninus. Suetonius, however, confesses that Octavian himself did not admit some of the charges made against him. The detailed version of Octavian's character given by Suetonius in Chapters XXXIII and LI–LVI is totally inconsistent with these casual charges of hardness and cruelty. We have to square the fact of the proscription with the equally certain fact that both Octavian and Antonius had reputations as good natured men. There is one way, however, of accounting for the intrusion of a cruel and malicious element into the proscription; and that

The Pro-scription

report; for the case which Antony could bring forward was so strong that Octavian could hardly have held out against it for two days. Cicero had been warmly and determinedly in favour of the murder of Caesar; his antagonism had been purely doctrinaire and political, for he had not, and confessed that he had not, a single definite personal reason for disliking Julius. So much the reverse that (as he himself admitted) he had received marked kindness and attentions from Julius: and—as we know quite as well, from his Letters, as Octavian and Antony could know—he recognized that Julius was a man of larger humanity and generosity than any man likely to succeed him. In the teeth of every consideration of common sense and common gratitude, Cicero had urged and encouraged the deed and had exerted his whole energies to protect the murderers. He had intended—who could doubt?—to wind up by betraying and destroying Octavian: and the latter would have been a much more remarkable example of selfless saintliness than he ever became, if he had struggled very long to protect such a man.

Case against Cicero

This was not the whole of the case that could be brought against Cicero. Marcus Antonius was prejudiced against him by much more than any merely personal irritation. All his family relationships connected him with men and women who had reason for disliking the great orator. After his father's death his mother (a Julia of the elder branch of Caesar's family) had married Cornelius Lentulus Sura, one

---

is, by accepting the statements made by some historians about Fulvia, Antony's wife. She, at any rate, had the character of a cruel and unforgiving person. See the story told by Maximus Valerius, and Appian IV, 29, about Casetius Rufus. Looking at his head, Antony said: "I don't know this man: this is something of my wife's." She is said to have pierced the dead Cicero's tongue with a bodkin. If we accept these stories, it is easy to see the source from which some elements in the proscription were derived. The Triumvirs, of course (like Pilate), have to accept the consequences of their actions.

of the alleged conspirators, friends of Catiline, whom Cicero, during his consulship, put to death without trial. This, as Plutarch suggests, was the first seed of the dislike which Antonius had for Cicero. The unfortunate Lentulus, while not a model of moral character and private virtue, was one of a group of men done to death under circumstances more than suspected of political partisanship and gross unfairness. . . . Tradition even had it that the body of Lentulus was denied burial until Julia, the sister and daughter of consuls, begged the corpse—but this was only a legend which illustrates the embittered feeling to which the execution of the Catilinarian conspirators gave rise. The death of Lentulus, his step-father and his mother's husband, was by itself enough to plant the seed of enmity in the mind of the young Antonius. But he was also a friend of Cicero's determined opponent, the famous Publius Clodius, **Antony's** and after the violent death of the latter at the hands of the **case** gangsters of the *optimates*, he married his widow, Fulvia, a woman of immense ability, verve and zeal, who was just the person to cultivate the seed into full flower. The hostility of Marcus Antonius towards Cicero was a pale copy of the hatred in the heart of Fulvia. Hence Antonius was disposed from the first to look darkly upon Cicero as a representative of those political forces which used subornation of perjury and judicial murder as part of their methods. He became finally and irrevocably an enemy when he realized that Cicero supported, praised and endorsed the assassination of Caesar, and advocated that of Marcus Antonius too.

The preface which the Committee prepared as an explanation of its actions may be described here, as it clearly shows the motives which inspired them. It begins by observing that if faithless traitors had not begged for mercy, and then became the murderers of the man who spared them (some of whom he made his friends and gave great benefits), it never would have been necessary for the committee to take this action. To placate the murderers of Caesar was impossible—so the Committee preferred to strike first rather than to let their enemies do so. After this preamble, it goes on to describe the actions which, beginning with the murder of Caesar, have led up to the present situation, and remarks that some of the murderers had already been visited with vengeance,[7] and with God's help, the rest should be brought to justice. Gaul, Spain and Italy having been settled, the next task was to pursue the murderers of Caesar beyond the sea. But the Committee thought it unsafe, in its own and in the public interest, to leave behind it enemies who would certainly seize the chance to make trouble. Seeing, therefore, that these people are the stirrers up of strife, the Committee considers it best to dispose of them for good.

Declaration by the Committee

The committee, however, does not propose to take indiscriminate vengeance on all its enemies, nor to aim at those who are rich in order to plunder their estates; nor does the Committee propose to slay as many as was done by a certain person who once stood in their shoes, and who was known as "The Fortunate." Only the principal guilty parties will be touched. It would be possible to arrest, but the Committee prefers to proscribe. The process of arrest is liable to abuse; but proscription makes it more difficult for the agents to exceed their orders. The Committee has therefore issued a proscription list.

No one must harbour or protect the persons named in this list. Any one who connives at their escape is thereby added to the list without appeal. Any one who produces

---

[7] It is very necessary here to remember one fundamental difference that parts this age from that: to us, vengeance is a moral weakness to which a man may give way—sometimes excusably; to them, it was a moral duty which ought to be performed as a matter of ethical right.

the head of a proscribed person shall receive, if a free man, **Rewards** 100,000 sesterces per head; if servile, two-fifths of this sum, **and penalties** plus his freedom, and the social grade of his master. Informers shall receive the same. The names of those who receive the rewards or give information will be confidential, and will not be put on record.[8]

Such were the contentions by which the Committee defended its action in condemning something like one-third of the senate to death.

IV

While the conference at Bononia was breaking up, messengers rode hot-foot to Rome. The day was the twenty-seventh of November. That night a number of the proscribed, whose names had been sent ahead in a special secret list, were sought for throughout the city. Four were taken at once, and slain; and when the news spread that people were being arrested and executed a panic began. In the absence of definite information, a very large number of persons entertained an inward conviction that they must be **The first** among the threatened, and desperate deeds of despair might **news**

---

[8] This very remarkable document (genuine or fabricated—but probably more genuine than fabricated) which Appian (*Civil Wars*, IV, 8-11) includes in his history, deserves some comment. The authors claim that they have proscribed fewer people than Sulla—which shows for one thing how extraordinarily deep Sulla's proscription bit, and how profoundly it was resented: and, for another, that the confusion of figures by which the Samnite prisoners of war were included as part of the Sullan proscription was already current. According to Appian, Sulla's list included 40 senators and 1600 equites. That of the Triumvirs, also according to Appian, included in round figures 300 senators and 2000 equites. The argument about arrest sounds curious to a modern ear; but it is unquestionably made in perfect good faith. The Roman government possessed no reliable prison service and any attempt to hold a considerable number of men in custody was to risk serious abuses which would render the Committee much more unpopular than merely killing them was likely to do.

have been done if Quintus Pedius had not hurried round to quiet the alarm. He urged the panic-stricken to wait for daylight. As soon as the morning came, Quintus, on his own authority, published the list of seventeen, believing it to be the full list. He pledged his word that there were no other names.

His efforts that night—and perhaps the news that he received during the following day—had so serious an effect upon him that he died on the night of the twenty-eighth of November. The events which immediately succeeded rolled over and obliterated the memory of a harmless and innocent man, who was as much a victim of the proscription as if he had been upon the list. The triumvirs were arriving in Rome, each on one of three successive days; and as they came Rome was filled with troops and standards. An Assembly was at once called, and was packed with military. A tribune, Publius Titius, moved the adoption of a bill creating the new magistracy, the Committee of Three for reorganizing the State, and nominating Octavian, Antonius and Lepidus as its first members. The crowded military electors passed it with acclaim, and the Committee at once came into being. That night the second proscription list was published, containing one hundred and thirty names: and thereafter, from time to time, fresh instalments of the list were published, until all the names had been made known.

Proscription lists published

The tales that were afterwards told about this proscription [9] throw much light upon the current state of society in Rome and upon the relation of father and son, master and servant, and husband and wife. Some of them, for poignancy, for pathos or for horror rank high in the repertory of good stories. It was a time in which many

[9] Appian devotes some thirty-nine sections to them (*Civil Wars,* IV, 12–51).

chickens came home to roost: in which the fate of cruel
and tyrannical men was suddenly put into the hands of
delighted slaves who gladly led the soldiers to their hiding
places, and in which men who had made themselves beloved found their servants laying down their own lives in
their defence. There is the grim tale of Thuranius, who
implored the slayers to wait while his son spoke to Antony.
The soldiers, vastly amused, assured him that his son had
already "spoken to Antony"—the other way round! The
old man asked them to wait yet another moment while he
spoke to his daughter: and to her he gave the advice not to
claim her share of his property, or her brother might go on
speaking to Antony. . . . And there is the story—a little
less grim—of Annalis, who hid in the house of a client who
kept the secret faithfully until Annalis's son, suspecting the
truth, led the slayer there in person. . . . It ends with the
son, returning home drunk after receiving the reward, becoming mixed up in a quarrel with the same soldiers who
had slain his father, and being killed by them too. Thu- The Terror
ranius's son also, the narrator is careful to assure us, took to
loose ways and came to a bad end. There was the wife of
Septimius, who got her husband put upon the list, and
married a new husband the day after he was killed, and that
of Ligarius, who hid hers to the best of her power, and
then, when he was discovered, followed the murderers cry-
ing out that she had sheltered him, and those who gave
shelter were to share the penalty—but no one would take
any notice of her. She even went in front of the triumvirs,
and called out the same thing; but they pretended not to
hear. There were men like Capito and Vetulinus, who defended themselves sword in hand to the last, and might
have gained a name like Achilles if they had had a Homer
to record them. Capito fixed his door half open, and for a
long time slew every man who sought to enter, until at last

he was overpowered by numbers. Vetulinus organized resistance in southern Italy, not only from among the proscribed, but from indignant citizens of the eighteen cities which were to be given to the Caesarian veterans. For some time he succeeded in holding his own, until such forces were sent against him that he was obliged to retire across the straits to Sicily. . . . And there were aged patriarchs like Labienus, who caused his chair to be placed at his door, where he received the executioners with dignity and state; and like old Statius, aged eighty, who with true Samnite spirit distributed his valuables among his neighbours and servants, and then closed his doors and set fire to his house, perishing in the flames. . . . Or there was Oppius, who, being too old to fly for his life, was carried out of the city by his son (who was not on the list) and half led and half carried (as Auchises was by Aeneas) all the way to Sicily.

Flight . . . Some men fled one way, some another. A considerable number took refuge in Sicily, where the ships of the exiled chief Sextus Pompeius were continually on the watch to pick up stragglers. There was a welcome from Sextus for all refugees, and a place in his army for every suitable person. Many, or most, sought the protection of Marcus Brutus in Macedonia. This last was the aim of Cicero.

Of all the deaths that followed from the proscription, that of Cicero was the most noteworthy. Sulla never slew any man one half so important to the world at large. The proscription of the triumvirs, indeed, would merit a peculiar immortality of its own, if only for the reason that in it appeared the names of two of the greatest of Romans—Marcus Tullius Cicero, the supreme master of the Latin tongue, and Marcus Terentius Varro, the most learned man of his age, and, on some aspects of Roman history and archaeology, perhaps the most learned man of any age.

Cicero was at Tusculum when the lists were published,

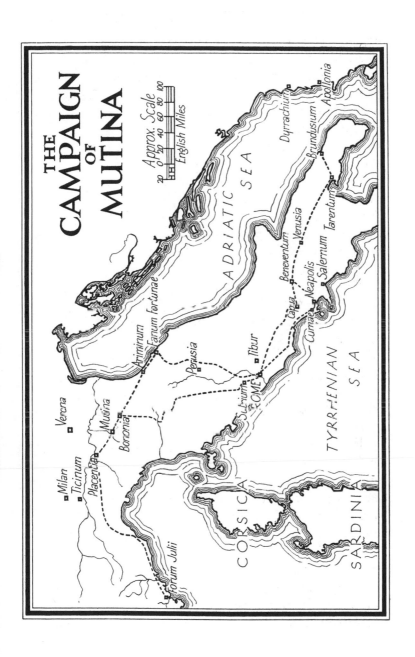

THE
CAMPAIGN
OF
MUTINA

Approx. Scale
20 0 20 40 60 80 100
English Miles

ADRIATIC SEA

TYRRHENIAN SEA

Milan
Verona
Ticinum
Placentia
Mutina
Boronia
Forum Julii

Ariminum
Fanum fortunae
Perusia
Tibur
Sutrium
ROME

CORSICA
SARDINIA

Capua
Cumae
Neapolis
Beneventum
Venusia
Salernum
Tarentum

Dyrrachium
Brundusium
Apollonia

in company with his brother Quintus, and his nephew, Quintus's son—the latter of whom had had a very bitter personal quarrel with Marcus Antonius, and had gone over to his uncle's party. He was sure to be on the list—and was. As we have seen, the Committee had hoped to surprise the chief persons whom they wished to remove, before any news of their intention could leak out. They failed in this aim. Cicero's friends and agents in Rome, who were alert, and were probably not altogether without suspicions of what was coming, sent him the earliest warning; and the party left Tusculum for Astura, intending to take ship there. Quintus, however, was quite unprepared for a long journey abroad—a serious matter in these days—and he decided to return to Rome, sure that he could remain in safe concealment until he was ready. Cicero himself, finding his ship waiting at Astura according to programme, went aboard and set sail.

Cicero warned

If Cicero's heart had really been set upon it, nothing now need have prevented him from making good his escape. It was not the chance nor the means, but the will that was lacking. He was always a bad sailor, a thorough landsman uneasy upon the water; and he began to grow restless when a rough sea and a contrary wind made things uncomfortable upon the little vessel he had chartered. He insisted upon landing at Circaeum, a short distance down the coast; and there he tarried, thoroughly undecided, not only as to what he ought to do, but even as to what he wanted to do. If it had been a speech or a treatise that was in question, he would have mapped out his plans with a Napoleonic hand; but since physical actions were concerned, he could not make up his mind. Should he flee to Marcus Brutus?— or to Cassius in Syria?—or to Sextus Pompeius in Sicily? It was all very difficult. He rather fancied that it might be pleasant to die.

Flight of Cicero

He has left us ample means of reading his thoughts upon this subject. . . . Let us copy here the passage which he himself, in the *Tusculan Disputations*, copied from Plato:

"There must follow one of two consequences, either that death takes away all sensation altogether, or that by death a passage is secured from these regions to another place. Accordingly, if sensation is obliterated and death resembles the sleep which sometimes brings the calmest rest, untroubled even by the appearance of dreams, good gods! what gain it is to die! . . . But if there be truth in the tale that death is a passage to those shores which are inhabited by the departed dead, that is surely happier still. To think that, when thou hast escaped from thee who wish to be reckoned judges, thou art coming to those who can really be called judges, Minos, Rhadamanthus, Aeacus and Triptolemus. . . . For my part I could feel in my heart the wish to die many times, that I might have the privilege of finding what I am speaking of. . . . For no evil can befall any good man either in life or in death, nor will his troubles ever be disregarded by the immortal gods, nor has my own lot come by accident." And then the last words of Socrates:— "The time has now come for departure: I to die, you to get on with your lives. Which of the two, however, is better the immortal gods know; no human being, I think, does know." [10] . . .

View of death

It was just such thoughts as these that preoccupied him. But he had other things to think of; he was not merely a simple individual person, but the head of a household, in whose hand rested the lives and happiness of many people whose rights to consideration he must not ignore. He allowed his servants, therefore, to persuade him to continue on his way to Caieta, where he once more went ashore for

[10] *Tusculan Disputations*, I, xli. (Loeb translation.)

a rest in his Formian villa. With his incurable habit of epigram, he said that he would die in the land he had so often saved. They could see that he was tired and despondent; but no doubt he had often been so before, and the servants put him into his litter, shouldered it, and made off to the ship. They took quiet ways through the grounds of the villa. Hardly had they left the house, when the soldiers arrived. The bird was flown, but it was easy to guess where he had gone,[11] and they pursued down to the sea.

Cicero gives up

The officer in command of the party was Popilius Laenas —a name that takes its place in history together with those of many other men of the tribe of Judas. Cicero had once defended him and saved him when he was charged with the murder of his father; and the man he had preserved now accepted the task of slaying the man who preserved him. Cicero had been a good master. The slaves put down the litter and prepared to fight. He checked their zeal. It was impossible for them to defend him without bloodshed—and he no longer valued his life to that degree. Leaning out of the litter, looking over the fields and vineyards that still stretch down to the blue Caietan bay, where Ischia lies in the distance and the blue mountains of Naples close the horizon, he gave himself to be slain. The swordsman was perhaps nervous and flurried; he was possibly disconcerted by the audience, for he had to strike three times before the head fell. By the express order of Antony the hands of Cicero—especially the hand that had written the Second Philippic with its incitement to murder—were also cut off, and with these prizes Popilius Laenas returned to Rome.

[11] There are alternative versions concerning this. According to Plutarch, a slave of Quintus, named Philologus, gave information—but he admits that Tiro made no mention of Philologus. Appian tells us that it was a shoemaker, a client of Clodius. These conflicting accounts seem to prove that no one was definitely known to have given information.

V

News of Cicero's death

Marcus Antonius was in the Forum, conducting an Assembly, amid crowds of people, when Popilius Laenas arrived: but when the latter signalled from a distance the nature of his errand, a path was at once cleft for him, and the happy Antonius bestowed upon him a crown of gold and, in addition to the reward, a special gift of a million sesterces. The head of Cicero was fixed above the rostra, with the hands on each side; and Antony is reported to have said that the proscription could end now for all he cared. He had very little further interest in its progress.

Other examples

And in fact the great proscription spent its main force and bitterness on Marcus Tullius Cicero. Old Varro remained concealed until things blew over. No one betrayed him. Indeed, his friends struggled for the honour of protecting him. One of the peculiarities of the proscription had been that, as far as the public could see, while Octavian surrendered Cicero to the vengeance of Antony, the latter gave up Lucius Caesar, his mother's brother, and Lepidus his brother Paullus; [12] and the Greek Plutarch, the biographer of the ancient world, more than once expresses his profound horror at the cold-blooded bargain. He need not have worried. The proscription of Lucius Caesar and Aemilius Paullus was no more than a pretence by which

[12] This is the famous beginning of Act IV, Scene I in Shakespeare's *Julius Caesar.*

"*Ant.* These many then shall die; their names are pricked.
"*Oct.* Your brother too must die; consent you, Lepidus?
"*Lep.* I do consent.
                    Prick him down, Antony.
"*Lep.* Upon condition Publius shall not live
        Who is your sister's son, Mark Antony.
"*Ant.* He shall not live; look!—with a spot I damn him!"

Had Shakespeare explored a little further, he would have found that neither of them was hurt, and we might have lost some magnificent lines.

the other members of the Committee saved the face of Octavian. Antony's mother looked after her brother, and on the only occasion on which she found it necessary to speak to Marcus he merely grumbled and apologized and dismissed the matter. Paullus survived the proscription. Nobody dared to touch him, and when it was over he found himself so comfortable at Miletus, where he had settled, that he decided to stay there permanently. Messalla Corvinus was pardoned, and rose to high office under Augustus. The distinctive note of this proscription was, indeed, the number of persons who successfully escaped it. The Committee showed a remarkable lack of energy in pursuing them.

The real aim of the proscription had been stated with accuracy in the preface already quoted: it was intended, not to destroy a party, but to leave Italy reasonably safe while the Committee led its armies overseas to meet those of Brutus and Cassius. This purpose was fulfilled if it drove out of the country, and into the camps of Brutus and Cassius, the leaders of the *optimates* in the senate. They could **Purpose of** be more easily dealt with there, than at Rome. The Com- **the Terror** mittee was much nearer to certain events in history than we are. It doubtless remembered very clearly the circumstances by which Cinna was prevented from crossing the Adriatic to meet Sulla, so that Sulla invaded Italy and fought the war on Italian soil. They had no intention of allowing this particular part of history to repeat itself. They meant to leave a reasonably secure and peaceful Italy behind them, and meet Brutus in Macedonia.

To achieve this aim, money was of the first importance. Like Sulla, Cassius was drawing upon the wealth of the Asiatic provinces. The Committee had only the less wealthy European provinces—and some of these were in the hands of Sextus Pompeius. If there had been any hope of gathering great sums from the sale of the confiscated estates of the proscribed, as Sulla had done, this fancy was soon dashed. Investors remembered the vengeance wrought by Sulla upon those who bought up the estates confiscated by Marius—and they hesitated now to buy. Such estates as were worth selling therefore changed hands at disappointingly low figures, and the Committee gained very little from the transactions. It found itself eight hundred million sesterces short on the amount required for the war.

Tax on women

One of the expedients it resorted to became famous. The Committee decided to require a return of property held by women, with a view to assessing it for taxation. Fourteen hundred of the richer women with property were served with notices. The women at once acted.[13] As this is almost the first occasion on which we catch a real glimpse of some of the women who afterwards were to play a great part in the story, it is worth while to pause and note their entry upon the scene. Of Octavian's sister Octavia we have already seen something; and of Julia, the mother of Marcus Antonius. Both of these, as we might expect, willingly undertook to do what they could. Fulvia, Antony's wife, made herself unpleasant to the deputation—which again is what we might expect. Fulvia was a clever and able woman, but an individualist. While she had been married to Clodius, Clodius had been great. Now that she was married to Antony, Antony was great. Clodius had come to an unfortunate end—and we all know what was to become of Antony. This individualism, which led her now to put her

---

[13] The Roman lady of the period was in a position very different from the average woman of the nineteenth century. Roman women (as we can see from the story of Clodius and the Bona Dea told by Plutarch in his life of Caesar) had their own organization, independent of that of men; and the college of Vestal Virgins, a corporation of the most select and exclusive kind, was one of the most powerful and influential in the city. It had once been able to put pressure upon Sulla: and that alone is enough to mark the extent of the power it wielded.

husband's interests before those of her sex, was to have further and more serious results later on, as we shall see. But the intercession of Octavia and Julia secured for the women's deputation an unwilling hearing from the Committee.

The spokesman for the deputation was Hortensia, the daughter of Hortensius the orator, Cicero's great rival. The speech which Appian puts into her mouth was a very re- Hortensia markable one. After a scathing reference to Fulvia's manners, Hortensia proceeded to say that the triumvirs had deprived them of fathers, husbands and sons who were supposed to have wronged them. If they, the women, had also done the Committee wrong, Hortensia invited it to proscribe them too; but if they had not, why should they suffer the penalty when they did not share the guilt? The objection they had to being taxed was that they did not share the privileges and offices which were the prizes of public life among men. The excuse that it was necessary for the prosecution of the war was groundless for there had always been wars, and yet women had not been taxed to pay for them. When, in the past, women had contributed, it had been voluntarily, from their personal property, not from their settled estates or dowries, which were necessary to their decent maintenance. No danger to the state was threatening them now. If the Gauls or the Parthians came, the women of the present day would be as good as their mothers; but to Civil War they would never willingly contribute. Neither Marius, Sulla, Cinna, Pompeius nor Caesar had ever taxed women; that was left to the present Committee, who professed to be reorganising the state.

The Committee, alarmed at this plain and effective speaking, ordered the lictors to show the deputation out. As Fulvia had already expressed her opinion, we may fairly

The Committee withdraws its plans

suppose that it was principally Antony who took up this attitude of hostility, and that it was his colleagues who, realizing that the speech had gone down extremely well with the general audience, hastily restrained him. The applause that greeted Hortensia's speech meant that her cause had triumphed. After a further consultation the Committee cut down from 1400 to 400 the number of women who were required to make a return. They made up the deficit by an order that all men who possessed property above a certain value should contribute one year's income to the war fund, and lend the state at interest two per cent of their capital. By such expedients as these the necessary money was raised to carry the struggle into Macedonia.

VI

As soon as the preparations could be hurried through, the care of Italy was left in the hands of Lepidus and Plancus, the new consuls, while Antony and Octavian took charge of the campaign in Macedonia. Octavian had done wonders in claiming and securing so great a status in the world at such an age, and against such competitors; but the time had not come yet when he could be sure of the permanency of his success. If it was rapid, it was rickety; and

Preparations

at any moment the swiftly won triumph might collapse under him and vanish.

He needed to make permanent the place he had won.

CHAPTER VI

THEY ALL MEET AGAIN AT PHILIPPI

I

IT was not Shakespeare who invented that dark and hideous spectre which, while Brutus was working late at night in his tent, grew into materialization at his side. Every historian who told the tale of Brutus had heard of the story, and of the question Brutus asked: "What are you?—divine or infernal?—and why do you come to me?" . . . The apparition answered: "I am your evil genius, Brutus. We shall meet again at Philippi." Marcus Junius Brutus

Cassius—a lean and hungry sceptic—laughed when he heard this story, and argued with Brutus. It was, he said, a hallucination, due to nervous fatigue, and he explained how it had happened. It may have been so: or perhaps Brutus had caught a glimpse of his own conscience, and was discouraged. A deep and heavy depression weighed upon him, inhibiting all his powers. Unlike Cicero, who had been a man of words and ideas, Brutus was a man of action; and his actions were paralysed and frustrated by some strange force which seemed to prevent him from his natural energy. He did nothing quite right; nothing was as good as it should have been.

Cassius was a competent officer, active and shrewd, sound in judgment and firm in purpose; he had proved his abilities before, in the days of Crassus and the Parthian wars. But of inspiration, of the divine afflatus, he had not one spark. He had acted throughout on a certain mediocre level of motive and policy. Upon his arrival in Syria he had Gaius Cassius Longinus found the whole province in a state of doubt and disorder. Julius had left large military forces ready for his projected Parthian campaign, and in the absence of any adequate control from Rome they had begun to get themselves into trouble. One of them had killed its commanding officer, and had had three legions sent against it to enforce disciplinary measures. As the three legions found some difficulty in carrying out their task, a further three were sent to their assistance from Bithynia, and thus when Cassius reached Syria he found seven legions there, busily involved in hostilities with one another. As soon as he presented the decree of the senate entitling him to the governorship of Syria, the seven legions, out of touch with events in Italy, at once admitted his title, and put themselves under his orders. In the mean time, four other legions of time-expired men, who had been collected in Egypt, entered Palestine on their way home. Cassius met them with his seven legions, and offered them the choice of fighting or joining him. They were not prepared to fight seven legions; they accepted the terms offered; and in this way, by a curious mingling of luck and promptitude, Cassius had gathered eleven legions under his command. His luck went further than this. A number of the famous Parthian mounted bowmen, remembering his good repute as a commander under Crassus, entered his service as mercenary troops.

Dolabella, on his way to take possession of Syria, ran into this hornets' nest before he fully realized the strength he had to deal with. He thought he could hold Laodicea *ad Mare*, the Syrian seaport, since he had command of the sea, and could withdraw at his discretion. But Cassius, with his restless energy, obtained a fleet from the Phoenician and Asiatic ports, cut off Dolabella's retreat, and captured Laodicea. Dolabella died rather than survive this disgrace, and his army went over to Cassius.

Cassius in Syria

The powerful forces and immense area that had thus **The war** come under the undisputed control of Cassius seemed to **chest** augur favourably for his future. All he needed now was money to feed and equip the Grand Army he had so successfully accumulated. Egypt suggested itself. The vast wealth of Egypt, its ample corn production and its naval power, all seemed to indicate it as the true base of operations. Cleopatra, also (whose connection with Julius was notorious), took up no very friendly attitude towards Cassius, and prudence would lead him to deal with a possible enemy in his rear before he went westward.

Cassius, however, never went to Egypt, for he received word from Brutus that Octavian and Antonius were crossing the Adriatic. It was high time to set out to meet them.

II

The haste with which Cassius had to bring his great army westward made it necessary that he should fill his treasury from sources other than Egypt. He had already imposed a heavy indemnity on the city of Tarsus. He now seized Cappadocia and took over the treasures and military supplies of King Ariobarzanes. Before he left Syria, he paid off his Parthian mounted bowmen, gave them a heavy bonus, and sent them back to ask for a larger body. Then he took the steep road into the mountains through the Cilician gates and joined the ancient Persian "Royal Road" across the table land, descending at last to the Aegean Sea by Sardis and Smyrna, where he met Marcus Brutus.

They held a conference at Smyrna to decide upon their **Cassius** plans. Brutus had eight legions, together with large aux- **joins** iliary forces, and a war chest of sixteen thousand talents. **Brutus** The suggestion of Brutus was that they should unite their forces and cross forthwith to Macedonia. The Caesarians had forty legions, of which not all could be available for the war; and of those that would be available, no more than eight were now in Macedonia under Decidius Saxa and Norbauns Flaccus. Hence it was important to throw their own superior forces—twenty-one legions strong— upon the weaker detachments of the enemy as they arrived, and defeat them piecemeal. This reasonable plan Cassius instantly opposed. He thought the best course was to let all the Caesarian forces cross into Macedonia. They would (he believed) soon find themselves in serious trouble in that barren and mountainous country, and would probably disperse for lack of supplies. Brutus and Cassius, meanwhile, would deal with the Rhodians and Lycians, who were in sympathy with the Caesarians; by this means they would both fill their treasuries (a very expedient step) and remove from their rear a very dangerous menace. Brutus agreed to this. After all, it was necessary to agree on something, and one thing was as good as another as long as they did agree. He asked, however, for a grant from Cassius's war fund. He had spent a large amount of his own money on creating the fleet that now held the Ionian Sea. Since Cassius was calling the tune, he ought to pay the piper.

Policy of Brutus and Cassius
This request caused some heart-searching on the part of the Cassians. Pressing advice was given to Cassius by his council, not to provide Brutus with the means with which to buy his way into popularity. Cassius, however, finally decided to make a grant of one-third. Thereupon they separated, Cassius to lay siege to Rhodes on its island; Brutus to reduce the towns of the Lycian mainland.

Brutus had a difficult time of it. The Lycians seemed to have no sympathy with his demand for money and volunteers. His attempts to win them over by kindness seemed to go awry. Either they did not respond to kindness, or he used the wrong variety. When at last he drove them into

Xanthus, they acted with a desperate violence that seemed
to suggest that they thought him a tyrant instead of a lib-
erator. At the storming of the city they set fire to their
houses, killed their women and children and themselves
leaped defiantly into the flames. Plutarch has preserved
some of the tragic episodes—such as that of the woman
who hanged herself with her baby hanging round her neck,
and the torch still in her hand with which she had fired her
house. Brutus wept—which was at any rate something. He
only gathered a hundred and fifty talents in Lycia.

Cassius was of sterner stuff. The attempts of the Rhodians to negotiate were turned down with characteristic
severity. He required unconditional submission. The Rhodians, stirred by their popular leaders, and remembering
the many glorious triumphs and defences of their city in
the past, resolved to hold out against this demand. They Cassius
sent one last message to remind him that he had once lived at Rhodes
and studied in Rhodes, and to appeal to the law of God
and the public opinion of mankind. Cassius replied firmly
that they had taken part with tyrants and oppressors, and
that they seemed to ignore the fact that he and his friends
were liberators and champions of freedom. He produced
his commission from the senate, which placed in the hands
of him and Brutus the control of the Roman dominions
east of the Adriatic. . . . As the Rhodians still seemed
reluctant to surrender unconditionally, the siege began.

Rhodes always had been, and for long continued to be,
a home of fierce fighting-men. The very air of the island
seemed to create a race of hotspurs. They flung themselves
into the struggle now, not perhaps with relish, but certainly with the skill and impetuosity which were historic
characteristics of the Rhodians. But fortune was against
them. Defeated in two naval engagements, they discovered
the awful fact that they had been caught unprepared. The

city was not supplied and equipped for a long siege. Dissensions broke out, for some of the citizens realized the probable results of conducting a useless defence to the last. It was believed afterwards that the gates had been opened by some of these dissidents within the walls; for the day came when Cassius appeared in the city, no man could tell how. He fixed a spear in the market place—the ominous sign that the city had been taken by assault. There was no **The levy** violence: his men were under firm discipline: but he pro-
on Rhodes ceeded to take what he wanted from Rhodes.

Cassius is not the only apostle of freedom and enfranchisement who has conducted a reign of terror against people whose orthodoxy he questioned. Fifty of the leading citizens were formally summoned to appear before him. They declined; and he ordered their execution, and the banishment of twenty-five more. All the gold and silver in the city treasury and the temples was confiscated, and a day appointed on which all that was in private possession should be surrendered. The penalty for concealing the precious metals was death; and a reward of ten per cent was offered to informers. At first there was much concealment; but when Cassius proceeded to carry out these conditions to the letter, there was a great change. More than eight thousand talents [1] was extracted from Rhodes. . . . If the proscription by the Triumvirs at Rome seems terrible, we must not forget that Cassius was conducting a very passable imitation of it at Rhodes.

Cassius followed the precedent set by Sulla. He imposed a general levy of ten years' taxation upon the province of Asia. With all the money thus collected, the armies of the oligarchy prepared to take the road across the Dardanelles

---

[1] A talent was not a coin, but a sum of money, like a lakh of rupees. We can trace the sums of 16,000, 1,500, 150, 8,000 and 500 talents, or 26,150 talents in all, apart from the "ten years' taxation of Asia" as gathered for the equipment of the armies of Brutus and Cassius.

into Macedonia. Their fleet, at the same time, sailed for
Brundusium in order to hinder the transhipment of the
Caesarian legions.

III

Age, experience and temperament all alike pointed to
Marcus Antonius as the obvious commander in chief for
the Caesarians. When, after a few weeks of festivities and
riotous amusement in Rome, he closed down his gaieties
and settled to work, the drive he could impart to things
became clearly visible. He had evidently thought that Sextus Pompeius, from the Sicilian harbours, was likely to take
an active part in the attempt to blockade Brundusium, for
part of the original plan of campaign was an attack upon
Sicily by Octavian, with the aim of pinning Sextus to his
home ports. This was not by any means a trifling task.
Sextus was now at the height of his power and popularity.
Besides Spain, he could draw upon the wealth of Sicily, and
utilize the island harbours and dockyards; the Campanian
cities fed him with volunteers and subscriptions, and the
half Phoenician, half Greek seafaring population of the
islands—a fierce, capable and desperate race—crowded to
his standards. A raid in force upon Brundusium while the
legions were crossing might be a fatal blow to the Caesarians.

It was difficult, no doubt, for Antonius to believe his
luck, or to credit that the lethargy and neglect of the
optimates had entirely omitted to establish any effective
link between the forces in the east, and those in Sicily. He
took no chances, but was careful that Octavian should
watch Sextus while the transportation proceeded. Octavian
despatched a fleet under the command of Salvidimus to
patrol the straits. The fleet of Sextus, issuing from its sta-

*Marcus
Antonius*

*Advantages
of Antony*

tion in Messina harbour, met that of Salvidienus at the northern entrance to the straits, where the promontory of Scyllaeum overlooks the sea and Pelorum, the north point of Sicily, rises opposite across the narrow water, and Aetna towers away to the southwest. A tremendous current scours through the straits—even stronger then than it is today, as the fame of Scylla and Charybdis testifies—and the big Roman ship became difficult to manage. The small local ships of Sextus, easily handled and manned by local men, had all the advantage. At sunset Salvidienus gave the signal to break off the engagement. Both sides retired to patch up their damages. The Caesarians were through the straits, but whether they could get back again was another matter.

Antonius, however, now sent to call Octavian and the fleet round to Brundisium, where he was in difficulties with the hostile squadrons from Asia that watched the port. The **Caesarians** latter withdrew at the appearance of Octavian. The Cae- **cross the** sarian legions were packed on board three-banker galleys **Adriatic** and sent safely across to Dyrrachium. Although Brutus and Cassius sent further squadrons, these contented themselves with harassing the supply ships of the Triumvirs and made no attempt to attack the transports in the course of their passage. The legions, once across, were pushed on rapidly across the mountains of the great Macedonian peninsula.

Meanwhile Brutus and Cassius came up from Sardis by the old coastal route—the route taken by Xerxes, centuries before, and, because it is the easiest route with adequate water supplies for an army's march, by nearly all great armies before or since. They crossed the Dardanelles from Abydos to Sestos, and took the road up the narrow peninsula to the place where the twin fortresses of Lysimachia and Cardia guard the way into Thrace. Just beyond them, in the valley of the Melas, they halted for a last review and

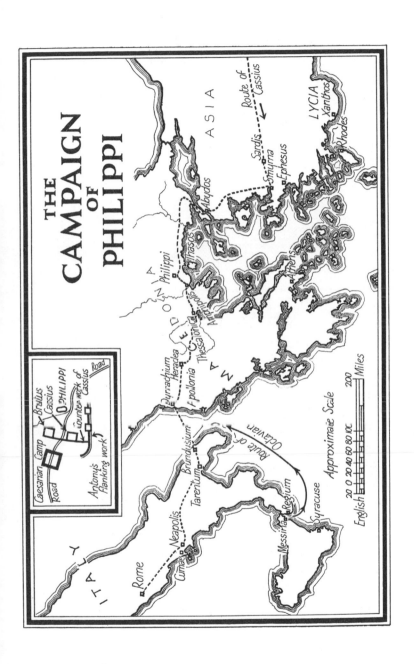

THE
CAMPAIGN
OF
PHILIPPI

inspection.

Nineteen legions deployed on the plain of Melas—most of them not at their full strength, but all of them composed of fully trained men, and some of them legions that had learnt their duties under Julius: making a total of something like eighty thousand Roman legionaries. In addition to these were a goodly number of auxiliaries, Spanish, Gallic, Illyrian, Tracian and Tessalian; a body of Parthian mounted bowmen, and Galatian levies from Asia Minor, descendants of the Gauls who had once sacked Delphi. It was a great army. After political speeches by the leaders, in explanation of where they were going and why they were going there, and their splendid prospects of victory, the army was paid its promised bonus: fifteen hundred drachmas to each soldier, and seven thousand five hundred to each centurion. As fast as they were paid they were put upon the road westward.

Saxa and Norbanus with the Caesarian advanced troops had seized narrow passes some way to the east of Philippi, which lies just about half way between Constantinople and Dyrrachium. Their business was to seize and hold favourable ground for fighting on behalf of Antonius, who was coming up rapidly with the main force of the Caesarians. Brutus and Cassius came groping westward, not perfectly certain what they were doing, nor whether they wished to drive the enemy before them or hold him where he was. Tillius Cimber, skirting the edge of the land with a fleet, outflanked Norbanus, who fell back, calling Saxa to join him, and the two held a strong position from which they could not be dislodged. With the aid of local advice Brutus and Cassius made a difficult circuit to the north, and after much hard work and discouragement forced their way across the hills with such success that they only failed by a narrow margin to cut off the Caesarian forces. The move-

Army of Brutus and Cassius

Contact at Philippi

ment being detected, however, Norbanus and Saxa fell back still further towards Amphipolis, and continued to watch the advance.

Appian describes Philippi. The town itself lies on the summit of a steep hill on the eastern border of the wide and fertile Strymon valley, guarding the passes through the mountains eastward. South of it, marshes extended a large part of the way to the Thracian Sea. North of it lay thick woods, and the whole valley sloped down westward in the direction of Amphipolis with a gradient which gave an advantage to an army on the higher ground. A couple of miles west of Philippi itself the old east and west route to Byzantium and Asia passed between two hills or rises which lay somewhat less than a mile apart, then curving away south behind the marshes, to cross the mountains by the principal pass close to the sea. It was these two hills that Brutus and Cassius now occupied; Brutus the lower, northernmost, and Cassius the higher, southerly hill. They fortified their camps on the hill tops in the usual Roman way, and then barred the road by a fortification stretching from one camp to the other. The whole constituted a powerful defensive position, with ample wood and water, and a market town in the neighbourhood. As the route was the only land route then available between Macedonia and Asia Minor (the mountains to the north, that some day were to be the provinces of Moesia and Illyricum, being still unconquered and unsettled) the Caesarians were completely cut off from the east except by sea—on which their foes had the supremacy. Hence a battle at this point was necessary to decide the issue.

Battle indicated

They were only just in time to seize this advantage of position. Marcus Antonius was coming up fast by the road from Dyrrachium through Heraclea Lyncestis, Pella, Thessalonica and Amphipolis. He was very anxious to secure

Amphipolis, and was vastly relieved to find that it had been occupied and fortified by Norbanus. Philippi was only so very excellent while Brutus and Cassius stood upon the defensive. If they were obliged to attack, they would find that the Caesarians, entrenched at Amphipolis, had a position no less powerful for defence.

IV

But Antonius, a man trained under the great Julius, had no idea of conducting a defensive campaign until obliged. He intended to strike hard, and quickly, and he wished both his own men and the enemy to feel that a Caesarian army was an attacking and a conquering army. Battles are won in the minds of men before a sword is drawn or a shot fired, and in the mind of Marcus Antonius the battle of Philippi was already won. He passed through Amphipolis, came right up to the twin camps with their connecting fortification, pitched his own camp, and dug in close to the enemy lines.

It was not everything he could have wished. Firewood was inadequate—only the light brushwood of the marsh was available—and the ground was liable to flooding. Although there was plenty of water in the wells, there might be too much on occasion. And all supplies had to be brought up from Amphipolis, some thirty miles off by road. Brutus and Cassius, with their main depot on the island of Thasos, opposite the shore below Philippi, could draw upon all the eastern provinces for supplies, while the Caesarians only had Macedonia and Italy, which could not long give them all they wanted. . . . But as Antonius had not the slightest intention of sitting still and waiting, these considerations were not so important as Brutus and Cassius may have thought them.

Plans of Antony

Seven days passed, while the troops of Antonius rested from their march, finished the defensive works of their camp, and waited for Octavian.

It was fortunate for Octavian that the main responsibility for the conduct of events did not rest upon his shoulders, for he was in no condition to bear it. He was young; he was always delicate, and he had been through a great mental strain and many changes of climate, including a sea-voyage. He was ill before he left Italy; at Dyrrachium, he had to take to his bed. But war will not wait on the convenience of invalids, and it was necessary for him to get to Amphipolis. He made the journey in a carriage. . . . Years afterwards Marcus Antonius, in his ribald way, jocularly alluded to this episode, with hints that Octavian's courage rather than his health was at fault; and Antonius certainly had to carry a double burden in consequence of Octavian's incapacity. But to have made the journey across the Macedonian mountains, even in a carriage, is a clear proof that whatsoever else may have been wrong, there was nothing wrong with Octavian's nerve and resolution.

Octavian arrives

Marcus Antonius had the kind of temperament that rises the higher in the teeth of difficulty. Realizing that Octavian was on the sick-list, he tackled the task of leadership with redoubled energy. The forces on each side were about equal—nineteen legions. Antony at once recognized that the plan of Brutus and Cassius was to keep him dallying while the season, and his supplies, and the patience of his men slowly ran out. He therefore paraded every day as if he meant to attack; and he forced Brutus and Cassius to parade similarly to meet this threat, and to concentrate their attention upon it. Meanwhile his engineers and their working parties were building a causeway through the marsh on the left, or southerly side of Cassius. Day and night they worked, cutting reeds and laying them down as

The road through the marsh

a foundation, throwing up an earthen bank on top of this, and revetting it with stone to prevent it from giving way at the edges. In the deeper parts of the marsh this road was carried on piles. It was, in fact, a complete Roman road, save that it was intended for a temporary purpose only. So rapidly and secretly did they work that in ten days the road was complete, and Antonius used it to throw a force across the marsh. Moving by night, they reached the other side, where they dug a line of redoubts opposite the southern flank of Cassius and occupied them.

Cassius—a competent, but not an imaginative commander —was astonished at the skill and secrecy with which this operation had been carried out. He, too, had engineers, and he instantly directed that a road with a defensive wall and ditch should be driven at right angles across the road of the Caesarians, cutting off the advanced troops from the main body. He crowded his own troops down to the danger point on the edge of the marsh, to protect the building of the road, which went on rapidly under their guardianship. This movement of the defending forces at once brought about a corresponding extension of the Caesarians, whose whole line began to hurry southwards. Antonius, consumed with suppressed impatience, let this southward tendency develop until Cassius was thoroughly committed to it. **Assault on** Then, taking charge in person, he led an assaulting party **Cassius's** straight up the hill for the part of the new fortified wall **camp** where it left the camp and began its course towards the marsh. The attack was so sudden and so totally unexpected that the Caesarians broke their way through the protecting screen of defenders, and some of them reached the wall. They had brought tools and ladders with them, and in spite of the showers of missiles hurled at them from the wall, they filled in the ditch, planted their ladders, and carried the wall by assault.

V

Meanwhile, the troops of Brutus, formed up upon the northernmost hill, three-quarters of a mile away, could scarcely believe their eyes when they saw the Caesarians opposite them draining away southward. The gap left by the southerly movement of the Antonians had to be filled by the Octavians. As Octavian himself lay sick in his tent, the operation was probably none too promptly or effectively carried out. The sight was too much for the legionaries of Brutus. Without waiting for the orders which Brutus was in course of issuing, they streamed out of their positions and fell upon the confused ranks of the Octavians. The attackers were in as great confusion as the attacked. The legion commanded by Messala Corvinus took the Octavians in flank and reached the Caesarian camp without any serious fighting. The Octavians, hearing the enemy in their rear, gave way. It seemed at that critical moment as if the star of Octavian, after its first bright twinkle, had set for ever; for his whole army was driven in rout, the camp was forced, Octavian's tent was invaded, and the men of Brutus were passing their javelins in eager anticipation through the litter he was supposed to be occupying.

Defeat of Octavian

But Octavian was not there.

Some uncanny instinct—he himself said in his memoirs that it was a warning in a dream: some said that a friend of his had had the dream—had inspired him to seek safer quarters at the first sign of trouble. Many of the soldiers believed him to be dead, and showed their bloodstained swords to Brutus in proof of it, with descriptive details of the man they had slain. . . . Brutus would have won the battle of Philippi if he could have kept control of his men, and had understood what to do with them. But they had got out of hand at an early stage of the proceedings, and now, instead of pushing their victory home by pursuit, they spent their time in plundering the camp. Hence the Octavians, though broken and routed, were not destroyed, and **Brutus at fault** were not driven too far for recovery. Though they had lost heavily, their defeat was not absolute. But—most fatal fault of all!—Brutus did not realize what was happening elsewhere, or that Cassius needed his help.

Returning from his victory, he glanced up at the southernmost hill—the higher of the two—on which the camp of Cassius lay. He was somewhat surprised to see it looking unlike its usual self. The great pavilion of Cassius, which was a conspicuous landmark, was absent, and other things also were different. Brutus, unlike a modern commander, had no field glasses, and his sight was not of the best. Some of his officers, who had keen sight, told him that there was a good deal of glittering armour and shields moving in the camp—and the armour did not look like that of the men who had been left as camp guards. But there was no sign of dead bodies lying about, as there would have been, had a battle taken place. Brutus became uneasy at this report, and sent out a general summons to rally to the standards.

The truth was that Antonius, having scaled the fortified wall, had been met by a charge of the soldiers who had **Camp of Cassius taken** been working on the wall, and who now picked up their weapons and came against him. In the wrestle that followed, he had the advantage. The defenders were driven down-hill into the marsh. While a battle was still raging furiously on the other side of the wall, Antonius and his men reformed and made another dash up-hill to Cassius's camp. The camp, being in a strong position and strongly fortified, was guarded by a mere handful of men, who were surprised and overrun. The battle below was by this time turning in favour of the Caesarians. As soon as the news spread that the camp was taken, the men of Cassius began to scatter. While, therefore, the Caesarian camp had been taken, and Octavian chased for his life, Antony had defeated the army of Cassius and sacked his camp—and that was the explanation of the strange appearance observed by Brutus.

But the fate of Cassius was not like that of Octavian. The latter was quite ready to run away and live to fight another day—but Cassius could not bring himself to this easy adaptability. Indeed, had he been able to do so, he would of course never have murdered Julius. With a few officers he hurried away to a knoll whence he could survey the field of battle. Not very much was to be seen, but from the north came a body of horsemen. As the troops on both sides wore much the same dress, Cassius despatched an officer, Titinius, to discover the identity of these. When Titinius met them, the foremost of the horsemen, who were friends, leaped down to congratulate him on his safety, and crowded around him. The episode, however, bore a very **Suicide** different and sinister appearance to those who watched it **of Cassius** from the knoll. To them, it appeared certain that Titinius had been seized by enemies. Cassius then said to his shield-bearer: "Have I waited for this?—to see my friend taken?" They retired to a tent; and no one knows what happened; but when Brutus arrived and hurried into the tent, he found Cassius dead, and Pindarus the shield-bearer was never seen again.

That, for what it is worth, is the story of the death of Gaius Cassius Longinus. The day was his birthday: the twenty-third of October.

VI

In this way ended the first battle of Philippi. It was a strange and inconclusive episode. The balance of loss was

against the Caesarians, who had lost sixteen thousand men,
whereas Cassius lost but eight thousand in the storming of
his camp. On the other hand, the death of Cassius himself
was a serious matter, for he was by far the best soldier of
his party. The night after the battle, Brutus abandoned his
own camp and occupied that of Cassius. Rain fell heavily,
and the Caesarians in the valley had a miserable time with
wet clothes, deep mud and tents flooded with freezing **Rain**
water. They were a depressed crew, until during the eve- **and mud**
ning came a man named Demetrius, who brought Antony
the garment, stained with blood, which had been taken
from the body of Cassius, together with his sword. This
was news indeed!—and the Caesarians responded to it.

Both armies were in an unhappy state, and everything
depended upon what fresh spirit could be lit in them by
their leaders. Brutus spent much time and labour on the
task of reorganizing both his own men and the defeated
legions of Cassius. He spoke to them, individually and collectively; he pointed out the vastly superior advantage of
their own position on the hills, as compared with the position of the Caesarians down in the valley; he promised large
and encouraging rewards, and distributed them to the men,
so that there should be no question about their reality. By
his efforts he created a much improved army; but he himself was the least cheerful of them in heart. When he had
seen the body of Cassius, he is reported to have said: "A
happy man, this!—freed from all the troubles that are leading Brutus—to what end, I wonder?" He continued to
wonder.

On the very same day—the twenty-third of October—on
which the first battle of Philippi was fought, another battle,
a sea-battle, was fought near Brundusium. In a dead calm
the transports of the Caesarians were attacked by the fast
galleys of the enemy squadrons. Seventeen were captured,

Disaster at Brundusium

and many were sunk with those on board. The news of this serious disaster was known to Antony and Octavian a few days later, but since they held the roads westward, they could at any rate prevent it from reaching Brutus, and this they were very careful to do.

They had reason. Their supplies—always their weakest point—were running short; the season was getting late, and if Brutus, with his comfortable position and ample supplies, could keep them waiting and wasting time for a few weeks more, they would be forced either to attack his entrenchments with the overwhelming probability of a serious repulse, or march away, with all the loss of prestige involved —perhaps to face a hostile public opinion in Italy as well as a discouraged army. And Brutus certainly meant to exhaust them in this way. Once he knew of the reverse in the Adriatic, his intention would be confirmed.

So the chess-play went on, the Caesarians striving to extend a chain of entrenched posts round the flank of Brutus, so that they might reach the road by which he brought up his supplies. If they could do this, he must fight or retreat. But it was a question whether they could achieve their aim before they themselves were starved out.

In such circumstances as this, Marcus Antonius shone at his best. His bounding spirits and exalting optimism kept

Antony on the watch

his own resolution up to fighting level and encouraged the spirits of others. He pointed out to his men with convincing force that the very reluctance of the enemy to come out and fight proved conclusively their opinion of who would win if they did. They must watch for the moment to strike. Brutus, with the curious despondence and melancholy which seemed part of his character, did not get on too well with his own men. They were anxious to fight, and confident of the result. They did not sympathize with his waiting tactics. His officers argued with him, and tempers grew a little frayed on each side—while Antony laughed and talked and exhorted, and kept his cold and hungry men watching for their chance with the intentness of a hungry cat watching a mouse-hole. Daily they walked up to the enemy entrenchments, and defied those within to come out and fight. At last Brutus weakened. He would not have weakened had he known the true position of affairs. On the fifteenth of November a deserter came in who reported that the Caesarian transports had been sunk outside Brundusium—but he was laughed at as a romancer. On the sixteenth, Brutus at last gave way and fought.

The night before the battle—so they say: but Plutarch admits that one of his best authorities does not mention it —the spectre once more appeared to Brutus, but disappeared again without speaking. Many strange omens and prodigies were afterwards alleged to have happened. More premonitory of the truth was the hesitance that overcame **Brutus weakens** Brutus when the ranks were formed in the morning. Reports were being brought him that shook his faith in his men: he had not much in himself. They were most of them old Caesarian legionaries, who had followed him and Cassius because of the high bonus paid. Few had much sympathy for the political theories that animated Brutus. The more clearly such ideas were explained to the common man, the less he liked them. He could see that the auxiliary cavalry were watching the legions to mark what happened. One well-known officer—Plutarch names him, Camulatus—walked across and deserted to the Caesarians in open day. Finally, at about three o'clock in the afternoon, Brutus gave the word to advance, lest worse befall. His men were confident—but it was a confidence in themselves rather than in their cause or their leader.

VII

The second battle of Philippi was one of those fierce infantry battles which were seen only in the civil wars of Rome: a hand-to-hand struggle of swordsmen who fell where they stood but never gave back. As fast as one man fell, the rear man stepped forward to take his place. At last the troops of Octavian, fighting on the northern wing, **The attack on Brutus** pressed back the line opposed to them, and swung it right round until they drove it against and past the fortifications of the camp. They seized the gates, enclosing those within and turning away any further fugitives from taking refuge there. While Octavian's men attended to the camp, those of Antonius drove the centre before them, and with the help of cavalry endeavoured to cut off all who fled by the mountain roads or towards the sea. Brutus was among those who took refuge in the mountains. Prodigies of valour were performed by the men who protected his retreat; and one of them, Lucilius, even surrendered to the Caesarians on the pretence of being Brutus. He was brought before a rather anxious Antony, who was so pleased and relieved at the knowledge that he was to be spared the odious responsibility of dealing with the principal murderer of Caesar, that he merely said to the disappointed captors: "You have done better than you thought, not worse—for you thought you were bringing me an enemy, but you have brought me a friend!" . . . And a friend of Antony Lucilius remained for the rest of his life.

The battle came to a stop as daylight faded, but the fighters bivouacked on the field. Octavian, being still an invalid, retired at midnight: Antonius remained under arms with his men. Brutus spent a similar but less happy night in the mountains. One or two attempts were made by his companions to ascertain how the day had really gone, and **Night on the battle-field** what the prospects were: Brutus himself had no illusions upon the subject. He probably realized much more clearly than he ever publicly admitted that he was fighting for an obsolete and antiquarian ideal, a system of government suitable for a country of small independent city-states, but totally useless to a great world-wide dominion. He never had entertained very high hopes that his resistance to the Caesarians would achieve any definite result. He had fought for a principle for which he himself, in his heart of hearts, had none too much enthusiasm. He had now definitely lost the struggle, and was, on the whole, glad to be relieved of a burden which had weighed very heavily upon him. He did not mean to survive it. His ideal was a poor one, but it had been his own.

In the evening he held a Council of War with such officers as he could collect. To his question whether they would join in a last effort to regain the camp and bring aid to those who were shut in there, they replied that it was best now for him to think of his own safety. They themselves could surrender without risk. This being decided, Brutus proceeded to take the only way to safety that he felt honourably open to him. He asked his friend Publius Volumnius to perform the friendly office—but Volumnius was very unwilling. After meeting with several other refusals, he gained a grudging assent from Strato the Epirote. **Suicide of Brutus** Strato held the sword steady, turning his face away as he did so; and Brutus ran upon it and died.

Marcus Antonius found the body of Brutus, and with a queer mingling of motives and feelings—a mixture of the good-humoured generosity he was apt to show, when Fulvia was not by, with a sudden recollection of Alexander the Great and King Darius—he took off his rich purple cloak and cast it over the body of the chief of Caesar's murderers.

He issued orders that the body, wrapped in that Tyrian purple, should be burned, and the ashes sent to the dead man's mother—the ashes of the famous son who had slain her still-more-famous lover. . . . A little later, he found that his orders had been disregarded. Relying on his well-known carelessness, his own servant had stolen the cloak, and poor Brutus had gone to his fathers without it. The justice of Antonius was stern and prompt, and the dishonest servant was soon carrying the cloak to Brutus in the Elysian Fields.

Some years afterwards, Messalla Corvinus introduced Strato the Epirote to Octavian, who received him with kindness and took him into his own service. Strato proved a faithful friend to the future Augustus, and was with him at Actium.

VIII

The two battles of Philippi were the end of the anti-Caesarian party as an effective force. Sextus Pompeius still survived—but there was never any likelihood that he would lead a Roman party or exercise a government at Rome.

Surrender to Antony With Brutus and Cassius the last of the possible counter-revolutionists passed away. The troops who surrendered after the death of Brutus were numerous. Some fourteen thousand legionaries, still in fighting trim, passed into the service of Octavian and Antonius. The fortified camp also surrendered, with all who had taken refuge there. The troops were received without hesitation. With the superior officers it was different. For many of these, who were involved in the murder of Caesar, there could be no reconciliation. Some escaped; some died fighting; some slew themselves. Those who were taken were executed; and in this the later tradition represented Octavian as the colder and more inexorable of the two Caesarian generals, when Fulvia was not by to egg Antony on. Such senators however as were not concerned in the murder of Caesar, had no difficulty in making their peace. A body of them who took refuge on the island of Thasos appointed Messalla Corvinus and Lucius Bibulus to conduct negotiations with the victors. The delegates carried out their task to the general satisfaction. The treasure and supplies in the great depot at Thasos was surrendered, and the refugees were received to mercy.

On the whole, in similar circumstances, many victors, before and after, have shown themselves less reasonable than Octavian and Antonius. The men who were executed had in most cases been condemned by a Roman court of justice, and their lives in any event were forfeit.

As soon as these matters were settled, it was necessary to arrange for the demobilization of most of the legions, and for the settlement of the eastern provinces. There could hardly be two opinions concerning the distribution of these tasks. The east needed a soldier who could deal with the Parthian menace, and who had authority and prestige: and Marcus Antonius was clearly the man best fitted for the purpose. Octavian was still a very sick man. It was urgent that he should go home: and as most of the business to be transacted in Italy had already been determined and described in formal acts of the senate, it could very well be superintended by Octavian. The two leaders therefore parted: Antonius to the east, Octavian to the west. Neither they nor those who followed them and admired, could have guessed the results that were to flow from that parting.

Antony and Octavian part

CHAPTER VII

THE RETURN FROM PHILIPPI

I

THE return from Philippi marked the end of one epoch and the beginning of a new. Julius was dead, his ashes entombed, his murder avenged; he belonged to the past, and the days he had lived in and the problems he had dealt with **The new** began to fade into the background of history. Even Mar- **era** cus Antonius had vanished into the east, towards the Parthian war, the plains of Mesopotamia and the Arabian desert. A new Caesar landed in Italy, with weary, bandaged, battle-worn legions dragging sullenly behind him. He was barely twenty years old; yet the burden of rebuilding a world lay upon him—and he knew it.

They all came back from Philippi with a dissatisfied sense that the world had gone wrong, and had to be put right. The Roman world had had this feeling for a good many years past—but there had always hitherto been some urgent necessity that prevented men from giving their full attention to the matter. Now the last of the urgent necessities had been dealt with. The ground was clear; the time had come. It was possible to survey the problem at leisure.

Among the prisoners taken at Philippi was a short, stout military officer of the name of Horatius Flaccus, but more familiarly known to us as the poet Horace—the man who, more than any other, transmits to us the typical spirit of the Roman: his common-sense, his mastery of the construc- **War-** tive art, his occasional sensuality, his fondness for a bottle **weariness** of wine and a pretty girl, and his fundamental justice, sim-

136

plicity and humanity, as such virtues were known in his day. No man was ever better fitted than Horace to express some of the feelings with which the army came home after Philippi—the weariness of war and strife, the longing for peace, and the tendency to picture a millennium in the shape of a bit of earth, not exclusively to make an income out of it, but also as a home, a little world, a spot where the retired warrior could sometimes take his afternoon nap in the shade of his own trees, listening to his own river rushing by. . . . This was the substance they had fought for, of which all talk about politics, and parties, Caesarianism and anti-Caesarianism, was merely the symbol and reflection. . . . The city of Rome never roared more loudly, or was crowded thicker than in the Augustan age; but this was quite consistent with the truth that the Roman was tired of city life.[1] Let the government, and the business men, and the shop keepers and the slaves dwell there; the serious Roman had finished with these things and hungered for the rural life.

The soldier who returned from Philippi was not dreaming of vast estates, with great responsibilities and equivalent risks. A small farm, that he could walk round in half an hour, and that half a dozen slaves or less could cultivate for him [2]—this was what he wanted. For one man like Horace, who could put this longing into perfect verse, there were tens of thousands who had the idea, but could not express it, and tens of thousands more who had the wish, without being able exactly to formulate it to themselves, much less to others. And there were (as indeed there always are in such cases) very serious difficulties in the way of realizing the dreams of the returning army. It never thought that,

---

[1] Horace, *Epistles*, I, xvi, 1–16; I, xiv; I, x.
[2] Horace's farm was cultivated by eight, as we learn from his remarks to Davus, *Satires*, II, vii, 101.

hard as it had been to fight the battle of Philippi, it was a
far harder task to produce the land allotments for the army
without raising the rest of Italy in arms and causing a
greater battle than Philippi had been.

II

The sickness from which Octavian had suffered throughout the campaign reached its culmination at Brundusium
on the way home. For some time he lay between life and
death, and rumours of his death did at one time spread. But
Providence had a use for him yet, and he did not die. He
recovered, to begin the second chapter of a long and successful life. As soon as he was well enough to travel, he
made his way north to Rome, where he laid before the
Octavian friends and allies of Marcus Antonius the details of the
shows his agreement he had entered into with his colleague. They
hand admitted them, and they made no objection to the terms:
but it must have been evident to Octavian from the first
that it would be their business to prevent him from acquir-
ing more influence in Italy than would suit the purposes of
their leader.

Marcus Antonius, when he divided the work with Octavian, had not acted upon any presumption that the latter
was going to rebuild a world, nor even that he was capable
of rebuilding one. He had made the division on terms very
favourable to Octavian. His reasons for this generosity he
never divulged; but it is not difficult to guess the conceptions upon which they were based. As he saw matters, he
was leaving Octavian—somewhat shorn of prestige after
the events at Philippi—to struggle with an insoluble problem in Italy while he, Antonius, went to gather fresh power
and new laurels in those lands which had made the wealth
of Lucullus a proverb and had founded the fortunes of

Sulla and Pompeius. He realized only too well by how narrow a margin the west had defeated the east at Philippi. A very little change—the difference even of one man, if that man chanced to be Marcus Antonius—might swing the balance. . . . Well—when he had finished with the Parthians he would return, just as Sulla had once returned; and he would pick up the supremacy where it was certain to fall from the hands of this boy, who did not realize the magnitude or difficulty of the task he was undertaking. . . . Every action of Marcus Antonius showed this to be his belief. He had communicated his thoughts on this head to his lieutenants and agents, so that they could adjust their actions to his policy. . . . And there was much to be said in favour of his point of view. Its one weakness was that he was taking his success against the Parthians far too much for granted. Before he could use the east, he had to become its master—and this was a proposition rather more difficult than he thought. It remained to be seen whether he could solve his own problems before Octavian had solved his. *The scheme of Antony*

At the first glance, the distribution of the land allotments seemed to be a task beyond the power of Octavian. The veterans demanded the fulfilment of the promises made to them, which involved the expropriation of eighteen Italian cities, and the redivision of the land belonging to them. There was no getting away from the fact that this promise had been made. But the owners who were to be expropriated—and who in some cases were themselves military colonists of an earlier settlement—demanded that they should be compensated. To refuse so natural a demand was not easy, without raising a further set of problems as serious as those it solved, for the expropriated owners were not large landlords, nor persons in irregular possession of public land, but were small proprietors whose title was beyond *Problem of the expropriated* reasonable question. But to assent to the demand for compensation was a flat impossibility. No fund existed from which the compensation could be paid. Octavian had no resources to which he could turn, save selling what might remain of the property confiscated under the proscription, and borrowing from the temples—both of them temporary expedients, and inadequate at that. . . . If he had had free access to the revenues of his provinces of Sicily, Africa and Sardinia, matters might have been easier—but Sextus Pompeius blocked the way. . . . The threatened owners suggested that alternatively the burden should be spread over the whole of Italy, and that the properties to be taken should be balloted for. They and their families came to Rome in crowds, and filled the public places with their presence, their arguments and their grievances. There cannot be many men who, at the age of twenty, are set to solve a puzzle of such an apparently insoluble nature. To

Rational solution necessary

cut physical knots is easy, though Gordius himself may tie them; but political knots are not susceptible of such treatment, and must be unravelled. Octavian entered upon the path that was to lead him to permanent fame and success when he set himself courageously to deal with this question in a way that should satisfy as many people as possible—and if he had to leave some dissatisfied, then to ensure that these should be the people who were least able to upset the settlement.

One of the serious dangers in the situation was the existence of a political party still able—and only too eager—to exploit the grievances of the threatened owners for their own purposes. The *optimates* gladly pointed out the evils engendered by a war which had been fought, as they contended, not for the common interest, but for the profit of a party. They preached the doctrine which Brutus had preached—that the land allotments were bribes given in order to ensure that the men who received them should be bound to support the new Caesarian dictatorship, just because they would live in continual terror of losing what had wrongfully been given them. It was an effective argument—not, indeed, with the Caesarian legionaries but certainly with the threatened owners, who were thus drawn into the anti-Caesarian ranks. Octavian's explanation of the impossible situation he was in did not satisfy either side. The legionaries were determined to have what they considered their rights, and they did not hesitate to take by force anything they thought they ought to have. They defied Octavian's efforts to restrain them.

The principal ally of the *optimates*—Sextus Pompeius, the pirate chief—threw the whole of his weight into the scale on their side, and it was no slight one. He stopped all the Sicilian and African corn ships. His complete blockade of Rome was all the more terribly effective because the immense number of men drafted into the legions, together with the unrest and unsettlement caused by the civil war, had caused a shortage of agricultural produce throughout Italy.

Such embarrassments needed to be met by a corresponding staunchness and unity on the side of the Caesarians; and it is certain that this was the feeling of the army. The unity of the party, however, was imperilled by the action of the Antonian leaders. Lucius Antonius, the triumvir's brother, was one of the consuls for the year, and he employed the power and dignity of his magisterial position to obstruct and restrain the proceedings of Octavian, nominally in the interests of the *optimates*, of whom he posed as a representative, but in reality with the purpose of delaying the land settlement until Marcus Antonius should return. Marius, the agent of the latter, assisted in this obstructive policy. The idea was that by preventing Octavian from

Sextus
Pompeius

effecting a successful settlement, they would all the more increase the prestige of Antony when the latter, upon coming home at length from the east, should proceed to accomplish, with majestic ease, all that Octavian had been **Obstruc-** unable to achieve. It did not seem to occur to either of **tion** them that Antony might find the solution as difficult as Octavian found it. They were relying, no doubt, upon the immense wealth of the east, which they expected him to bring with him.

The agreement between Octavian and Antony provided that Octavian should have full powers to nominate whom he liked as the leaders of the new colonies: and Antony, when he made the agreement, must have known what he was doing. Lucius and Manius, however, insisted that friends of Antony should be chosen to fill these offices. Octavian prudently gave way: but the men so chosen intrigued on behalf of Antony, and deliberately relaxed the discipline of the troops with the object of rendering the position of Octavian invidious when he endeavoured to restore it. The result was that the new colonists made depredations on their neighbours which brought a fresh set of angry and well-justified complaints to Rome: not only the dispossessed, but even those who had not been dispossessed, but who lived too near the new colonies, were seething with semi-revolt. One thing certainly was clear. Either Octavian would have to resign and retire into obscurity, a baffled and beaten man who had undertaken a task too large for him, or he must throw every ounce of his intelligence and determination into the work of accomplishing it. If there were power in him, it must be shown now.

The army How little real truth there was in the contention of the **decides** **policy** *optimates* that the Caesarian legionaries were the bribed hirelings of a tyranny can be seen by the helplessness of the

so-called tyrant in the hands of the legionaries. The wonderful discipline which made them the finest soldiers in the
world had its reverse side in an unequalled power of thinking and acting in unison. It was the army itself which laid
down the policy and compelled its execution. Over the
army, at least, Octavian had nothing remotely resembling
the authority of a tyrant. He did indeed possess exceptional legal powers; but he had received them only in order
to enable him to carry out measures that were demanded
by the army. The land allotments they were determined
to have. If there were difficulties, then it was his business
to devise methods of overcoming such difficulties. . . .
They were his soldiers and he was their commander, when
it came to fighting; but in matters of politics they were his
masters and he was their servant. They understood their
own indispensability to the man who led them. If their
protecting hand were once withdrawn, how much was the
life of Octavian worth? Very little!

He had not such an extraordinary personal ascendancy
as Julius had exercised over the troops; and the particular
kind of ascendancy that Julius had exercised he never possessed at all. The influence he was destined to gain over
them later on was a totally different one. Several times in
these days his life was in danger from their unruliness.
There is a well-known story, preserved in more than one
version, concerning a soldier who, on entering the theatre
when Octavian was present, found all the third-class seats
full. He therefore proceeded to impose himself upon one
of the second-class seats appropriated to the *equites*. On
this being pointed out to Octavian, the latter, in the interests of discipline, had the offending individual turned out.
There was no reason why anything more should have been
heard of this quite proper action; but by the time the per-
formance came to an end an extraordinary rumour had per-

Octavian
in danger

vaded the third-class seats. The expelled man had been (so it was said) arrested and tortured. Octavian, issuing from the theatre, found himself in the midst of an excited and dangerous mob of soldiers who called for the restoration of their missing comrade. He was accused of having made away with the man; and matters were saved only by the appearance of the unconscious cause of the trouble. Questioned, the soldier, to the indignation of his friends, flatly denied that he had been arrested, tortured or murdered. They accused him of truckling to the aristocracy; but after an exchange of language at least as vivid as would have ornamented a similar occasion today, the mob began to disperse. It was evident that a mistake had been made. But if there had been any delay in finding the individual concerned, the mistake might have had serious results for Octavian.

Facing the unrest
He learnt to face and subdue this rebellious tendency, as successful commanders in all ages have subdued it—by personal influence. A great meeting was called in the Campas Martius, at which the subject of the land allotments was to be dealt with. The proceedings, according to the Roman custom in an age in which artificial lighting was expensive and inadequate, were timed to begin at daybreak, and the veterans were in their places before dawn. Octavian was late; and this was adversely commented upon. To fill up the time, a centurion named Nonius took the platform. He reminded his hearers that Octavian was still an invalid, and this, and not disrespect for the meeting, was the probable cause of his absence. These very reasonable remarks were received with hostility and disorder by a section of the audience. Nonius too was called a truckler and a flunkey. Stones were thrown. Finally, Nonius was driven from the platform and chased into the river, whence he was dragged out and murdered.

MARCUS ANTONIUS
the husband of Cleopatra
(*From a coin in the British Museum*)

"THE SERPENT OF OLD NILE"
Cleopatra, Queen of Egypt
(*From the same coin*)

The murderers left the body of Nonius in the road by which Octavian was expected—no doubt to encourage him. Octavian's friends, on finding the body and hearing the story of what had happened, implored him not to go on. He, however, was wiser, and saw the absolute necessity of facing up to threats of this nature. When he spoke to the recalcitrant meeting, he did so very quietly, on the assumption that he himself had no connection whatsoever with what had taken place, but that it had been entirely a matter of private quarrel among the men themselves. He gave them a little good advice on the subject of mutual forbearance—good, commonplace advice, such as every one inwardly agreed with. Under his coolness, the temperature of the meeting rapidly fell. When he proceeded to read out the distribution of the awards, together with the extra rewards, *honoris causa*, and some additional gifts to soothe the impatience of the trouble-makers, the meeting underwent a striking change of feeling. The real sense of justice and good-will, that was never far from the surface in Roman citizens, urged them to apologize, and to tell him that it was their own wish that the murderers of Nonius should be punished. He answered quietly that he knew their identity, but would leave them to the condemnation of their own consciences and to the general opinion of their fellows. This went down excellently with his audience. They appreciated his appeal to their discipline and orderliness. The meeting, which had begun so badly, ended well, with something like a reconciliation between the rank and file and their leader.

The first effective distributions of land therefore resulted in a new spirit of confidence in their leader. Some of the impatience and unrest, if not all, died down; those who still awaited their allotments felt a renewal of trust that they would not be forgotten, and a general return to

Octavian as conciliator

His ascendancy

normal feeling began.

And this had been gained without any concession to the *optimates* or any such turning towards them as should shake the faith of the army. Octavian stood, in its eyes, as the unswerving and incorruptible champion of the Caesarian policy.

III

In the meantime, what had become of Marcus Antonius? While events were pushing Octavian inexorably along the path that led to the complete development of his peculiar character, they were doing the same to Antonius. Fate refused to be satisfied until she had wrung from them both all the possibilities of which they were capable.

But the primrose path of Antonius was very different from the hard and apparently ungrateful path of Octavian. Marcus Antonius was at the height of his prestige when he passed through Greece after the battle of Philippi. Universally regarded as the real creator of victory, the hero of the great struggle, he had nothing to do but to bask in the admiration, the worship, the servility of the subject population. They guessed some of the reasons why he had come. Having been stripped to the skin by the exactions of Brutus and Cassius, they were anxious to temper the process of being flayed by Antony. To Greece itself he was mild enough. Greece was always a privileged land to the admiring Roman. But as soon as he had crossed the Aegean to Asia, the triumphal progress began. Youth at the prow and pleasure at the helm had always pleased Antony, and high and low alike, throughout Asia, joined hands to flatter and amuse and propitiate the man whom they so deeply and justifiably dreaded. While kings (as Plutarch vividly puts it) waited at his door, and queens struggled with one an-

Antonius in the east

other for his smile, the musician with a new piece or the danger with a new turn, who could induce in him a pleasant mood, were public benefactors. His obvious delight in these things was an encouragement. He was by no means unable to enjoy the finest art, or to show excellent judgment: but his real pleasure was in the things of lightness and thistledown—the light music, the light feet, the light ladies who were so perfectly trained to the petty enchanting arts that a very old civilization like that of Asia has a way of bringing to perfection. . . . They needed every help that would lighten the burden upon them.

It only occurred to them later on that they were making a miscalculation. Marcus Antonius remorselessly swept into his net the treasures of the kings and the charms of the queens; and he gathered from helpless Asia itself the money he scattered so enthusiastically among the pipers and dancers. He was naturally the sort of man who never counts his change or adds up the items in his bill. But Asia was the home, not only of matchless musicians and enchanting courtesans, but of some of the shrewdest brains in the world. The orator Hybreas—a famous man in his day, who in a luckier age might have gone down to history in company with Miltiades and Themistocles—penetrated the secret of Antony's character. To flatter him was not the right way to his heart: flattery was only a pleasant jest to him. To talk to him as one man to another, with faith in his good feeling and his sense of justice—that was the way: and Hybreas discovered it. *Attempts to propitiate him*

The conversation between Hybreas and Antony was a striking one.

"So we are to pay you two years' taxation?" said Hybreas, in effect. "Well and good! There should be no difficulty, since you are doubtless able to give us two summers and a double harvest to pay it with."

Antony woke up, at that.

"Do you know," said Hybreas, "that Asia has raised two hundred thousand talents for your Romans? If you haven't got it, ask your collectors where it is. If you have got it, and have spent it, heaven help us, for we are done."

This was the way to deal with Marcus Antonius. He listened to Hybreas, and appreciated the common-sense of the situation as Hybreas laid it before him. His aim had not been the mere purposeless accumulation of money. He had had an object in view—the financing of the Parthian War, and of the land-settlements. Nor—when the case was fairly put to him—did he wish to tax Asia past the danger-point. From the moment of his conversation with Hybreas, he looked about for another source from which to obtain the financial support he wanted.

His search was destined to have historic consequences, for it brought him into touch with Egypt.

IV

One of the first measures he had taken after his arrival in Asia was to call Queen Cleopatra of Egypt to answer the accusations that had been brought against her, of having given assistance to Cassius. In the circumstances, the summons was equivalent to demanding ransom from Egypt; and at the time he looked, no doubt, for no result much more memorable than a large sum down (which Egypt could well afford) in aid of the Parthian War, and perhaps some pages of excuses and denials prepared for Cleopatra by the Egyptian Government. As a matter of fact, it is not very probable that he entertained any serious beliefs that Cleopatra had sided with the anti-Caesarians. The government which had murdered Pompeius, and the queen who had delighted and enchanted Julius, and was the

mother of his son Caesarian, were not very likely to have
entertained any passion for Brutus and Cassius. He knew
the queen personally, though slightly. She had lived for
some months in Rome, and had left only after the murder
of Julius. He had known her long years before, when he
commanded the cavalry corps that accompanied Gabinius
into Egypt. He had admired her then. What she had grown
into, of course, he could not tell. Julius had set a proper
value upon the women who, from time to time, had hon-
oured him with their interest; he never had shown any
disposition to share their company—especially with rovers
of the type of Marcus Antonius—and Cleopatra had respected his preferences. Hence Antony, at this juncture,
had only imperfect ideas respecting the material with
which he was dealing. Greek women aged quickly.

Dellius, his envoy to Egypt, had far clearer ideas upon
this subject than his chief. The moment he saw Cleopatra,
and had heard her speak, he realized something of what
might be in store. Marcus Antonius was incapable of harsh-
ness to a woman such as this. Her magic lay not in physical
beauty, but in the charm, the lovely voice, the enchanting
cleverness, the power of entering into other people's minds
that was shown even in her striking gift for languages. So
clearly did Dellius perceive the probabilities, that with **Her**
great wisdom he hastened to make friends with the mam- **powers**
mon of unrighteousness. He assured her of the distinguished virtues of Marcus Antonius—his manliness, his gen-
tleness and his generosity. He urged her to go herself to
Cilicia to meet Antony. Cleopatra had been able to catch
and hold Julius while she was an inexperienced girl. She
was now a mature woman with a large and varied knowledge of the world and of the men who dwelt in it. She
perfectly understood the man that Dellius was describing
to her, and the policy he was advising her to follow. She

made ready to catch and hold the successor of Julius—the man who, in that year and day, was the most famous man in the world. She had dexterity, brilliance and self-confidence; and she had money. There was hardly another person the whole world through who possessed the financial resources of the monarch of Egypt. . . . She had conquered Julius with nothing but her charm and a roll of carpet. She had a good deal more than a roll of carpet to equip her against Antony.

Cleopatra at Tarsus

While Cleopatra was making preparations for the voyage to Cilicia, she allowed Antony and his staff to keep on wondering why they received no answers to their communications. They wrote again—and still they had no answer from Egypt. Then one day, as they were at Tarsus, the news came! Antony, sitting in the market place, saw the crowd dissolve and disappear; and not only the crowd, but his own entourage, too. In a short time he had the unusual experience of finding himself sitting there alone. All he knew was that someone had passed a watchword: "Aphrodite has come to feast with Dionysus!" What it portended, he could not guess.

The historians have omitted to tell us whether Marcus Antonius went on sitting in the agora of Tarsus, or whether, at last, he too arose and followed the crowd down to the wharves that bordered the river Cydnus. Whether he saw it himself or not, he must have heard in full detail the story how the great Egyptian galleys, flashing with African colour and gold, spreading great sails of Tyrian purple, as we can still see them in the wall paintings of the Pharaohs, came gliding with measured stroke of oars up the river, to the music of flutes and harps and pipes; while under an awning of cloth of gold, surrounded by little Cupids, reclined Cleopatra, in the crossed cincture and patterned robe of the goddess. . . . As far as the onlookers

could see, as they followed along the towpaths of the Cyd- The ship of love
nus, or poured out of the gates of Tarsus, this vessel was
manned entirely by a bevy of beauties in keeping with the
scene: nymphs and graces stood at the steering oar, and
clustered around the ropes. This was the way in which
Cleopatra came to Tarsus.

Some things, which the modern age has to learn out of
books, were still living and current tradition in the age of
Marcus Antonius and Cleopatra. There were probably few
small children in Tarsus so ignorant as not to know the
stories of Aphrodite and Dionysus, which were as familiar
to them as those of Cinderella or Bluebeard to the modern
child. Every one in Tarsus therefore could enter into the
spirit of this gorgeous and most amusing pageant, and could
fill in the missing words. Antony, unexpectedly crowned
as Dionysus, could chuckle a little at the compliment!
After all, he had done a little to deserve it! He asked her
to dinner. She answered by suggesting that he should come
to her. He was not unwilling to satisfy his curiosity by
going. His reception blew away into forgetfulness the efforts of the Asiatic cities to amuse and flatter their lord.
This was the real thing! The splendour was beyond com-
parison; and it culminated in something new and dazzling
to a Roman, whose acquaintance with artificial lighting was
not great. At a given instant the whole ship was illuminated
by lights arranged in patterns. A modern, accustomed to Illumi-nations
Piccadilly Circus or Times Square, might have thought little of it; to a Roman, it was an enchanting novelty, the
memory of which was handed down among the stories of
Antony and Cleopatra.

Dellius had calculated with marvellous accuracy the results of bringing them together. Antonius insisted upon
entertaining her, and he put forth the whole of his power
to do it well; but the results fell so lamentably short of the

standard Cleopatra had set that he was the first to laugh and to apologize for them. She met him with exactly the right response to his mood. It was the man himself she was after; and with exact judgment she knew that it was the woman herself who must do most of the work of catching him. Like Catherine of Russia and Elizabeth of England, Cleopatra was a ruler who used her sex as part of the game of statesmanship; and of the three, Cleopatra was probably the greatest artist and the most successful player of the game. She was doing on a large scale what the Asiatic cities had imperfectly attempted; and she meant it to be successful in her case. She meant to absorb this man and all his power into the interests of Egypt. She needed him to make good her own deficiencies. And he could only be absorbed by a power as great as his own. There was something in Marcus Antonius that responded with amused and malicious glee to all these trimmings of outward show and fantastic exuberance; he loved a little light-hearted, light-headed lunacy; but inside him there was something which could not be grappled or held save with considerations of high statesmanship. He might be drunk for a week—nothing was more likely—but when he awoke he would start thinking about the Parthian War.

Antony
a complex
problem

The peculiarity of Cleopatra was that she not only penetrated to this truth, but could detect the time and the place at which these alternating moods changed into one another. He was a curious mingling of the sensualist, the soldier, the jester, the statesman, the jolly good fellow and the simple, affectionate man. To treat him as any one or two alone of these was to be certain of failure, but to consider them all, and allow for their change and alternation, needed a mind that had a touch of genius in it. Cleopatra had that touch. . . . It remained to be seen if Octavian possessed it also.

V

Hence, while the problems of Italy were pressing so hard upon those at home, Marcus Antonius left Asia (much to its relief) and went the golden and scented journey to Egypt with Cleopatra. Fulvia? He had forgotten about her! Out of sight was so often out of mind with Marcus Antonius, that we need not be surprised if the memory of Fulvia scarcely crossed his thoughts.

That winter in Egypt was famous, and has been described again and again. To say that it was one round of extravagant gaieties is one way of describing it; but perhaps the truest way of describing it is to call it a fantastic play, of which Cleopatra was the playwright and producer, and in which she herself played the leading part. So entertaining was the play that Marcus Antonius (who, as we have seen before, had a strong inborn histrionic sense) instinctively took the part he had been assigned, and proceeded to play it. At the time it seemed to many observers to be a comedy; later ages decided it to be a romance; modern students incline to fancy it a tragedy; but any play that contained Antony would tend to become a mixed one. *The Inimitable Life*

It even had a title—"The Inimitable Life"—chosen by Cleopatra; and the Inimitable Livers were the actors. The members of the caste entertained the company in turn in some inimitable way: the inimitableness was the sole condition, limit, bound and rule. The principle of inimitableness tickled the soul of Marcus Antonius. It was not the kind of notion that would appeal to a stupid or brutal man; and Cleopatra might have exercised her charms in vain upon the propraetor Verres (who had been in the triumvirs' proscription list—he, as well as Cicero!) or upon some Romans of his type; but there was something great in this idea of Inimitableness. There was something varied in it too, for as they explored the principle, they found out in how many curious ways it was possible to be inimitable: from mere profusion upwards.

Some of the stories come from sources which can be named, and the value of which can to some degree be estimated. Plutarch quotes the stories told by the physician **The fan-** Philotas of Amphissa, who was a friend of his grandfather. **tasies of** Philotas, then a medical student at Alexandria, used to dine **Alexandria** with Antyllus Antonius, Fulvia's son, and happened one day, in a friendly wrangle, to reduce a very loud-spoken person to silence. Antyllus, delighted, waved his hand at the side-board and said: "Philotas, all you see there is yours!" Philotas was polite in his thanks, but all the same was considerably astonished when, soon after, the plate was brought to him. At first he flatly refused the risk of accepting it. The value was too large for a boy to give away. The man who brought the articles reassured him. It was all in order. The boy had authority to spend what he liked. As a little friendly advice, however, he thought Philotas might be wise to take the value in money, since there might possibly be articles of specially valued workmanship that the boy's father would prefer to keep.

This was one form of Inimitableness. Philotas is our authority also for another. At the invitation of one of the palace cooks, whom he knew, the young student visited the royal kitchens. There, among other things of interest, he saw eight wild boars roasting whole. The cook laughed, however, at the suggestion that a great banquet was in preparation. Only twelve persons were expected, he assured his friend. Then he explained that Antony was highly **Profusion** temperamental. Dinner must be served with absolute perfection—and just when he was ready for it. If he changed his mind and put it off for any reason, no excuse was accepted for an imperfect or late meal. Hence these vast preparations. They were intended to provide for all possible eventualities.

Roman and Greek ideas of what constituted inimitableness differed a good deal. Antony and his friends did not always live up to the Greek standard. Drinking, hunting, dice-playing and horse-play appealed to them rather more deeply than eating, dressing up, and listening to music; it was the richness of the staging and the abundant profusion of expenditure that formed the common ground—the ideal of doing things upon a larger scale and with more complete disregard of consequences than any one had ever attempted before. Cleopatra had no objection to experimenting with some of the Roman dissipations that perhaps had the charm of novelty for her. She hunted and gambled; she dressed up as a maidservant and accompanied Antony on those "rags," or raids into the low parts of the town, which, with all their accompanying excitements of teasing the women and fighting the men, are usually the perquisite of free countries. She is probably the only reigning queen— and certainly the only queen of Egypt—who ever did take part in such recreations, which often enough ended in Antony and his friends being knocked about and driven home the worse for wear but still full of enthusiasm by the Alexandrians. There is a famous legend concerning the culmination of the Inimitable Life, when she herself performed the crowning act that no one else could rival, by dropping her pearl ear-ring into the wine-cup, watching it dissolve, and drinking it up: the most costly drink in all the long history of Man. . . . That was the story, at any rate. . . . It may have happened! [3]

Riot and Reason

But all this had a very definite purpose: and the purpose

[3] Augustus, in later years, preserved the other one of the pair in his museum on the Palatine.

was to keep fast hold of Marcus Antonius. As spring approached, she knew she could not keep him by her side, and that she ought not even to try. If anything, she must urge him away. . . . He had had an experience that could never be wiped out of his memory. He would never forget these days. She would always be able to appeal to them. And in this she was right. . . . She herself put into his mind the decision to go. It happened when the Inimitable Life, rather exhausted with its exuberances, had softened down to fishing matches in the Nile. Since the Romans got the worst of these contests, Antony paid a diver to go down and fasten fish to their hooks. Astonished and suspicious at the sudden improvement in the Roman skill, Cleopatra made enquiries and discovered what had happened. Next day she sent down one of her own divers, who affixed a large salt fish to Antony's line—and he had the grace and the good humour to join in the roars of laughter that saluted his catch when he drew it up! Cleopatra came across

They terminate the Inimitable Life

and said: "Leave fishing to us poor people of Pharos and Canopus: cities, provinces and people are the fish for you!"

So they terminated the Inimitable Life—for the time being. It had been a great winter!

VI

Marcus Antonius had seen no harm in playing the part and enjoying the fun. He was not quite so foolish as some people afterwards supposed. He had wasted time, no doubt: but he was in no hurry. He did not mean to return to Italy just yet—not until Octavian was much deeper in the slough of confusion. The boy had got through once, with the aid of Hirtius and Pausa; and twice, by the aid of Marcus Antonius. He was not likely to get through a third time, if Antony only kept well out of the way. Time and money were not so scanty in Egypt that Antony need trouble too much over them. The most serious waste was of attention. He should have kept himself in touch with all that went on elsewhere during that fateful autumn and winter—and he did not. The same cloud that had descended upon Julius and caused him to forget the world for half a year had now descended upon Antonius. He should have been laying his plans for the Parthian War, and obtaining from Cleopatra the money he needed to equip the armies. She would have raised no objection. She followed his moods with an intent watchfulness, playing up to them, forestalling them, continually delighting him with her infinite variety; her one object was to tie him to herself, not to determine his policy or his plans. Her success seemed so perfect, he was so completely charmed and conquered, that she had no suspicion of any mistake in the reckoning. And there would indeed have been no mistake if Marcus Antonius, like Julius Caesar, had been the only man of his kind in the world. Everything, in that case, would have happened as Cleopatra was counting that it would happen. The disturbing factors that threw out her reckoning and destroyed her work were the existence of Octavian—of whom she had perhaps barely heard—and of the brother and wife and agent of Antonius away in Italy. While she was charming Marcus Antonius to her own purposes by the methods that had proved so effective, the whole situation was being changed by catastrophic events, of which neither she nor Antony knew anything.

Marcus Antonius made the same error about Octavian that Pompeius Magnus made about Julius—he under-rated his opponent. Had he realized the real character of the man he was dealing with, he would at once have forced the Parthian War to a crisis. Egypt, which could find money to be wasted, could have found money to be used, and

Cleopatra's mistake

Antony and Octavian

Marcus Antonius, as he was in the days immediately after the battle of Philippi, was strong enough and hardy enough to have won two victorious campaigns and then to have faced Octavian with the additional glory and prestige earned by these new laurels. History, in such an event, might have been different. But he never conceived the necessity of any such precaution—and certainly Cleopatra could not tell him. She was a woman of charm and cleverness—but she was not a soldier, nor was she a Roman politician. She had no means of knowing the ebb and flow of affairs at Rome; and she guessed nothing of the quicksands waiting for Marcus Antonius.

The difficulties between Lucius Antonius and Octavian had increased as the year wore on. Lucius openly made friends with the dispossessed proprietors, and showed sympathy for their plight. He had no right to do this unless he was prepared to restore their lands to them, or to pay them compensation—neither of which steps, however just and desirable they might be, he was able to promise. The Antonian troops disapproved of the conduct of Lucius.

The departure of Antony for Egypt was a heavy blow to Fulvia. She had been foolish enough to let him go to the East without her, though she must have known the instability of his temperament on the subject of women. Up to this point she had opposed the policy of Lucius, on the ground that it created the danger of civil war while Antony was absent from Italy. When Manius made the malicious but convincing suggestion that nothing would bring Antony back to Italy so quickly as a civil war, the shot went home. From this moment the three representatives of Marcus Antonius were united—and their unity sprang direct from his visit to Egypt.

Fulvia is jealous

It is very difficult to believe that Antony himself, had he been in touch with his representatives, would have approved the course they adopted, or would have allowed its continuance. They were especially unwise in ignoring the opinion of the army, which should have been decisive— and would have been, had Antony been there to note it. Moreover, they were precipitate in forcing the issue. Their leader would not be ready to return to Italy for something like two years to come. They were quite capable of forming an intelligent opinion concerning the military power of the Parthians and the length of time it would take to complete the campaigns upon the Mesopotamian border. But it is probable that the ineffectiveness of Octavian during the campaign of Philippi was now bearing its strange fruit. It had convinced the Antonian leaders, as well as Antony himself, that Octavian was not a man to be feared. And, as we have just seen, the journey of Antony to Egypt and the winter of Inimitable Living completed the vicious circle by enlisting Fulvia on the side of those who **The** were now hastening to embroil Italy in another civil war. **vicious circle**

CHAPTER VIII

THE REMARKABLE PROCEEDINGS OF
THE ROMAN ARMY

I

WE should do the army the greatest injustice if we supposed that it either welcomed the prospect of fighting, or idly allowed civil war to develop through any lethargy or indifference on its own part. So far from this being the case, the army took every possible step it could think of to calm down quarrels within the party, and to mediate between the rivals. Nothing could be done as long as the dissensions were indefinite; but as soon as there was something that could form a subject of arbitration, the leading military officers intervened.

While Octavian was superintending the last of the new settlements in Campania, Fulvia sent Antony's children with Lucius, in order to keep them before the eyes of the veterans. It was an irritating and quite an unnecessary thing to do, as no one was attempting to do any harm to Marcus Antonius, or to obscure his glory. It was probably intended to be irritating. While the business of settlement was on foot, Sextus Pompeius made a naval raid upon the coast of Bruttium; whereupon, naturally enough, Octavian sent a body of cavalry to patrol the coast and drive off any raiders whom they could intercept. The gentle art of screaming for help is a very old one; and Lucius seized this opportunity to resort to it. He took refuge in one of the colonies which had been settled with Antonian veterans, and began to enrol a bodyguard on the ground that his life was in danger, and that Octavian was conspiring against Antony. Octavian replied that he was on perfectly good terms with Marcus Antonius, and that Lucius was trying to make mischief, and to upset the triumvirate which had been instituted to carry out the land-settlements. The cavalry were in Bruttium on proper and lawful business, and were not directed against Lucius or his life.

This was a suitable subject for mediation and the superior officers at once tendered their services. Octavian welcomed these peacemakers. His attitude may have been unqualified in its sincerity, or it may have been an example of enlightened diplomacy; but in any case it was a wise one. We should make a grievous error if we pictured to ourselves an Octavian who was in calm control of this stormy situation, riding the whirlwind and directing the storm. The reality was lamentably otherwise. He was a worried and harassed individual by no means seeing his way out of the tangle he was in, and far from certain that he was going to make a success of his work. He must have known, indeed, that only a certain amount of luck—and perhaps only a certain amount of blundering by his opponents—would enable him to win through. He could not afford to show an irreconcilable spirit. If he ultimately obtained the support of the majority of the veterans, it was by invariably accepting these offers of mediation, and making clear his wish to avoid strife. He realized that the army did not want another civil war, and would not forgive those who made it inevitable.

Arbitration offered

Octavian accepts

The Antonian leaders showed some obtuseness on all these points. None of them shared the infallible instinct for public opinion which Marcus Antonius himself possessed; and they were three, not one. Their triplicity caused a confusion of will and policy. Lucius Antonius was proceeding upon the assumption that, in addition to the enthusiastic backing of the army, he could obtain also the sympathy and support of the still powerful party of the *optimates* by talking Caesarianism to one and anti-Caesarianism to the other. Manius believed in the insincerity of Octavian, and thought he could play trick for trick—not realizing that he was going far too fast in showing these convictions, which were neither admitted by Octavian nor agreed on by the army. Fulvia added to the confusion by possessing a third and totally irrelevant motive—she wanted to frighten Marcus Antonius to the point of leaving Cleopatra and returning to Italy. The more threatening the spectre of civil war, the more likely he was to return. The interplay of these three different policies fatally weakened the Antonian cause. The army became restive at the idea of an anti-Caesarian policy supported by the *optimates*. Many of those who would not actually side against Antony became sullen and nerveless in his support. They thought Manius himself cynical and insincere; and they had not the least interest in cutting short Antony's enjoyment of Cleopatra's company. But the policy of Octavian was single and unconfused. It was his intention simply to carry out the terms of his agreement with Antony. The army, rightly or wrongly, gradually got hold of the idea that he would listen to its point of view rather than insist upon his own; that he was willing to give them what they wanted, and was single-minded and straight and trustworthy. And no doubt, if he saw it to be worth his while, Octavian could show all these virtues. It is extremely unlikely that even he himself at this time could have told where he was following and where leading; where he was single-minded, and where duplex. They were all of them moving together upon a current none of them could resist.

The board of arbitration agreed upon seven articles which were submitted to the parties concerned. The only two that we need concern ourselves with are the first and

Antonian
cause
weakened

the last; the first provided that the triumvirs should not interfere with the customary duties of the consuls; while the seventh laid down that Lucius was to dispense with his bodyguard and go about his magisterial duties without fear. . . . It is obvious that the arbitrators considered the complaints of Lucius Antonius to be without foundation.

Lucius, however, refused to accept this finding. He retired to Praeneste among the hills, complaining that he was an unprotected person, while Octavian was armed to the teeth. Fulvia supported him by expressing the terrors of a devoted mother on account of her darling children—on whom Octavian, presumably, was supposed to have designs. Both wrote to Egypt to complain of the treatment they were receiving—and it was probably the receipt of these letters that aroused the surprised and mystified Antony to start on his return home to find out what was amiss. The superior officers again attempted to mediate, and to secure the execution of their award.

Lucius Antonius

Lucius refused to state his case before this voluntary body of arbitrators. Octavian, wiser or more wily, took good care to do so. He warmly denounced the conduct of Lucius and the Antonian leaders. The *optimates* now took part in the dispute by sending a deputation to Lucius to implore him to avoid any risk of a civil war, and to consent to arbitration. If he were not satisfied with the award given by the officers, they offered their own services. Lucius hesitated: but now Manius came to the front.

The articles of accusation which Manius drew up are an interesting version of the work Octavian had been carrying out in Italy. They charged him with endeavouring to seduce the loyalty of the army to himself alone; they declared that he had taken the control of Cisalpine Gaul out of the hands of Marcus Antonius; that instead of the eighteen cities previously agreed upon, he had divided almost

Manius

the whole of Italy among the soldiers; that only twenty-eight legions, which had been at Philippi, were entitled to take part in the allotments, but Octavian had allowed thirty-four to participate; that he had not used for its nominal purpose the money he had borrowed from the temples for the defence of Italy against Sextus Pompeius, but had employed it to suborn the soldiery to the prejudice of Antony; and that the property confiscated during the proscription had not been sold as it should have been, but distributed to the troops. If Octavian wished for peace, Manius invited him to give a full account of what he had done, and for the future to do only what should be agreed upon collectively.

This was a very insolent production—and the demand that Octavian should in future do only what they collectively agreed upon was equivalent to tearing up the agreement Octavian had made with Marcus Antonius, and cancelling the law by which the Committee for the Reorganization of the State had been appointed. Such a demand was unreasonable beyond all the bounds of toleration; and after it was made, Octavian thought it time he began to prepare for a military struggle.

Before matters reached this issue, a further intervention was made by the army. The military colonists at Ancona, veterans who had served under Julius and Antonius, sent deputies to beg for further consideration. Octavian replied that their appeal must be made to Lucius. The combined deputation and arbitration commission then addressed Lucius Antonius. They asked him to submit to the arbitration of a tribunal, and they left him in no doubt of their view of the case if he refused. Lucius consented, and Gabii, half way between Praeneste and Rome, on the Praenestine road, was fixed.

Octavian arrived first, sending forward a detachment of

Further inter-vention

cavalry to see that all was clear. Oddly enough, these men ran into a similar detachment sent forward by Lucius Antonius. There was a collision: some men were killed, and Lucius retired, declaring that he feared a trap. The arbitrators had made all ready at Gabii, and had prepared a judgment hall in which the case could be considered with all due seriousness. They pledged their word that Lucius would be safe; but he would not put in an appearance. Whether his fear was real, or whether he was glad of the opportunity to refuse the arbitration, we are all at liberty to judge for ourselves.

II

This was practically the end of any organized attempt to arbitrate. Only too obviously, the Antonian leaders would welcome a war, and were confident of its outcome. Their opinion was not so widely shared nor so warmly greeted as they thought. The majority of the Caesarian legionaries were on Octavian's side, and even those who were still devoted to Antonius were lukewarm.

Octavian himself made a last attempt to avert what was coming. At a joint meeting of senators and *equites*, the upper and the middle classes of the Roman state, he appealed to the gathering to intervene. He told them that he fully appreciated that his appeal might look like fear and unwillingness to fight; but he had strong backing, and was well equipped with everything except a desire for strife. He hated civil war, and most of all a civil war in the midst of Italy itself. He had no fear but that if they failed to bring Lucius into a better mood, he could soon prove that his own motives had been pure love of peace, and not doubt of the outcome of war. To this he asked them to bear witness.

Octavian's final effort

A mission of the two orders therefore set out for Praeneste in obedience to this request. Lucius was not to be moved. He assured the members of the mission that war had already begun, and that Octavian was deceiving them, for he had already sent a legion to Brundusium to prevent a landing by Antony. This was an oblique way of suggesting that the return of Marcus Antonius was imminent —and possibly the insinuation made the desired impression on some of his hearers. Manius also refused arbitration, and the negotiators returned unsuccessful. They had had no collective reception, and they made no formal report. It was clear to every one that further attempts to preserve peace would be useless, and that the issue must be decided by arms.

Octavian, regarding the breach as absolute—at any rate, so far as Fulvia was concerned—took the serious and con-
Clodia sent home clusive step of sending back to her her daughter Clodia, who had been betrothed to him at Bononia when the Committee was founded. The young lady had been so very young that there never had been any question of an immediate marriage, and she now went back intact to her mother. It is very probable that Octavian was not altogether sorry to be free from such a relationship to Fulvia, whose peculiar character had its drawbacks. Clodia herself, too, belonged to a world which Octavian never at any time in his life found very sympathetic—a world of aristocratic radicalism, at once free-thinking in its opinions, exclusive in its social tone, and revolutionary in its politics. He was far too much a man of the sober middle-class to relish the mixture; and he never showed any regret for Clodia.

Most of the *optimates* supported Lucius, even though their enthusiasm may not have been overwhelming. They had their reasons.

As the parties sorted themselves out into opposing camps, they were conscious enough of the nature of the war they were undertaking. It was a war for supremacy between (on the one hand) the consul for the current year, the constitutional magistrate whose office was as old as the republic itself, and (on the other) the Reorganizer of the State—that new and remarkable magistrate who since the days of Sulla had been coming more and more to be the real pilot of the commonwealth and the real representative of the people. Was it wise for the *optimates* to fight this issue in circumstances so unfavourable to their own cause? If the new magistrate won, there would be an end of the consulship as the supreme magistracy. If, on the other hand, the consul were victorious . . . what would happen? . . . Octavian was not the only person concerned. Marcus Antonius (as well as Lepidus) shared the office and the responsibility and might have a word to say about the result. . . . There must have been serious and urgent questions addressed to Lucius, for he took the first opportunity of publicly announcing his views on the subject.

His march upon Rome was the first act in the war. The gates were opened to him by night, and he entered without striking a blow. Lucius, speaking to the assembled citizens, asserted the superior claims of his own historic office, undertook the punishment of Octavian and Lepidus for their dictatorial government, and promised—and here came the important point—that Marcus Antonius would resign his seat in the Committee of Three and accept the constitutional and traditional office of consul, in accordance with the ancient laws of Rome, instead of the illegal tyranny he at present held. This speech gave great satisfaction in certain quarters, and the rule of the Committee was believed to be at an end.

But had Marcus Antonius ever given any authority to

Lucius exceeds his authority

Lucius to make such very remarkable undertakings on his behalf? We may safely doubt it. It is probable that Octavian at the time doubted it. The attitude of Lucius moreover was very far from creating wild enthusiasm among the Antonian veterans or their leaders. He had made the profound mistake of plunging into armed conflict with a doubtful cause, under highly suspicious pretences, and after earning the disapproval of a large proportion of the higher officers of the army. He had earned, instead, the warm support of a class which had never yet supported any cause without wrecking it.

III

The campaign of Perusia

The campaign which followed bears signs of having been planned by a strong and trenchant mind which only at this point becomes clearly visible to us—that of Marcus Vipsanius Agrippa. It had a unity, a skill and a vigour which Octavian himself did not display in military matters. Agrippa had from the first been among the young officers whom Julius picked as suitable companions for his grand-nephew. He had been at Apollonia with him, and had followed him to Italy and to Philippi. He was himself very little more than a youth; he and Octavian had been born within a year of one another. The great advantage of his close association with Octavian was that he had seen exactly the same story unrolled before him and had seen it from the same angle, so that his reactions had been the same, and his very different mind attacked the problems in the exact way Octavian required. Far indeed from Agrippa were the coldness, the reflectiveness and the physical timidity of Octavian! He was a stern, unbending man, a typical Roman plebeian in his firmness and decisiveness, his downright character and robust frame. Without one spark

LIVIA

wife of Augustus and mother of Tiberius and Drusus

From a Sculpture at Oxford,
by courtesy of the Visitors of the Ashmolean Museum

of originative genius, he had the perfect equipment of the Agrippa
lieutenant—the man who could carry out the ideas of
others. As soon as hostilities broke out, the young Octavian, as if by magic, seemed to double himself, and another young man, with a jutting chin, hard grey eyes and
compressed lips, stood by his side—just the man he needed
to make good the peculiarities of his own character.
Agrippa had the gift for making men work. He even made
Octavian work with more conspicuous energy than we
have hitherto noticed in him.

The moves followed one another like the moves in a
game of chess. As Salvidienus with his army of six legions
marched back from Gaul to the assistance of Octavian, he
naturally took the great main highway that stretched from
Placentia on the river Padus, to Ariminum on the Adriatic.
The route was quite as fixed as if it had been a railway. He
was cautiously followed by Ventidius and Asinius Pollio
—who were allies and friends of Antonius: that is to say,
as far as it was safe to be. They were not—and could not be
—the sort of allies who are loyal to death. Their men were
not enthusiastic about the war, and might not follow them.
When Salvidienus reached the junction of Ariminum, he
would leave the Aemilian road for the Flaminian, which
cut back across Italy and over the mountains from Fanum
Fortunae to Rome. Ventidius and Asinius Pollio, still following, would then seize Ariminum and block his retreat. Lucius
out-
The plan of Lucius was to set out from Rome and meet manoeu-
Salvidienus on the Flaminian way, where Salvidienus vred
would be surrounded and could be destroyed before Octavian could join him. This plan Agrippa promptly shattered by marching upon Sutrium, one of those old Etruscan fortress-cities standing among the volcanic mountains
of southern Etruria, guarding the Cassian road on its way
to Florence. As soon as Lucius heard the news, he came to

a halt. Agrippa had only to go on, and he would reach Florence—whence, by a pass across the undefended mountains, it was possible for him to cut Ventidius and Asinius off from Gaul. Hence Lucius halted, and compromised by camping beside the great fortress of Perusia, the modern Perugia, on its height above the Tiber valley and the Flaminian road. There he might think himself moderately safe.

But a much more determined and skilful opponent than he dreamed of was at his heels. Agrippa had only wanted to detain Lucius and in this he had perfectly succeeded. He now left the Cassian road at Clusium and turned towards Perusia, while Octavian closed upon the same objective by the Flaminian road. As Salvidienus was also on the road, farther up beyond Perusia, coming down from Fanum, the tables were completely turned, and it was now **Lucius** who was surrounded. Moreover, this encirclement **forced** (as a good diplomatist could easily have calculated before-**into** hand) at once produced its effect upon Ventidius and **Perusia** Asinius Pollio. Instead of being spurred to prodigies of valour they distinctly cooled.

To have tied up Lucius Antonius like this at the very beginning of the war was a great triumph, which promised to localize the struggle. But it was only the beginning. The task now was to capture him and his army. Octavian sent out for all the support he could gather, and one of those great engineering struggles began, the conduct of which the Romans had first learnt centuries before from their sieges of the old Etruscan cities in this very district. The siege of Perusia, indeed, was to be almost the very last great siege of ancient Italy.

Octavian—or rather Agrippa, for the latter was the man with the engineering mind—proceeded to draw works of circumvallation round Perusia, with a mound, a palisade and a ditch, some six and a half miles in circuit. He extended flanking walls right down to the Tiber, to complete the blockade. Lucius built a work of contravallation round the foot of the hill to face this, and sent out a call for help. Fulvia threw herself into the contest with energy, doing her utmost to collect allies. But a kind of lethargy or un-willingness lay heavy upon the Antonian troops. Calenus, who had eleven legions—a great army—at Milan, did not **Perusia** move at all. Asinius Pollio, Ventidius and Plancus, aroused **surrounded** out of their hesitation, made tentative steps towards the relief of Perusia: but they hastily gave up and retired when Agrippa and Octavian moved against them. There was no zeal in them. Meanwhile the Caesarians, busy at work, in-creased the ditch that surrounded Perusia to thirty feet in depth and width. The wall was similarly raised and strength-ened with redoubts and with wooden towers and the whole circumvallation was doubled, to face both the defenders within and the armies of relief without. Sorties had no ef-fect. Finding his own men too untrained to make much headway against the Caesarian veterans, Lucius employed a corps of gladiators, trained professional fighting men, as storm troops; and the Caesarians had the worst of it in hand-to-hand fighting with these men. Still they were not numerous enough to decide the issue. The ring around Perusia seemed too strong to be broken.

The great advantage of having induced Lucius to defend an unprepared stronghold rapidly became obvious. Perusia had not been equipped for a siege. Hunger grew into fam-ine. But the besiegers themselves were only a little better off under the strangle-hold of Sextus Pompeius. On the last day of the year, the last day on which Lucius Antonius remained consul, he attempted a great sortie from Perusia. His attack on the circumvallation was thrown back by the **Food-** reserves of Octavian; and on the same day there was riot- **shortage** ing in Rome on account of the shortage of food. . . . The next day Lucius Antonius was no longer consul. His term of office had expired; but Octavian was still triumvir.

IV

Early in the new year, urged on by the pressure of their friends, Ventidius and Asinius Pollio made another attempt to relieve Perusia. Pollio was one of the new consuls; but after the events of the past few months the prestige of the consulship had dwindled. Moving down the Flaminian way from Fano, they reached Fulginium, which was their station for Perusia. Here, however, they met the forces of Agrippa and Salvidienus, barring their farther road. The great smoke signals rolled their volumes of smoke skyward to announce to Perusia that the relieving army was at hand. A council of war found Ventidius and Asinius willing to advance; but Plancus was more prudent. He pointed out to his colleagues the difficulties of their position as they advanced upon Perusia—the likelihood that they would be caught between the army of Agrippa and that of Octavian. Little by little the fires died down, and no relieving army appeared at hungry Perusia. Another sortie was repulsed; and Perusia settled down to starve under the blockade. Lucius could not believe that help would not come.

No relief

But the garrison of Perusia preferred to die fighting rather than to die of hunger. One of the measures of Lucius had been to put the slaves off the rationing list. He did not allow them to leave Perusia, for they could have divulged fatal truths about the state of the defenders. So they slowly died, and were buried in long trenches—and since common human nature and common human sympathy are much more substantial realities than artificial abstractions about a man's legal status, the troops grew restive at the spectacle. They demanded to be led to another attempt to break out. They felt sure they could achieve it. At least, they said they did.

The last great sortie was accordingly planned, and a very great and Homeric battle it was. The attacking parties were equipped with every possible means of crossing the ditches and escalading the mound and palisade; and in order to conceal the real point of attack a general assault on the wall was ordered. Under cover of this general assault, a desperate storming party fought its way across the thirty-foot ditch and scaled the thirty-foot mound, and did those things which, when we come to look at them in cold blood many years after the event, seem beyond human power. They might have broken through the circumvallation, had not Octavian perceived in time that the front on which this attack was made was a limited one, and that the rest of the wall could be neglected. He at once concentrated his men upon the limited front—and the sortie was repulsed.

It was the last effort. As it had failed, the time had come to surrender.

Three envoys waited upon Octavian to ask what terms they might expect. Octavian replied, publicly, that on account of his regard for Marcus Antonius, he would admit the Antonian veterans to terms, but all others must surrender unconditionally. In private, he had a little conversation with one of the envoys, to whom he gave a secret message. He would be severe, he said, only to certain persons. All others, including Lucius, might expect friendly treatment. *Surrender of Perusia*

This private conversation did not escape the notice of certain persons in Perusia who were expecting some such discrimination against themselves. They waited upon Lucius Antonius and urged him to insist upon a general settlement in which all would be protected. But Lucius had done all that he felt like doing. He said that he would visit Octavian himself. Without further ado he walked out of the defences alone towards the spot where Octavian was standing. Seeing him approach in this remarkable manner, Octavian walked out to meet him; and they concluded the surrender by a personal conversation between the lines. Those who watched their faces saw that whatsoever they may have agreed upon, it was evidently satisfactory to both parties.

In his history of the Civil Wars, Appian places in the mouths of the two leaders appropriate sentiments which he inferred from the statements about the conversation which Octavian himself, in his memoirs, afterwards made. Lucius said that he had acted on principle throughout, in the interests of the ancient political constitution of Rome, and he now surrendered unconditionally, placing upon Octavian the responsibility for all that followed. Octavian replied that he could not accept the contentions of Lucius, but he would accept the responsibility, which he thought Lucius would have no cause to regret. The two then parted amicably. In this way Perusia was surrendered.

v

The next morning the surrender was given effect. The defenders began to march out past the tribunal where Octavian sat. Nothing could better illustrate the real opinions of the army about the civil wars than the scene which immediately followed. The Caesarian troops almost at once broke their ranks and fraternized with the Antonians. Although they had been wrestling in ferocious strife with these very same men, only a few hours before, the moment the surrender was made they intervened to obtain for them the full honours of war. Octavian, quick to perceive the currents of feeling, was gracious, if not enthusiastic. He abandoned any idea of differentiating between Antonian

Lucius and Octavian (marginal note)

The troops fraternize (marginal note)

veterans and other troops. All alike were dismissed without punishment. Lucius Antonius and the other men of responsible rank were then called forward. Lucius was given a seat beside Octavian, and remained in his personal custody. The other officers were taken over by men of equivalent rank, who would answer for them. A general pardon was granted to the citizens of Perusia, with the exception of the council and magistrates, who (for reasons unknown to us) were all save one thrown into prison, and were later on executed. A small number of individuals—four or five—whom Octavian considered dangerous mischief-makers were also executed; but this was the limit of the punitive measures. Octavian had intended the plunder of Perusia to be the reward of his troops—but some citizen (supposed, for quite inadequate reasons, to be mad) set fire to his own house; the fire spread, and the whole of Perusia perished in the flames.

This was the end of old Perusia; and it was the end, for all effective purposes, of the civil war in Italy. Asinius Pollio and Ventidius withdrew with their armies to the Adriatic sea-board and remained passive. There was a general rush of refugees to the camps of the opposition: among them Tiberius Claudius Nero, his wife Livia, and their little two-year-old son Tiberius, the future emperor. Fulvia with her children took refuge at Puteoli, whence she made her way to Brundusium, and so to Athens.

Asinius Pollio and Ventidius had thirteen legions with them, in addition to auxiliary cavalry; and Calenus, in Cisalpine Gaul, had eleven legions under his command. It is clear, therefore, that the Antonians were not suffering from lack of numbers. It was leadership that was lacking. Marcus Antonius was expected back, and in anticipation of this event Asinius and Ventidius made preparations at Brundusium and established supply depots. But still he did not

Lack of
leadership

come; and the delay lost him yet further points of advantage, for Calenus died, and Octavian not only took over the eleven legions, but Spain and Gaul besides. When at last Antonius sailed from Alexandria, the situation in Italy had been transformed. The prestige he had won at Philippi had been lost again, and Octavian, by patience and skill, had gathered more and more united power into his own hands. Octavian was beginning to command general confidence —and what is more, to deserve it.

Marcus Antonius and his lieutenants were all alike involved in one common mistake. They did not allow for the possible effect of advisers upon Octavian. Conscious of his own individual strength—that he himself did the thinking, and his subordinates executed the directions given them—it never seems to have occurred to Antony, and still less to his representatives, that a man might exist who had a peculiar gift for assembling round himself a group of minds whose abilities he could harmonise and blend—and that Octavian was this man. As he slowly emerges from the haze of history after the battle of Philippi, we begin to be more and more certain that Octavian was habitually the figure-head of a group. He had taken his first steps under the powerful guidance of Aulus Hirtius, Vibius Pansa and Cornelius Balbus; now we catch the first glimpses of Marcus Vipcanius Agrippa and of the thrice famous Maecenas, whose name, like that of Lucullus, grew to be fabulous and proverbial. Antonius made his crucial error when he thought of Octavian merely as a person. Octavian was far more than a person. He was a committee; he was a pool, into which a dozen men threw their special intelligence; he was a movement, a type of government. The boy Octavian, merely as such, would not have lasted a week. Octavian, the presiding member of the Friends of Caesar, was immortal and indestructible.

The advisers of Octavian

VI

As we have already seen, Marcus Antonius sailed from Alexandria in the spring of the year 40 B. C. While his ship is ploughing its way across the sea to Tyre, let us glance for a moment at the situation as it revealed itself to him.

Although he had received letters, and a deputation of veterans, which told him that there had been some dissensions in Italy, he had at this date no idea at all of the disastrous events which had culminated in the surrender of Perusia. The chief reason why Cleopatra had encouraged him to go, and why he was now upon the sea, had nothing to do with Italy, but concerned the state of the Asiatic provinces, which called imperatively for action. Ever since the defeat of Crassus at Carrhae, the Parthians had been doing almost as they liked along the Mesopotamian border. It was, of course, much easier to destroy a Roman army in the desert than to occupy and organize a Roman province, and the Parthians were finding it a very long job to reduce Armenia, Syria and Asia Minor. There was yet time for active intervention by Roman troops. The task of Marcus Antonius, as he set out from Alexandria, was that which Sulla had faced and carried out forty-three years before—to clear the oriental enemy out of the Greek lands, to restore Greek culture and Greek supremacy everywhere, and to re-establish it in strength under Roman direction, so that it need fear no foe. There was no reason why Antony should imagine that the task would be particularly difficult. The Parthians were no more dangerous than Mithradates had been—or so it seemed to the Roman onlooker. If anything, Antonius seemed to have the easier task. And after the work had been accomplished with the expected success, Antonius—again like Sulla, whom he

Antony leaves Egypt

seemed to resemble in so many ways—would face the west ready to reconquer it and return to it as a master.

At Tyre, however, he heard the fuller reports which told him that he would need all his military resources against the Parthians. After the battle of Philippi the renegade Labienus, the able son of a famous father, had fled to the Parthian court, and now was invading the Roman provinces, from the Euphrates as far as Lydia and Ionia, with a Parthian army. If Antonius were to gain from Asia the resources he wanted to enable him to assert his supremacy in Italy, he would need to hurry, or the Parthians would have got off with the golden eggs and killed the goose into the bargain. Once he was roused, Antony was a rapid and effective worker. He set sail with a fleet from Tyre, touched at Rhodes, and reached the Aegean coast, where he intended to establish his depot. Here, however, the astounding news reached him which shattered all his plans and entirely altered his position: the story of the civil war in Italy and the fall of Perusia. He was furious when he heard the tale. Whether he would have worried very much if it had been carried off with dexterity and success we need not stay to enquire: but he would have been more than mortal if he had not been enraged at the mingling of crass folly, incredible presumption and scandalous inefficiency which had disgraced the proceedings of his representatives in Italy. Did any one suppose for a moment that such policies would have been adopted had he been personally present? Even Octavian did him more justice! Antony cursed Lucius for a fool; he cursed Fulvia, and above all he cursed Manius. Fulvia had reached Athens. Crossing the Aegean, Antony met her there.

The scene between Antony and Fulvia has not been recorded for the benefit of history. It was probably not of a nature which either of them wished to remember or per-

The
Parthian
menace

Fulvia
and
Antony
meet

petuate. We must remember that Fulvia was herself a very remarkable woman, of unusual strength of character, and that she had been successful in making two husbands famous. Publius Clodius and Marcus Antonius had owed their meteoric rise and immortal celebrity to her inspiration. Marcus Antonius had been nothing until he married her—and he was destined to fall back into tragic impotence after he lost her. Cruel, savage and unforgiving she may have been:—we do not know:—they said she was, and many able women are: but there can be no doubt of her power. She had blundered over the Perusian War because, like so many other women, her wits had been blinded by jealousy. But jealousy itself is a testimony to the devotion of the person who feels it: and perhaps the ridiculous excess which led her to play straight into the hands of Octavian was a measure of her devotion to her husband.

But Marcus Antonius, coming straight from Cleopatra and Egypt, was very sensitive about jealousy. The more of it Fulvia felt, the more deadly a charge it seemed to be against him. He was just in the mood to lash out against any hint that he had been wrong, and to resent even the implication that he had failed in loyalty. . . . Besides, to him, fresh from Cleopatra, it is very possible that some of the Roman angularity of Fulvia stood out with unpleasing clearness. After a winter of companionship with the nightingale voice and subtle enchantment of Cleopatra, he saw with exasperation that Fulvia was a virago. In any case, he was trapped by the very thing he had done: his own actions tangled his feet and tripped him at this particular critical instant. . . . There can be no doubt that the interview was a very violent one, in which both husband and wife spoke their minds with unqualified freedom. And there cannot be much doubt that it killed Fulvia. She died at Sicyon soon after the meeting—and if she did not die of a

Mood of Antony

broken heart, she got as near to it as most people have succeeded in doing. He did not even see her again before he sailed for Italy. . . . It was a heavy punishment. . . . But then (as he found, before very long) when she died, his luck died with her. Marcus Antonius realized that he had killed her, and he was not a happy man. So many things had already occurred, about which remorse seemed useless.

The very circumstances in which he came back to Italy had an odd effect of making him seem a traitor. His mother, after the flight from Perusia, had taken refuge with Sextus Pompeius. That gallant, though piratical gentleman—a true predecessor of Captain Blood—had at once despatched the lady to her son at Athens, with a great assembly of *optimates* and an escort of warships. Serious efforts were made by those who brought her to persuade Antony into friendly overtures with Sextus. He answered, morosely, that he would repay the favour in due time, and that if he were involved in a war with Octavian, he would welcome the alliance of Sextus, but that if he and Octavian remained friends, he would try to reconcile Octavian with Sextus.

Antony tempted

It was a long time since Antony had been the champion of Julius and the Julian cause!

VII

Octavian heard these stories—and others like them. They roused in his mind certain doubts of Antony's good faith that were not soon laid to rest. He was in a difficult situation. From the military point of view he had not very much to fear; but he had no navy of any sort or description, and his trouble was the possibility that Pompeius and Marcus Antonius in conjunction might establish a sea-blockade and starve Italy into surrender. It was, indeed, more than a mere possibility. . . . In the circumstances, his best defensive move was to turn towards Sextus Pompeius, and this he proceeded to do.

He did something much more dexterous than merely to open negotiations with Sextus, with all the difficulties and drawbacks that this would involve. He, or his advisers, perceived a far better diplomatic opening. L. Scribonius Libo, the father-in-law of Sextus Pompeius, had a sister who was now a widow for the second time. Her husbands had been men of dignified consular rank; the widow herself, therefore, was a suitable match. There had been much discussion concerning the marriage of Octavian, which every one recognized to be necessary and imminent, though no one so far had succeeded in suggesting the right person. Octavian now commissioned Maecenas to approach L. Scribonius Libo. The old gentleman, perceiving the possibilities, jumped at the offer—so it was formally settled.

Octavian marries Scribonia September, 40 B. C.

Antony, therefore, arriving at Brundusium with his fleet and army, reached an Italy defended by an Octavian who had allied himself with the family of Sextus by one of those ties which are so much more convenient to a states man than a political treaty ever can be. For one thing, it was entirely non-committal. Neither Octavian nor Sextus bound themselves to anything. But it automatically warned Antony of what steps Octavian might take, if pushed to it—and that is perhaps all that Octavian ever wanted it to do.

The citizens of Brundusium not unnaturally closed their gates to the formidable armament. Antonius regarded their action as an act of hostility towards himself and at once blockaded the city.[1] He occupied various places on the

[1] The city stood on a peninsula. A double mound and ditch across this peninsula cut the city off from all communication with the mainland. Octavian, when he arrived, found it impossible to reach the city or to raise the siege.

Adriatic coast, and invited Sextus Pompeius to co-operate.

Sextus fulfilled his engagements. He seized Sardinia, and besieged Consentia and Thurii, the two fortresses that guarded the toe of Italy. So rapid and vigorous was their joint action, that the heel and toe of Italy were soon in their possession.

Octavian was already in consultation with Agrippa concerning the measures to be taken against this menace, when once more the army intervened. There had been a certain amount of "fraternization" between the opposing armies at Brundusium, if such a term can be applied to the angry charges and counter-charges exchanged between the troops. The old Antonian veterans had been very unwilling to follow Agrippa when he tried to raise them for the defence of Italy, and they were determined to stop the war. At the first checks to the progress of the invasion, when Sextus Pompeius failed to capture Thurii and when Agrippa succeeded in taking Sipontum, and so cutting Antony's road north, a rapid change came over affairs. Opinion in the army, as so often before, forced peace upon the leaders. Lucius Cocceius Nerva acted as a diplomatic go-between. Maecenas, as a friend of Octavian, and the consul, Gaius Asinius Pollio, as a friend of Antony, mediated. A committee of officers from both armies approved a scheme of reconciliation. Octavian, as always, readily accepted the scheme, and Antony, wiser than Lucius and Fulvia, hastened to subscribe to it.

The terms of the reconciliation provided for an amnesty for all that had happened in the past, and friendship for the future. As there seemed to be a general agreement that Fulvia was to blame for much of the bad blood created in the past, a plan was arranged for avoiding any similar danger in the future. Octavian had a half-sister, Octavia, a charming and accomplished woman who was universally liked. She had recently become a widow through the death of her husband Gaius Marcellus. The plan evolved by the Committee of officers was that Antony, a widower through the death of Fulvia, should marry Octavia, and that every one should live happily ever after.

For Marcus Antonius to refuse to marry a charming and beautiful woman was unthinkable. He accepted the proposal with alacrity, and the betrothal was immediately accomplished. Octavian and Antony then publicly embraced before the delighted view of the assembled armies, which proceeded to celebrate the occasion with great enthusiasm for a day and a night on end. . . . It was, after all, far better than fighting.

The reconciliation thus effected at Brundusium was much more successful, and had far more solid and permanent results, than might have been supposed from the apparently artificial conditions of its origin. The wedding of Antony and Octavia took place at Rome amid general congratulations. Antony was, at any rate for a time, a model husband; and Octavia seems to have been one of those discreet women who expect very little, and are seldom disappointed. The senate obligingly dispensed with the law by which a widow was not allowed to marry until ten months after her husband's death. So every one had a share in the festivities.

Octavian and Antonius recast their old agreement together. The former distribution of the provinces, made during the conference at Bononia and revised after the battle of Philippi, was cancelled. A new agreement was made. Beginning at the town of Scodra, a little way north of Dyrrachium, a line was drawn down the Adriatic and the Ionian Seas. This line divided the Roman world into two, omitting Africa. As Africa had already been given to Lepidus by Octavian it was agreed that he should keep

Marriage of Antony and Octavia November 40 B. C.

it. The rest was divided between Antony and Octavian. All to the east of the line was to be the sphere of Antony; all to the west of it, the sphere of Octavian. Then, as to details, it was agreed that both should be entitled to raise troops in Italy, in equal numbers. Antony was to attend to the Parthian War—Octavian, to Sextus Pompeius. Finally, Octavian was to make the same agreement with certain of the anti-Caesarians that Antony had already made, and was to be reconciled with them. Antony's further suggestion that Octavian should come to an accommodation with Sextus Pompeius was, however, not proceeded with at that time.

So another great stage in the history was reached. It remained now to see whether the Roman dominion would remain permanently in two parts, or whether one would prevail over the other—and if so, which: and why.

Future problems

CHAPTER IX

THE GREAT PLAN OF MARCUS ANTONIUS AND THE LITTLE PLAN OF OCTAVIAN

I

THE Treaty of Brundusium must have seemed a much stranger event to those who shared in it than it does to us. Marcus Antonius had bulked so big in men's eyes; the cloud that was gradually dimming his reputation was so gradual, and so unaccountable, that there was something a little bewildering in the advance of Octavian to an equality with him—and perhaps some men did not perfectly realize that equality. The problem concerning the real causes of the steady advance of Octavian was quite visible to his contemporaries. Was it luck or a profound dissimulation? Had he climbed upon the shoulders of other men? Had his youth aroused a paternal sympathy in the breasts of Cae sar's veterans, and led them again and again to interfere on his behalf? He had cut such a poor figure at Philippi, when Marcus Antonius was the life and soul and inspiration of the army! Very few Romans had much sympathy with Octavian's physical delicacy. They were robust men who regarded it as a fault rather than a misfortune. . . . And yet in some way—it was hard to say how—this youth, with everything against him, persistently maintained himself in the struggle, and was tending slowly, inexorably, to eclipse Marcus Antonius.

The truth seems to have been that Octavian had a natural genius for all those passivities, hesitations and redirections which are much more clearly comprehended by the average

The rise of Octavian

Its cause

onlooker when they are embodied in a system of physical wrestling like jujitsu, than when they are a part of a system of statesmanship. The very force and power of Antonius had been used against him. And now they must sit down for a while hand in hand and let the world see them as brethren. The army had demanded it. Gone was the time when Octavian thought of marrying Antony's stepdaughter. Antony had now married Octavian's sister—and brothers they were indeed. . . . And when the time came and they started their contest afresh, they would start level. Antony had lost the advantage he had possessed after the battle of Philippi.

If we could look into the mind of Marcus Antonius in the days just after his marriage to Octavia, we should be very much wiser than we are. But it is possible to infer what we cannot see. As we have already noticed, Asinius Pollio, who that year held the consulship, had been one of the chief intermediaries in arranging the reconciliation of Antony and Octavian. As a friend of Marcus Antonius, he occupied a favourable position for impressing upon him the necessity of the step. Pollio, himself a distinguished literary critic and a devoted student of Latin style, had made the acquaintance while governing Cisalpine Gaul for

Virgil

Antony, of a young man who lived near Mantua, and whom he believed to be a poet of promise. During the land allotments this young man's holding had been seized for reallotment. He had appealed to Pollio, who befriended him. Maecenas, who was then the right-hand man of Octavian in civil affairs, had been communicated with, and Maecenas had decided that such a poet deserved to possess a portion of the land of Italy. The young man was Publius Virgilius Maro, who some years later became the author of the Aeneid.

Nothing could be more natural than that Virgil, rightly

grateful for Pollio's help, should address to him a poem in celebration of his consulship. He chose as his theme the marriage of Octavia with Pollio's leader, Marcus Antonius. The poem so written was the famous Fourth Eclogue. . . . Pollio's consulship had not been tremendously exciting. It was, perhaps, when intently surveyed, somewhat lacking in incident—especially incident of a kind suitable for treatment by a lyric poet. Virgil might conceivably have composed a poem on the Treaty; but that may have been delicate ground, and in any case, it may have seemed too prosaic. So Virgil chose the wedding as his theme.

It would be very strange if bride and bridegroom should never have read or heard of Virgil's eclogue. We may take it for granted that the well-satisfied Pollio hastened to present both them and all his friends—including Octavian—with copies of the poem: that Virgil read it at the wedding-feast, and that every one concerned was familiar with the ideas it expressed. Much as these ideas have puzzled the commentators since, they were probably clear enough to those for whom the poem was intended.

Virgil says that the last age of the Sibylline prophecies has now arrived, and a new age is beginning. The Virgin Astraea (i. e., Justice) who left the earth with the end of the Golden Age, is returning now with the beginning of the new one. A new race of men begins: the old iron brood shall fail and die out and the golden race shall arise. The Sun is King. . . . Everyone knew what this meant. Virgil was delicately alluding to the Civil Wars, and the long disheartening strife; and he was foretelling the return of peace to the world. If some of his hearers perchance had little faith in the fulfilment of his prophecy, they all of them heartily approved and admired, and thought it a noble ideal.

Then, turning to Pollio, Virgil goes on to say that in this

present consulship of Pollio the new age starts with the conception of a child who shall receive the life of the gods, and with his father's qualities shall rule a reconciled world.

The child whose birth Virgil thus foresaw was the prospective son of Marcus Antonius and Octavia—"dear offspring of the gods, mighty child of Jove." . . . And Virgil made a magnificent picture of the thought, glowing with colour and imagination, and lifting the whole idea to a level of high inspiration. . . . The poem is a short one, consisting of sixty-three lines.

Antony is impressed It is very evident from what followed that this poem made a great impression upon Marcus Antonius. The thought Virgil had suggested fixed itself deep in his mind. It has, indeed, fixed itself deep in the minds of numberless readers of Virgil since that day. Devout Christians have seen in it a prefiguration of the birth of the Christ. If it could produce this effect upon strangers to whom it was not addressed, and who had no personal interest in it, we need not wonder if it touched even more profoundly the mind of the man who was most closely concerned. Antony was in a mood to be influenced. During the months that followed his marriage, he had leisure to reflect over Virgil's thought.[1]

II

The weakness of Marcus Antonius had always been what Stoics and Quakers would have agreed to call his worldly nature. He seemed absorbed in the external experiences of life. Even his virtues had been those of a good fellow and a stout one, always preferring to be jocund with the fruitful vine rather than to sadden after none or bitter

[1] See W. W. Tarn, *Alexander Helios and the Golden Age*, in "Journal of Roman Studies," Vol. XXII, p. 135. (1932.)

fruit. We may guess that it was his women who had educated him—first, Fulvia, and then Cleopatra. The latter had
not spent her millions upon him, and drunk her pearl ear-
ring into the bargain, altogether for fun. There had been
shrewd business calculation in all she did, and certainly Influence
there had been profitable little intervals in the round of of
pleasure, when they had talked together of much more Cleopatra
substantial things—such as the future of Egypt, the future
of Rome, and the form of government Rome would evolve
from her civil wars and the struggles between her rival
classes and interests. Cleopatra was descended from one of
the most distinguished and successful of the Hellenistic
dynasties which had their origin from the brilliant band
of lieutenants who surrounded Alexander the Great. Secure and solid success had marked Ptolemy Lagos and his
race. What Cleopatra could have divulged to Antony in
those interludes of serious conversation might well have
come as a revelation to that intelligent, if careless, man: the
tradition of political science which had been handed down
in the family since Alexander's days. It was a very high
and elaborate science, which at this date was still kept away
from the knowledge of the multitude; and the Egyptian
branch of it was touched with a good many influences derived from the still older tradition of the Pharaohs. Antony
would have heard things that astonished him about the
Divine Monarchs, and the peculiar office of reconciliation,
which it was their task to occupy, and the nature of their
divinity, and the political function it fulfilled, and all manner of things of this nature. He is hardly likely to have
asked no questions at all about such queer facts as the
brother-and-sister marriage which the Lagids had derived The
from the Pharaohs: and the answers would have led up Hellenistic
naturally enough to the thought which Cleopatra most of tradition
all wanted to plant in his mind—why should he not become

a King of Egypt, a divine monarch, deriving his title through her and using the vast wealth and security of the ancient kingdom to give him control of the military power of Rome, and of all the lands of the Roman dominion? . . . All this, and many more thoughts like it, had been in the mind of Marcus Antonius when he came back from Egypt. He saw that he had been casual, careless and neglectful of systematic planning. He had drifted from one day to another, when he ought to have thought out matters from the beginning, and possessed definite principles to direct his actions. . . . At the time of his marriage to Octavia he had not made up his mind to accept the notions of Cleopatra. He was after all a Roman, and in his heart preferred Roman ways. Hence he had a double reason for feeling interest in Virgil's poem. It seemed as if Virgil had voiced all these things that Cleopatra had been hinting at, yet had kept them hearty, healthy, Roman thoughts. . . . Marcus Antonius make up his mind to take these ideas as his principles. . . . He, a descendant of Hercules, and proud of his divine ancestry, would be a new Alexander, a conqueror of Asia and a reconciler of mankind under one sway, as Alexander had been—and his son should be the King of the Golden Age, beneath whose rule the world should be peaceful and happy again.

It was a splendid dream, and no idle one. True—there was work to be done first. Sextus Pompeius had to be got rid of, and the Parthians reduced, as the Gauls had been. But as soon as that was finished, what prevented the realization of the dream?

The child

Much, therefore, came to hinge upon the birth of the child of Octavia and Antony. Perhaps the whole future of Octavian himself hinged upon it. If the child proved (as every one hoped) a boy, Octavian might find himself falling into the background. The prestige of Antony would increase, and the probability that his power would become permanent would verge upon certainty. Octavian himself, up to this point, had no principles, no propaganda, nothing that he could set against this wonderful dream of Virgil's. The eclogue may well have inspired him in turn with a desire to possess such an ideal.

III

Marcus Antonius was busy in Italy throughout the winter and the spring of the year 39 B. C., raising and training troops for his coming Parthian expedition—the one that was to restore the empire of Alexander—and providing for their replacement and their equipment.

Sextus Pompeius had shown his opinion of the reconciliation by suddenly tightening his stranglehold: and the blockade of Italy became a more menacing reality than ever. The seizure of Sardinia meant that Rome was now enclosed by a ring of fleets which stopped all sea-trade towards Spain and Africa, or through the Sicilian straits eastward. Prices rose higher and higher, and public opinion laid all the trouble at the door of the Committee of Three, which was spending its time in rivalry and internecine strife. Peace with Sextus was called for. . . . But Octavian was very unwilling to make a peace which would split the western Roman world into two, and put it permanently into a position of weakness and inferiority. He was perhaps all the more unwilling when he knew Antony to be revolving schemes for reuniting the east into one great consolidated monarchy.

Marcus Antonius had kept his word in attempting to persuade Octavian into an agreement with Sextus; but having failed, he now gave the obvious advice that his failure called for, and urged that if Octavian would not make

Sextus
Pompeius
and Sicily

definite peace, he should make definite war—but at any rate something definite.

The difficulty, as usual, was the question of money. The treasury was empty, and an attempt to raise money by a new tax resulted in serious disorders. Violent criticism of the Committee, its selfishness, self-seeking and incompetence, was followed by rioting. Octavian, attempting to reason with a crowd in the Forum, was struck by stones, **Rioting in Rome** and was in some personal danger. Seeing him practically besieged in the Forum, Antony was obliged to come to his assistance with armed force. His attempt to reach the Forum through the Via Sacra was blocked by the rioters. They did not at first stone him, since he at least was known to be in favour of peace with Sextus Pompeius, but they warned him off. When he refused to go, they stoned him also. Antony, always prompt in action, hurried back and called in troops from outside the city. With their aid he forced a way down the Via Sacra, charged the mob, and drove it into the side streets. Many of the rioters were killed. Octavian was rescued just in time, and taken to Antony's house.

The passion, the ill-feeling and the violence that were provoked by these events, the dead bodies that were thrown into the river, the cowed but sullen state of public opinion, all combined to shake the resolution of Octavian, who was not naturally a man fond of defying the general feeling. . . . Antony urged the family of L. Scribonius Libo to call him to Rome to talk to his son-in-law. He promised that he himself would furnish the safe-conduct. This was a dexterous turning of the tables upon Octavian, who had never contemplated the idea of his marriage with Scribonia being used to force him into compliance with a situation he thoroughly hated. He did not want to condone the independent power of Sextus Pompeius in Sicily; and Antony

THE YOUNG GAIUS OCTAVIUS
(*From a coin in the British Museum*)

MARCUS VIPSANIUS AGRIPPA
as a young man
(*From a coin in the British Museum*)

was eager to make him do so. . . . Scribonia and her rela- Pressure upon Octavian
tives, unconscious of these unconfessed struggles behind
the scenes, saw no reason why they should not do as Antony suggested—the more so since it appeared to be in the
interests of Octavian. So they hastened to obey: Sextus
raised no objection, and Libo came as far as the island of
Ischia off Naples. The pressure of public opinion was too
strong for Octavian to resist. Reluctantly he gave way.
Libo suggested a personal conference of the principals. Octavian and Antonius went to Baiae accordingly, and there
Sextus met them. He came in great pride and power, with
a squadron of his finest ships, himself in his huge flagship,
a six-banker. When, one nightfall, he sailed past Puteoli in
the full glory of his might, there must have been some
spectators who bethought them that this son of Pompeius
Magnus was the greatest ruler that Sicily had known since
the days of Dionysius. What if he, after all, were destined
to do what Dionysius so narrowly missed accomplishing?
What if he founded the sea-empire of Sicily which history
had repeatedly been upon the point of creating, and might
yet create? It was a thought to reflect over!

The next day, the conference took place. A pier, or Conference at Puteoli
landing stage, had been built out from the shore; and on the
platform, at the end, Antony and Octavian took their seats.
A few yards away, seaward, another platform, an island
amid the sea, had been built. Hither came the huge flagship
of Sextus, and when it was moored, he and Libo crossed
the gang-plank and took their seats opposite Octavian and
Antony, with just the strip of water to separate them. In
this way the Conference took place.

Nothing immediate came of the Conference. Sextus
wished to be admitted to the Committee of Three; and if
it had been possible to grant the demand, it might have
been a happy solution of the difficulty. But too many things

had come to pass since the days when Julius and Pompeius Magnus had been faithful colleagues with Marcus Crassus. The murder of Julius lay like a bar preventing the possibility of faith in the oath or the honour of the *optimates*. The meeting broke up without agreement; but friends of both sides were busily at work with unofficial negotiations which had a better result. The Committee granted that any persons implicated in the murder of Julius, who had taken refuge with Sextus Pompeius, should be allowed to go into exile without interference, and that refugees not so implicated who had fled to him after the confiscation of their property should be restored to their citizenship and that one-fourth of their property should be returned to them —the Committee (not very enthusiastically) undertaking to be responsible for the cost. The refugees accepted these terms, and implored Sextus to strike the bargain. He was none too eager to do so, but at their request finally he consented.

Diffi-culties

The conference therefore met once more on their platforms on the water at Puteoli, and agreed upon a treaty. The war was to terminate; trade to be free; Pompeius to remove all garrisons from Italy, and to harbour no fugitive slaves; Pompeius to retain the government of Sicily, Sardinia and Corsica, paying the corn-tribute (with arrears) due from these lands, together with the Peloponnesus; he might nominate consuls, and might be a member of the college of Augurs; all exiles to return, save those condemned for a share in the murder of Julius; the land of exiles not so condemned to be restored in full; persons proscribed by the Committee to receive one-fourth; slaves who had served in the army of Pompeius were to receive their freedom; and veterans of his armies were to receive the same rewards as those of Antony and Octavian.

This very generous and satisfactory treaty was signed

and sealed, and placed in the care of the vestal virgins, who usually acted as custodians of documents of such a nature. Treaty of Misenum

Sextus, Antony and Octavian then exchanged visits—not mere formal visits of courtesy, but good solid feasts at which the wine flowed. They drew lots to settle the order of the visits, and Sextus drew the first place. The entertainment which he provided on his great flagship is the subject of a famous story. At the height of the festivities a dark figure bent over Sextus, and a voice whispered:

"Shall I cut the cables—and leave you master of the whole dominion of Rome?"

It was his Greek captain, Menas.

Sextus thought over it, and made answer: "Menas, you should have done it without consulting me. Now we must let things remain as they are, for I cannot go back upon my word."

So Sextus Pompeius ultimately died in exile, a failure, as the world counts failure; and Octavian lived to become Augustus, and the King of the Golden Age.

IV

The Treaty of Misenum was received with great rejoicing throughout Italy—save by those veterans at whose expense the exiles would be restored to their native country. But these, at the moment, were silent. Octavian also was silent: but he chose this significant moment for dissolving his marriage with Scribonia. He could not get over the part she had been made to play in forcing the treaty upon him. The possibility of so utilizing her was based upon the complete lack of sympathy and confidence between the young husband and his older wife. The marriage had been a purely political one. Octavian had never cared in the least for Scribonia, and he had never confided his motives Scribonia divorced or his reasons to her, nor dared to do so. The excuse he now gave for parting from her was that he could not stand her temper—an excuse which we need hardly take seriously. No man who cared much for a woman ever troubled about her temper. It was, however, for this very reason, the most tactfully chosen cause he could have alleged, and was much better than impugning any of those virtues which the world —certainly the Roman world—really valued in a wife. He assuredly could not say that she was barren, for she was expecting their child. . . . And this was the one consideration that held Octavian's hand. If the child were a boy, the marriage would need to hold. . . . But when the day came, the child proved to be a girl: and the notice of divorce was served upon Scribonia that same day.

Birth of Julia
Under these strange auspices Julia was born. We shall see more of Julia presently. For the moment we can leave her to get over this peculiar entry into the world. . . . Whether the circumstances attending it left any mark upon her later character, we can only guess. Scribonia, for her own part, did not break her heart over the matter, but lived to see many strange events and unexpected happenings in days to come.

Octavian might—for his own reasons—range himself with the veterans who looked with disfavour upon the treaty of Misenum; but for the moment it seemed as if Antony's star were in the ascendant. A great crowd of exiles flocked back into Italy, and the Committee was once more popular and praised. To Marcus Antonius, if to any one, this result was due. He might well be elated at the favourable signs. It needed only one more touch to bring him back to the supremacy. If Octavia's child were a boy, the victory was won!

Her time wore; and in August or early September the great event came to pass. The Wonder-Child, the mighty

offspring of Jove, was born—
   And alas!—like Julia, it was a girl!

There is something comic, and a great deal that is tragic, in the collapse of Antony's house of cards. The daughter so born to him—Antonia "major"—was destined to grow up into an accomplished and charming woman, who made a very dignified figure at the court of Augustus; but she was not the Wonder-Child, the King of the Golden Age. . . . And whereas the sex of Julia was a matter of very little immediate importance to Octavian—and, indeed, encouraged him in his attitude of hostility to Sextus Pompeius and the independence of Sicily—the sex of Antony's daughter was a serious disaster which affected his future. The unity of the east was not to be established so easily as he had hoped: and Octavian still set his face resolutely towards the unity of the west. Luckily, Marcus Antonius had not proclaimed too loudly to the world his hopes and fears; so he had very little now to wish unsaid.

He had already sent Ventidius ahead of him to organize the first stages of the Parthian War, and a little later in the year he sailed for the East to be near the scene of action. Wiser than Fulvia, Octavia took care to go with him; and as far as the world could see, they were a happy and contented pair, who had no quarrel with fate. They passed the winter at Athens. Antony was quiet enough. He dressed in the Greek fashion, and lived like a Greek, attending the philosophical lectures which were one of the special and distinctive features of life in Athens. He had plenty of reason to study philosophy—at any rate, political philosophy. An effective conquest of Asia involved both some study of the current ideas which were the basis of public opinion, and also the exercise of such influence over them, and control of them as should convert them into supports of the government he was planning. Antony, in fact, was studying the art of propaganda. Although he had been disappointed once, he still hoped for the birth of a son to Octavia.

Other considerations kept him at Athens. The city was within very convenient distance of Peloponnesus, and he wished to prevent Sextus Pompeius from occupying the territory ceded to him before he had fulfilled the conditions of the treaty. No urgent necessity called him to Asia. Ventidius had been very successful, and had driven the Parthians out of Asia Minor and killed the traitor Labienus. Social life was, of course, by no means confined to philosophical lectures. Antony took care that the victories of Ventidius were appropriately celebrated, and took a prominent part in the festivities. So the winter passed away. With the spring, Antony visited Asia himself, and made some important redistributions of power; but he did not go very far.

v

Octavian, meanwhile, gave him little cause for concern. If the treaty of Misenum had been carried out as it should **Octavian** have been, Antony might have felt it necessary to press **and** on with the work of establishing his own advantage; but **Sextus** while Octavian and Sextus Pompeius still remained at daggers drawn, he could take his own time. Sextus still unofficially seized the corn ship and informally prevented the traders from pursuing their lawful errands. The rejoicings in Rome had been premature.

It is difficult to see what Octavian, in the absence of an adequate fleet, could have done to remedy this new stringency. Fortune played into his hands. A quarrel between Sextus and his admiral Menodorus ended in the latter's making overtures to the Roman government and surrendering

Sardinia and Corsica into its possession, together with sixty ships. Sextus demanded the return of these ships, and Octavian, seeing his opportunity, answered by denouncing the treaty of Misenum on the ground that its terms had never been carried out. His real objection to it—his deeply rooted and ineradicable objection—was that it divided the western dominion of Rome into two parts and put it into a permanent position of inferiority. Octavian was determined to preserve it under one government and one tradition. Somewhere in his mind—dimly, perhaps, as yet—was stirring the concept of the "good European": the will to defend and maintain the western idea, the Roman idea, of life: and he meant to maintain it whole and unbroken, as it had come down to him. With the sixty ships of Menodorus, and a number that were built on the Adriatic coast, Octavian determined to try the issue.

Octavian denounces the treaty

The plans were laid with skill. The fleet from the Adriatic was to attack the straits of Messina from the southern end, while that of Menodorus attacked from the northern end; and during the struggle, while the attention of every one was diverted, a strong force of troops was to be ferried across the straits into Sicily. But the defence of Pompeius was strong and vigorous. His admiral Menecrates defeated the northerly fleet, the ships of Menodorus, near Cumæ, drove them on shore, and destroyed most of them, losing his own life in the battle. So upset was the second in command by the death of Menecrates, that he withdrew the victorious fleet, with the natural result that the Roman admiral, gathering together what still remained to him of his beaten squadrons, set out for the straits to meet the fleet from the Adriatic. As long as he could reach his objective and hold the straits for the crossing of the army, it mattered very little whether his fleet were nominally "victorious" or not. His only trouble was that he would be late at the trysting spot.

Attack on Sicily

Octavian proceeded to throw away his unexpected advantage by a characteristic bit of imprudent prudence. Although his practical fighting men, seeing their chance, exhorted him to rush in and get Pompeius, who was inside the harbour of Messina, he steadily declined to attempt it. He would not act until he was joined by the fleet from the north, so that his combined forces should have an overwhelming superiority. As the northern fleet, for the reasons just given, was delayed, he went to meet it, sailing past Messina on his way. He probably knew of no reason against such an operation. There were, however, very serious reasons, known to trained seamen, against it. Sextus Pompeius, ensconced in the harbour of Messina, at once seized his opportunity. Coming out of the harbour in his fast ships, with a following wind, he caught up the rear of Octavian's fleet, brought it to bay and then proceeded to attack each of the ships in turn with two of his own. Octavian's fleet, unable to manoeuvre with equal effectiveness against the wind, was cut up, driven on shore, or sunk. Octavian himself had to leap overboard from his beached vessel, and take refuge up•n the rocks. He did what he could to save the men and material of his beaten fleet; but there could be no doubt that beaten it was. Only the approach of the

The invasion fails

northern fleet saved it from complete destruction. Military success did not seem to be among the natural gifts with which the gods had endowed Octavian. The survivors of the disaster spent the night on shore as best they could, their leader among them. Next day one of the terrible storms which haunt the Sicilian waters sprang up and overwhelmed everything that was left. It raged throughout the afternoon, and most of the following night. When it cleared, there was no further question of fighting Sextus Pompeius.

Octavian was deeply discouraged; and any man who (as he did) defers much to public opinion and guides his policy by the degree of support it evokes, must necessarily be more readily discouraged than the bull-tempered men who push on against all opposition. Opinion in Rome, restive under the influence of high prices and short supplies, looked upon Octavian's failure as a judgment upon him for tearing up the treaty of Misenum, and it demanded a new treaty. Taxes were not being paid regularly. The financial stringency was the most difficult part of a difficult situation. In these circumstances Octavian was anxious to force a decisive result and to clear up the whole matter. But could he? That was the question!

Octavian in diffi-culties

The problem was all the harder to deal with because Marcus Antonius in the meantime seemed to be doing very well. While Octavian was failing to defeat Sextus Pompeius, Ventidius had won a great victory in Syria over the Parthians, in which Pacorus, the son of King Orodes, was slain. It was so much the greatest victory that the Romans had ever hitherto won against the Parthians, that it seemed to wipe out the memory of the defeat of Crassus at Carrhae: it certainly drove the Parthians back into Mesopotamia. . . . Ventidius was the first Roman general to establish a genuine military ascendancy over the Parthian power. . . . Too wise to over-do his success, he refrained from pursuing the enemy beyond the Euphrates. He turned, instead, to the task of reducing the minor powers who were still uncertain whether they owed their allegiance to one side or the other. King Antiochus of Commagene, shut up in Samosata, offered a thousand talents for pardon and peace. Ventidius referred the matter to Antony. The latter, conscious that he was being outshone by a subordinate, said that he would deal with the matter in person.

The first slip in Antony's good luck had been the birth

Antony also in difficulties

of a daughter instead of the expected son. The second came over the business of Samosata. The defenders, thinking that their offer had been refused, put up so stout a defence that when Antony at last arrived, he found that he would have to accept a much smaller sum than had at first been offered. He had to take three hundred talents—and this was a serious humiliation. He felt it necessary to recall Ventidius, who was sent home to receive the honour of a triumph—the first triumph ever celebrated for a victory over Parthians. . . . So was removed the only general who hitherto had shown any ability to deal with the new Parthian power.

But the third slip in Antony's luck was fatal: Octavia's second child was born—and it was another girl! The Wonder-Child was as far off as ever. From the moment of the birth of Antonia "minor," Antony must have realized that his hopes were in vain. Octavia was not destined to produce the Wonder-Child. He could wait no longer. . . . And why need he wait, when he had known for some time past that he was the father of a fine man-child, the son of Cleopatra? . . . He had hardly left Egypt three years before when Cleopatra gave birth to twins, a boy and a girl. . . . This, perhaps, had been part of her reason for sending him away. Why need he trouble any more, when here was

The children of Cleopatra

the Wonder-Child and when Cleopatra was a rich and worthy mate for him, and the kind of woman he liked and enjoyed, well able to enter into his schemes and to help him to realize them?

But one or two things needed to be considered first. He wanted a son; and he wanted the backing of wealthy Egypt; but in order to use both, he needed Roman troops. Now the Committee of Three would come to an end on the last day of December next following, when the five-year term would be up. Consequently, he could not break away from Octavia just yet. Besides (the case of Fulvia notwithstanding) Marcus Antonius was not the kind of man to hurt a woman's feelings unnecessarily. When he did it, he would do it as politely as possible, with as little gratuitous pain as he could help. . . . He must first of all see Octavian and renew the Committee. *Then* he could act.

Besides—he had heard, by this time, that Octavian was not going to sit down idly under his reverse from Sextus Pompeius: a reverse which, no doubt, in secret gave Antony a good deal of quiet amusement. Maecenas had already come to see him and talk to him. From Maecenas, even if from nowhere else, he is sure to have heard of Marcus Agrippa's great victory in Gaul, that summer, which came to Octavian as a sudden ray of hope in the gloom. Agrippa had repressed a rebellion, had crossed the Rhine, and had showed himself once more a strong and competent soldier. . . . Octavian had made up his mind to break altogether with Sextus Pompeius, to spend a year or two in reorganizing, and then to bring Agrippa down to deal with the Sicilian problem. If any man could beat Sextus, Agrippa was that man. . . . Hence, while Antony was casting off Ventidius,[2] Octavian was pushing forward Agrippa into the work he seemed born to do: and the results which followed will show which step was the wiser one.

Octavian perseveres

VI

It was the peculiar and distinctive note of the Sicilian problem that it suggested to Octavian a train of thought, the results of which are visible in his actions. He was still

[2] Ventidius was a self-made man who rose from being a successful army contractor. If the instances given by Frontinus (*Stratagems*, I, i, 6; II, ii, 5; II, v, 36, 37) are any guide, he was an astute psychologist whose success was due to a very shrewd judgment of what the other man was likely to do or think. A contest between Ventidius the psychologist and Agrippa the engineer would have been worth watching.

young, and it would be surprising if he did not marry again. We have seen the circumstances in which Scribonia was used against him, with the result that he dissolved the marriage. The stupidest man—and Octavian was far from being that—might have reflected over the lack of confidence between husband and wife which had been the primary cause of the whole affair. Next time, he would choose a very different wife—some one in whom he might repose such implicit confidence, that she would know all his thoughts and intentions, and would direct her own activities to helping, not hindering, them. . . . And there was another point which the difficulty over Sextus Pompeius had brought to light. Hitherto, Octavian had been purely a party leader.

Octavian's position He had been foremost in insisting upon vengeance for the murder of Julius, and in stipulating for the pure milk of party doctrine. He had (as we know) criticised Marcus Antonius for his compromise with the oligarchs; though probably he had been unable to deny the truth of Antony's defence. But the problem of Sextus, and the question of the unity of government and tradition throughout the Roman dominion, almost insensibly moved him towards that position which politicians call the "centre," away from exclusively party considerations. He wished to establish friendly relations with the classes who would sympathise, and who could help, but who hitherto had been remote from his social circle. . . . What better method of doing so could be thought of, than marrying into those classes? The only question was, Was there a woman who perfectly fulfilled both requirements of being a wife he could trust, and a woman of the aristocracy?

There was such a woman.

Among the refugees who left Perusia after its surrender, we have already noted Tiberius Claudius Nero and his wife Livia, with their little son, the future Emperor Tiberius. It is possible that Octavian saw Livia then. Tiberius Nero and his wife and son had an exciting time while escaping from Perusia, reaching Sicily, and making their way ultimately to Antony in Greece. They returned with Antony, and after the treaty of Brundusium they settled down in Rome, where, apparently, they remained. Of their social affiliations there could be no question whatsoever. The Claudians were one of the very oldest and proudest houses in Rome. Livia

Livia was a beautiful, brilliant and very strong woman, who possessed many of the characteristics most noticeably lacking in Octavian. She was tall, majestic and impressive in personal appearance; she belonged by birth to the famous house of Livius Drusus, and had all the aristocratic breeding, the high intelligence and the liberal feeling which had distinguished that remarkable family. Livia was thus capable of bringing Octavian right into a world which he had barely touched before, and of bringing him into it under the most favourable circumstances. She had immense competence socially, and vast capacity for all those wars, battles and counterplots which take place among women in drawing rooms and at dinner parties. The high degree of organization which existed among the women of older Rome made it very necessary that Octavian should be represented in the intimate proceedings of that half of the community; and here, too, Livia could be invaluable. Such a man as Octavian, a man's man who spent most of his time in the company of men and in the transactions of politics and government, could hardly fail to find Livia a most fascinating companion. She completed his personality in a wonderful way, so that the two of them together presented the aspect of a predestined pair. . . . They evidently thought so themselves. A pre-
destined
pair

It is easy to see what Octavian found in Livia. Less easy

is it to see what she found in him. He was not the kind of man to sweep a woman off her feet. He was only the head of the Caesarian party, the *populares*—an Octavian by birth, without ancestors or connections—a rather common person, who wore a beard. At this date it took an act of faith to detect the coming Augustus in Octavian. Yet evidently she could see in him something that induced her to part from Tiberius Nero and to go over to this coming man. Some ideas they held in common, some mutual sympathy respecting the old Roman tradition, the tradition of Cincinnatus and Cato. Some affinity of temper, taste and touch they must have had, for the jealousy and malice of Roman society, which spared none and treated some with savage spite and ferocious hatred, passed them over very lightly. It did indeed say that Livia acted as a procuress for her husband—but this, in the circumstances, was almost playful, and it never pretended that he ever sincerely cared for any one else, or that she did.

Marriage of Octavian and Livia
Tiberius Nero—one of the silent men of history—made no objection. His marriage with Livia was dissolved, when she was not far from the birth of her second son, Claudius Drusus. Her marriage to Octavian at once followed, and the second son of Tiberius Nero was born to Octavian's wife. . . . There were comments of varying degrees of maliciousness. But the marriage of Octavian and Livia, if startling in its abruptness, did not end as abruptly as it began. It was a life-long alliance, which lasted until his death fifty-two years later. They were a splendidly matched pair, and they lived in peace, prosperity, and a reasonable amount of happiness for the whole of that fifty-two years. If Antony destroyed his own luck when he broke with Fulvia, Octavian as surely made his fortune when he married Livia. . . . Without her, he might never have grown into the man who became Augustus.

VII

Hence, by a noteworthy dispensation of Providence, both Marcus Antonius and Octavian were at this juncture brought into a mood to agree with one another. Their interests, diverse as they might be, converged upon one point: they must renew the law which gave the Committee of Three its legal existence. While Marcus Antonius was already entitled by the treaty of Brundusium to raise troops in Italy, it was not the easiest thing for him to exercise this right if Octavian were unfriendly. An agreed settlement would make everything simpler and easier. Antony, in return for the troops he would need for the Parthian War, could give Octavian the fleet he needed for his Sicilian campaign. Antony had ample naval resources. Marcus Antonius accordingly sailed for Italy in the December of the year 38 B. C., to meet Octavian and to discuss these things. *Antony and Octavian agree*

Owing to the completeness with which the business had been arranged beforehand, there was comparatively little to do at Tarentum when the two men met. The comedy which was staged there seemed a very serious matter to some people at the time, as it has done to many people since: but most of it was by-play. The essential points had been worked out beforehand by Maecenas.

To begin with, Octavian took good care that Marcus Antonius should not land at Brundusium, and so occupy the main port of communication with the East. Antony, somewhat annoyed, went to Tarentum instead; and he evidently chose to make a good deal of fuss over the rebuff, for Octavia was alarmed. Receiving permission to visit her brother, she met Octavian some distance from Tarentum. Agrippa and Maecenas were with him, so that there could be no mistaking the importance he attached to the coming *Meeting at Tarentum* interview with Antony. The three were profoundly affected by her picture of herself, the wife of one protagonist and the sister of the other—the one person who was certain to be the loser in a struggle. Octavian behaved with great tact. He had quite a string of complaints respecting Antony's conduct, which he allowed Octavia successfully to refute. It must have given her the greatest satisfaction to see the friendly temper in which he then continued his journey to Tarentum. . . . Nothing less than a personal interview would satisfy him. . . . It was indeed touching to observe the warmth with which Antony came to greet his brother-in-law. He had established his headquarters in the town of Tarentum itself. The harbour was crowded with the ships of his fleet. The army of Octavian, arriving at the banks of the river Taras, at once fraternized with Antony's naval force; all was friendship, cordiality and festivity. The barges of the two leaders met in midstream, and after a brotherly wrangle respecting which should be host, and which guest, it was allowed that Octavian should be the guest on this first day, so that he could visit his sister. This being agreed, the assembled army and fleet beheld their commanders climb into a carriage together and drive off to Antony's quarters in Tarentum, with vast friendliness and mutual confidence. . . . When they *did* agree, their unity was indeed wonderful! Octavian spent the night at Tarentum, without bodyguard or formal guarantee, showing his complete confidence in Antony—who paid him a visit in like manner, as a proof of absolute trust.

Their unity is wonderful

When, after these preliminaries, they got to business, it was still agreed to regard Octavia as a peace-maker reconciling two inveterate opponents—and it is likely enough that she, at any rate, took her function seriously. It was settled that the law constituting the Committee should be renewed for another five years, beginning on January 1st,

37 B. C. The arrangements already standing between them were similarly continued. Octavian however undertook to furnish Antony with twenty thousand trained Italian legionaries, while Antony supplied Octavian with a hundred and twenty ships, which he delivered complete upon the spot. Octavia, with Antony's approval, presented her brother with a squadron of ten three-bank vessels of an unusual pattern. In return, Octavian gave her a thousand men—a praetorian cohort, or commander's bodyguard—to be picked by Antony at his pleasure. This was no trifling gift to make, if Antony were really to exercise his choice. It implied the thousand best fighting men in Italy.

They part on their ways

So they parted. Marcus Antonius—why should he not?—deposited in the care of Octavian his most precious possessions, his wife and children, including Fulvia's children, before he sailed. Then, bidding them farewell, he left Tarentum for the East . . . with what plans and purposes we shall presently see.

Did Octavian suspect anything? There was no reason why he should do so: and at the moment it was convenient to close his eyes tightly to anything he did not wish to notice. Octavia evidently suspected that it was necessary for her to stand well with her husband—but we may judge that she would not have let him slip away quite so easily had she guessed his intentions. As for Antony—he had got all he wanted, and he left Octavian to carry on the endless and apparently hopeless war with Sextus Pompeius, while he sailed for the lands of sunshine, wealth and success.

VIII

While Agrippa was busy in those vast preparations which heralded the attack upon Sicily, Marcus Antonius reached Syria and fixed his headquarters at Antioch. He had made

up his mind and drawn up his programme. He despatched
Fonteius Capito to Egypt to see Cleopatra. Did she expect
the message? It is probable that she did. It is probable that
she already knew that Antony meant to cut adrift from
the West—for the time being—and to carry through the
Parthian War in partnership with her. She went to Syria
fully primed to carry out her share in the arrangement.

Antony marries Cleopatra Autumn 37 B. C.

In the autumn of the very year of the renewal of the
Committee, therefore, Marcus Antonius, receiving the
Queen of Egypt in great glory and state in Syria, married
her. His marriage was worthless in the eyes of Roman
law; but neither he nor any one else troubled much about
that. The twins, his son and daughter by Cleopatra, he
solemnly recognized, and in honour of the occasion they
were re-named by the names under which they are known
to history—Alexander-Helios and Cleopatra-Selene. These
strange names had a meaning which was not lost upon the
Greek East. Antony had decided that Alexander Helios
should be the Wonder-Child of Virgil's dream and his own
—the Sun-King in whose name he would appeal to all the
East for unity. He aimed at re-establishing (where he could,
by appeal to the great tradition of Alexander the reconciler of nations; and where he could not, by appeal to the
Roman sword) the empire of Alexander that had once
stretched from where his (Antony's) rule began in Macedonia, to the Oxus and the Indus and the mountains of
Afghanistan. That was the programme.

The great plan

To mark what he was doing, he bestowed upon Cleopatra, in trust for the two children, the lost Asiatic provinces of their ancestor Ptolemy II, which had included Palestine, Syria, Cyprus and a great part of Cilicia—in fact most
of the lands that were to be his starting point for the attack
upon the Parthians and the conquest of the East. . . . He
had obtained his twenty thousand Roman troops from Oc-

tavian by paying for them with ships. He obtained now the backing of Egypt's immense wealth by this marriage with Cleopatra and this gift to her children. . . . The Romans might hate those proceedings—but dare any of them say that the scheme was not greater, deeper, more magnificent, more likely to succeed than the miserable little plans of Octavian?

CHAPTER X

THE STRUGGLE BETWEEN THE LITTLE PLAN AND THE GREAT PLAN

I

THE prospects of the struggle against Sextus Pompeius took on a very different aspect as soon as Marcus Vipsanius Agrippa grasped the nettle. As consul for the year he had powers which he added to those of the triumvir Octavian. He at once put in hand the creation of a powerful fleet. Under his personal supervision the ships were laid down; the crews were trained; a new port was built close to Puteoli, where the new ships could lie up in perfect safety, secure from weather. Agrippa's new harbour attracted the interest of both Horace and Virgil,[1] who have left allusions to it embedded in their work. . . . He was one of the commanders who gave the Roman army its historic reputation as an engineering army, habituated to fight with the spade, the hammer and the trowel as much as with the sword. Right at the innermost end of the Bay of Baiae, with Misenum and ancient Palaeopolis guarding the entrance, and Baiae and Puteoli smiling at one another across the water, lay two lakes with the old Greek port of Cumae not far off, northwestward, on its rock. These lakes bore famous names. One was the Lucrine, famous for its oysters; the other, farther in, was Avernus, with those signs of sinister volcanic agency about it which made the ancients think it the mouth of hell. Agrippa dredged out the Lucrine, repaired and altered the breakwater, and drove a

Marcus Vipsanius Agrippa, consul, 37 B. C.

Preparations

[1] Horace, *Art of Poetry*, 63; Virgil, *Georgics*, II, 161.

channel inland to join up Avernus to form an inner harbour. With characteristic dislike of sentimentality and superstition, Agrippa swept away the dark woods that hedged Avernus in and helped to make it proverbial for gloom and deathliness. . . . Port Julius [2] rapidly filled with waiting ships, while the training of the crews proceeded.

The plan had been for Agrippa to act under his powers as consul, and he arranged his scheme according to the old method which had given such good results in the past. After his year as consul, during which he made his preparations, he entered Sicily with the proconsular powers which had now become a matter of course upon laying down the consular office. The organization was worthy of him in extent and thoroughness—and it certainly needed to be.

II

The invaders of Sicily set out all together on the first day of July: Lepidus from Africa with a thousand troop-ships and seventy galleys: Statilius Taurus from Tarentum with a hundred and two of the Asiatic ships which Antony had given: Agrippa from Portus Julius with Octavian and the main armada. What they were chiefly afraid of can be seen from the sacrifices which Octavian offered up when setting out: to the Favourable Winds, the Waveless Sea and Neptune the Securer. They had reason to fear—for the grim powers that guard Sicily were alert, and up came the southerly gale with all its force. Statilius Taurus was blown back to Tarentum, whether he would or no; Octavian, strung out in a long line, lost part of his fleet in rounding

Agrippa invades Sicily 36 B. C.

[2] Port Julius was still visible in 1538 A. D., when it was blotted out by the great earthquake which raised Monte Nuovo and half filled the Lucrine Lake. It may have been during the work on the port that Virgil made the intimate acquaintance with the Lake Avernus which he afterwards used to immortalize it in the sixth book of the Aeneid.

the Sorrentine peninsula, and himself, with the main fleet, was driven to take refuge in the open bay of Velia, where the mountains afforded a partial shelter. The wind, with frightening malice, then shifted to the southwest and began to blow the fleet upon the rocks. To get out was impossible in the teeth of wind and sea, and the destruction was very serious. Only Lepidus, with some damage to his troop-ships, managed to effect a landing and to reach Lilybaeum.

It seemed at first as if the expedition would have to be abandoned—at any rate, for that year. But a very tough and grim man was in charge of it, and after a pause the campaign was reorganized. True—the time of year was uncomfortably late, and to recondition the fleet would take a month. But Rome was starving. The strangle-hold of Sextus must be broken at all costs. Maecenas therefore was despatched to Rome to keep his finger upon those who **Disaster** would at once begin to decry Octavian and to damage his reputation and influence, while Agrippa took in hand the reconstruction of the expedition. The dead were buried; the living were rescued, cared for, reclothed and equipped: ships were collected and repaired. Crews who had lost their ships were sent to Tarentum to man ships which had no crews. And while all these matters were being put in hand, Octavian himself made a tour of inspection through the new land-allotments, to calm the doubts of those of the veterans who had been disturbed by recent events.

The attack upon Sicily which followed was a very different affair from its predecessor two years before. The huge northeastern spur of Sicily, Mount Pelorus, lay almost touching Italy like the bow of an enormous ship, divided from the Italian mainland only by the straights of Messina. At Messina itself, watching the toe of Italy, Sextus Pompeius lay with his main force. The son of Pompeius Magnus was as good a soldier as his father—and that was a pretty good one.

Agrippa's first step was to bring Statilius Taurus down from Tarentum, this time more cautiously, the ships coasting along, while the troops, screened by cavalry, marched along the shore. When in due time they reached Scylacium, they were within easy distance of Vibo across the mountains on the west coast, where Octavian had his headquarters. Barely fifteen miles separated the two places. After inspecting the troops at Scylacium and approving their condition, Octavian returned to Vibo and gave the word to proceed. Second attempt

Sailing west from Vibo with his main fighting squadron, Agrippa took up his post at the island of Strongyle. The scouts reported that the coast of Sicily was strongly held; and the natural deduction was that Sextus was himself there in command of his main forces. Octavian therefore returned swiftly to Vibo, crossed the mountains to Scylacium, and brought the army and fleet of Statilius Taurus right down to the extremity of Italy, where they faced the town of Tauromenium across the straits. In order to pin down the forces of Sextus on the north coast, Agrippa now moved out from Strongyle in force, and came south to Hiera, prepared to fall upon the fleet of the Pompeian commander Demochares at Mylae. Agrippa and Octavian had been mistaken in thinking that Sextus was present in person; but now the threat of the action taken upon the erroneous supposition brought about the reality. Sextus, believing the main attack to be coming from Agrippa, sent forty-five ships to reinforce Demochares, and himself, with a further reinforcement of seventy vessels, followed. Agrippa despatched the news to Octavian, and cleared for action.

The sea-battle of Mylae was the first of the three great battles that built up the fame of Marcus Vipsanius Agrippa

Mylae

and the power of Octavian. He had the bigger ships and the fiercer fighting men, and he had the drive and the vigour to make the best use of his advantages. All day long at Mylae the big Roman ships bore down upon the lighter Sicilian Greek vessels, overwhelming them with their shooting, grappling them, boarding them and clearing them. Agrippa's own ship went for the Sicilian flagship, rammed it and sunk it, and he cheered his captains on to the fray. Sextus, watching the battle from a hill on shore, gave the word to withdraw; and the Sicilian ships retired to the shallows in-shore, where the larger Roman ships could not follow. Agrippa at first proposed to anchor off shore and pursue the advantages he had gained; but he was persuaded to consider discretion the better part of valour, and he sailed away again to harbour. Sextus had lost thirty ships.

But Sextus had no doubt that an attempt was being made to cross the straits farther south, while his attention was concentrated upon Mylae. As soon as Agrippa had retired, Sextus had his supper and started back for Messina. In the meantime Octavian heard of the victory at Mylae, and with the incurable prudence which fatally disqualified him as a soldier, while it was his greatest virtue as a statesman, he decided not to risk crossing the straits in the dark, but to wait for daylight. The delay enabled Sextus to reach Tauromenium in time. Octavian's troops had not dug in. It was necessary for Octavian to fight a sea-battle in de-

Attack on Tauro-menium

fence of his land forces. It was an obstinately contested struggle, which ended in the victory of Sextus. Some of Octavian's ships escaped; many were captured and burned. Octavian himself in an exhausted condition was brought, by a few faithful rescuers, to the camp of Messalla Corvinus. . . . Appian notes, as a matter honourable to the Roman character, that Messalla had been on the proscription list, and had only escaped with his life by flight; and

CAMPANIA

Here Cicero died

Formiae

Caieta

Minturnae

Sinuessa

Allifae

Callifae

Teanum

Cales

Telesia

Beneventum

Casilinum

To Brundusium & the East

Capua

Calatia

Spessula

FALERNIAN PLAIN

Atella

Nola

Portus Julius

NEAPOLIS

Cumae

Puteoli

VESUVIUS

Baiae

Herculaneum

AENARIA

Miserium

Pompeii

PROCHYTA

Nuceria

Salernum

CAPRI

C. Minerva

To Bruttium & Sicily

Approximate Scale

0   5   10   15   20   English Miles

that now he saved and befriended in desperate adversity
one of the men who had proscribed him. . . . And it is
certain that if Messalla had taken a different view of his
duty, the world would never have heard of Caesar Augustus. . . .

Octavian might not be a successful soldier, but he knew
how to keep his head in emergencies. He sent instant word
to Agrippa to organize help for the troops left behind at
Tauromenium and he sent Maecenas again to Rome to
check any attempt to make political capital out of his misfortunes.

He had left behind a capable commander at Tauromenium. Gaius Cornificius, seeing what had happened, collected his troops, placed in the centre the unarmed refugees
whom he had saved from the fleet, and set out to march
across Sicily to find Agrippa. Ignorant of the way, strangers
to the peculiar conditions of Sicily, dogged by enemies and
possible enemies, they strayed into the volcanic region of
Etna, crossed a lava field where they nearly died of heat
and thirst, and after great hardships, courageously borne,
were met by a column sent out by Agrippa to look for
them. Agrippa had sailed westward while Sextus was at Agrippa
Tauromenium, had effected a landing at Tyndaris on the lands at
north coast, and his first step had been to rescue Cornificius. Tyndaris

It was Agrippa's energy and promptitude which forced
a way into Sicily. As soon as Agrippa had got a hold on
Tyndaris, Octavian could rush up the troops by sea to pour
in to support him. Sextus fortified the mountain passes, and
proceeded to turn the range of Mount Pelorus into a huge
citadel.[3] But Agrippa, by a feint eastward with his ships,
persuaded Sextus that he meant to attack there; and Sextus
rushed his men eastward after him, throwing open the de-

[3] Both Christians and Moslems, in the later history of Sicily, successfully defended the recesses of these mountains against their enemies.

files to the west—and Octavian at once seized them, and began to throw a long line of posts right across the hills to the foot of Mount Etna. The flames and rumblings of the huge mountain were particularly trying to the Germans among the troops, who—being new to this kind of thing—sprang up from their hard-earned sleep anticipating the worst; and heavy rain added to the difficulties of the situation. But they held their ground, and cut Sextus off from the source of his supplies.

Sextus isolated

Sextus saw that the game was up. He could not maintain his armies without adequate supplies: and he was far too good a soldier to fancy that he could. He elected to fight a big battle while his men were still fresh and well fed, rather than drag things out and be forced into it when they were starving. As he thought he had more chance at sea than on land, he communicated his views to Octavian, challenging him to have matters out on the water.

There was a famous precedent at Vercellae when Gaius Marius, asked to name a day, replied that Roman commanders chose their own time and place for battle. But Sextus had judged the circumstances rightly: Octavian also had an interest in forcing a quick decision. Possibly Octavian realized to the full the difficulty of his position in Rome if Sextus managed to drag the war out. Agrippa, too, may have felt more confident of his power to win a decisive battle than a long guerilla war with the possibility of having his own resources cut off by political events in Italy. Hence, Octavian, though he was no sailor, and rather dreaded the sea, accepted the proposition of Sextus, and the preparations were begun.

III

The battle of Naulochus was the kind of battle, fought between men of like race, like abilities, and like equipment,

which is almost necessarily doomed to be a fruitless slaughter ending in a drawn contest, unless some new idea can
be introduced into it to produce a decisive result. It was **Naulochus**
the peculiar virtue of Agrippa that he clearly saw this necessity. While the commanders on both sides were making all
the conventional preparations—the towers, the catapults, the
grappling irons, the boarding bridges, the stores of weapons
—Agrippa bent his mind to designing a novelty. He thought
out a new kind of armour-plated grappling apparatus
which, like a harpoon, could be shot from a mechanical
catapult trailing ropes behind it. By this means the dodging
and manoeuvring of the expert Sicilian pilots could be
brought to an abrupt end by seizing their ships at a distance, and drawing them in by means of windlasses—when
the boarding bridges and grappling irons would do the rest.

It was this long-distance grappler which won the sea-
battle of Naulochus. While the long lines of ships, strung
out across the sea, were locked in a struggle that was only
too often deadly without being decisive, Agrippa with a
chosen squadron drove into the fight with the new grappler, and cleared ship after ship. So blind was the struggle,
that even Agrippa could not tell how it was going—but he
cheered his men on with unflinching energy until he saw
the enemy drawing out of the battle and breaking their own
line. Seventeen ships, the vanguard of Sextus's fleet, got off
clear and sailed for the straits and safety. The rest were
rounded up and captured or driven on shore: some were **Agrippa's**
set on fire and burned, others surrendered. Except the **victory**
seventeen that escaped, the whole of Sextus's fleet was
destroyed or captured, with the loss of three of Agrippa's
vessels.

A vast audience—the armies of Octavian and Sextus,
drawn up on shore—watched this fierce gladiatorial combat
with cheers, shouts, groans, and all the manifestations of

excitement and suspense. The decision was final. As soon as he saw that all was lost, Sextus slipped away quietly to Messina. Finding that their general had gone, the troops of Sextus surrendered on terms to Octavian. A few hours later a fast galley, that had been made ready beforehand against emergencies, swept out of the harbour at Messina and made for the East. It carried Sextus Pompeius on board. With him went the seventeen ships that had escaped from the battle.

He never came back. He went to join Marcus Antonius, hoping that in return for the kindness he had shown Antony's mother, he might expect a little himself. . . . With his flight he ceased to be a man whose actions influenced the course of history.

IV

And now Lepidus entered upon the scene. He had done nothing towards the defeat of Sextus Pompeius, but he now appeared at Messina, received the surrender of the town and the garrison, and faced Octavian with more than a suggestion that the time had come for a reckoning between them. He had twenty-two legions with him—a great army, more numerous than that of Octavian, and perfectly fresh. His claim was that he had been the first in Sicily, and had done much to bring the island over to the Committee. He claimed Sicily as his.

Lepidus

The revolt of the mild and inoffensive Lepidus was indeed surprising; and like some other episodes, it had its root in a vague conviction that Octavian was not much of a fighting man, and that no one need be afraid of him. This remarkable belief was one which it took many years totally to root out.

A personal interview between Octavian and Lepidus—a rather angry one—led to no result. But Lepidus had not merely misjudged Octavian; he misjudged the whole situation, the whole trend of the times, which Octavian, beyond any other man, personified. The mere suggestion of another civil war between their leaders exasperated the army, which was sick, tired and weary to death of unending and unnecessary war, and which simply would not follow any leader who appealed to it without reason. Lepidus had no conception of the strength or extent of this feeling; but Octavian perfectly understood it. While Lepidus sat down **War of** to wait, the emissaries of Octavian hastened to the camp of **propaganda** Lepidus, and one of those campaigns of whispering, argument and unobtrusive propaganda began which had once before overthrown the hopes of Marcus Antonius, and was now destined to do the like even more effectively to Lepidus. The troops of Sextus Pompeius were persuaded that their terms of surrender might not be valid unless Octavian endorsed them. In the midst of all this, Octavian himself arrived. He addressed the assembled soldiers in small separate groups, his theme being his unwillingness to take part in civil war, and his regret at the compulsion put upon him to resort to it. He was welcomed with respect and approval. The troops of Sextus asked his forgiveness for having put themselves on the wrong side. He answered by asking why, in that case, they did not do what their interests indicated. This was clear enough. They began to pack up ready to go over to Octavian. Some of the men of Lepidus intervened. Octavian was threatened, struck, and driven out of the camp. But it was now too late. The rot had begun. First the Pompeians went over; then others; and when the alarm was given, and Lepidus, aroused to his danger, sent troops to stop the process of desertion, these very troops joined the movement they had been sent to suppress. . . . Lepidus presently found himself deserted and forgotten in his camp—but alas! not because any Cleo- **Lepidus** patra was arriving there. . . . The last men who left him, **surrenders**

before they departed, sent to ask if they should kill Lepidus.
. . . Octavian forbade any such idea. . . . So at last Lepidus was left without help or hope, despondent and alone.

He made the best of it, put off his military equipment, changed into private dress, and went over to Octavian too, accompanied by a curious crowd, anxious to see what would happen. As he approached, Octavian sprang up from his seat, and stayed him from performing the act of obeisance and surrender. After all, the old gentleman was old enough to be Octavian's father. Lepidus was sent back to Rome as a private citizen; he was deprived of his military command, but not of his other offices, and that was the last of him as a soldier and a statesman. He lived several years more in safety and retirement, a harmless and quite unnecessary man.

V

The defeat and flight of Sextus Pompeius, and the pacification of Sicily, threw open the gates that for so long had been barred and bolted in the face of Octavian. For the first time for many years the Roman world was at peace, and the rule of her magistrates extended over the whole of her dominion. The stranglehold was broken, and once more traffic was free, and the corn of Africa and Sicily could be poured into the Roman market. The change might have come slowly, by degrees, so that men hardly noticed it; but as a matter of fact it came suddenly, like a glorious dawn, a dropping off of fetters, a wonderful delivery, a dramatic tableau. The great bound of exaltation and enthusiasm which lifted up the hearts of the Roman people may have been foreseen by Octavian—or he may only have realized it when he reached Rome and saw the sudden popularity into which he had leaped at one bound. . . . He might almost have thought that *he* was the King of the

**Effects of
conquest
of Sicily**

Golden Age! . . . The senate in a body went out to meet him, with garlands, followed by a great concourse of citizens, and this startling and unusual reception committee, the like of which Rome had not seen for many a day, marched beside him to the temples, to return thanks, and escorted him home to his own house. . . . If they did this in the green leaf, what would they do in the dry? His policy had been justified. Though they had complained and opposed him and begged him to make a peace that would have been no peace, he had held out steadily for the policy of destroying the power of Sextus Pompeius, and making a peace that should be a peace indeed.

Yet all his tact and skill were needed to survive the results even of this triumph. With forty legions in arms in Sicily, the problem of demobilization was a very serious one. He had managed, so far, by one expedient or another, to avoid the necessity of grappling with the worst of the problem. The troops insisted upon equality of treatment and upon the substantial nature of the rewards promised. They refused to be fobbed off with honours alone. It was useless to threaten them; he had no power to repress by severity opinions which were universal among the legionaries. *Octavian and the army*

The only resort was to treat the whole problem with the subtlety and forethought which great statesmen devote to great problems—and certainly this was such a problem. He discharged, at their own demand, the veterans of longest service, the men of Mutina and Philippi, and took steps to provide them with land allotments. The newer troops he partly demobilized, but retained where he could. He needed a definite plan by which he could utilize the men he retained and he secured this by a project which certainly (as things then were) looked very far ahead: the conquest and organization of Illyria. The reason why Illyria should occupy the thoughts of a Roman statesman, and the question of what beneficial results might be obtained by absorbing it into the circle of Roman civilization, were probably not very apparent to the average citizen. Octavian, nevertheless, foresaw what would become necessary in the remote future. By taking the work in hand now, he was able to find a use for a good-sized army, for which accordingly he need not just yet find land allotments. Sicily and the rich newly recovered lands would furnish the money required at the beginning; and he hoped subsequently to make his venture self-supporting. Finally—and this was not the least important consideration—he would have a trained army at hand when the break with Antony should come, as come it would.

Policy
imposed
upon
Octavian

Even if he had had no other aim than a narrowly selfish one, he would have been obliged, by the most elementary considerations of his own safety, to strive his utmost to form a great solid bloc of united public opinion in his own support. This imperative necessity of unity governed all his conduct, and inspired all his thoughts. It forced him on when he might have been too slow; it held him back when he might have wished to insist upon his own private views and desires; it guided him through the crazy labyrinth of hopes, fears, prejudices, ignorances, passions and fantasies which constitute public opinion. Now, when all was enthusiasm around him, he took care not to let it carry him away. He accepted such harmless compliments as the institution of annual games in honour of his victory, and the erection of a gilded statue with a naval trophy as pedestal, and with a complimentary inscription to him as the Restorer of Peace: such things had their practical utility in fixing in the public memory the remembrance of what had happened. But he accepted no privilege which might alienate any important section of opinion. He refused to

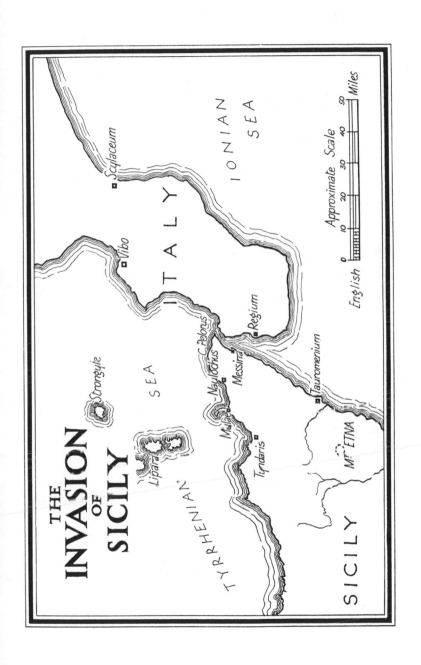

THE
INVASION
OF
SICILY

Scylaceum

IONIAN
SEA

Vibo

ITALY

Approximate Scale

Regium

Strongyle

SEA

C. Pelorus

Naulochus

Messina

Tauromenium

Lipara

Malae

TYRRHENIAN

Tyndaris

Mᵗ ETNA

SICILY

English

0 10 20 30 40 50 Miles

countenance the execution of Lepidus, and he declined the office of Pontifex Maximus, which Lepidus held. He burnt the papers of Sextus Pompeius unread, so that the past might be forgotten: his new power he used to restore pub- **Prudence** lic order throughout Italy, and to suppress the bands of robbers and kidnappers who had been secure of impunity during the time of disturbances. Now that he had in his hands the disposition of the vast revenues of Sicily and Africa, he treated them as a trust. When he settled his veterans round Capua, he set an example by building them a magnificent aqueduct—a lead instantly followed by Agrippa, who thoroughly grasped the principle of using wealth for the public benefit. . . . Only one thing personal to himself he accepted—and that was the grant to him in perpetuity of the sanctity of the tribunician power.

There was a particular reason for this grant. He had expressed the view that when the Parthian War was over, Antony would probably join him in dissolving the Committee, resigning his special position, and restoring the old constitution—in fact, resigning the collective dictatorship Republicae Constituendae Causa exactly as Sulla had resigned the individual one. But every one knew the difficulty in the way—which was the possibility of the ex-Dictator's being murdered, either judicially or extra-judicially, as soon as he divested himself of power. The Sanctity of the Tribuneship formed what we should now call an Act of Indemnity, a permanent protection guaranteed by the constitution itself.

VI

The reader who has followed this narrative up to the present point may well pause and ask: But what made Octavian express opinions which, on the face of them, were

so improbable?—and what can have made him take pro-
vision against an event so unlikely to come to pass? Knowing what he knew, he cannot possibly have believed that
Marcus Antonius was preparing to retire, like Sulla, into
private life. . . . And the explanation is that he possessed
information not shared by the general public, or even by
the majority of the senate. He knew the real truth about
Antony's Parthian expedition, which had been in progress
while Octavian and Agrippa were in the midst of their
Sicilian campaign. The news of Antony's great victory had
arrived: the senate was ordering days of thanksgiving: the
people looked forward to the end of the war: the world
at large wondered: and only Octavian and the inner circle
of his friends knew the truth, which was that Antony's
expedition had been a disastrous failure.

The grand army, a hundred thousand strong, including
sixty thousand Roman legionaries, had marched a thousand miles through the mountains and foothills from Syria
to the borders of Armenia, where it was joined by an
Armenian army of thirteen thousand men. Marcus Antonius
learnt by the fate of Crassus, and took good care to avoid

the desert. He arrived in Armenia rather late in the year.
There he was given good counsel—to stay where he was
over the winter and begin his campaign next spring. But
luck was now flowing adverse to Antony. He could not
persuade himself to stay away from Egypt so long: he decided that he must strike one blow for the sake of prestige,
and go home. . . . He did not, indeed, display the dangerous prudence of Octavian; but he showed a dangerous im-
prudence no less fatal. Leaving his siege train behind him
under Oppius, he advanced to capture the city of Phraata
in Media, failed to capture it, lost his siege-train to a flanking raid by the Parthians, was abandoned by the angry
King of Armenia, and had to march the thousand miles

back to Syria as best he could. . . . He was still too good a soldier and too good a fellow for the retreat to be as fatal as the Retreat from Moscow: but in some of its effects it was not unlike that great disaster. He lost more than a fifth of his magnificent army, and, tramping through the snow-storms of autumn, arrived back in Syria with a hungry, freezing and disheartened army. Cleopatra hastened thither with money and clothes—and she can never have been more welcome.

If the world at large did not realize the meaning of this disaster, it is largely because Marcus Antonius realized it only too well, and exerted every effort of which he was capable to hide its magnitude. But Octavian knew—though it was no part of Octavian's policy to publish the news too broadcast—and he saw from the first some of the great changes it foreshadowed in their relative positions. . . . Antony's Agrippa had won the decisive battle of Naulochus by in- position venting a new tactical device. Marcus Antonius had lost the Parthian campaign because he still had no answer to the tactical novelty of the armoured Parthian horse-soldier and the mounted Parthian archer working in unison. And there were probably soldiers around Octavian who were capable of telling him that no answer was likely to be found just yet. In such a case, Antony would never win the Parthian War. He would never come home again like Sulla with the glory of an Asiatic triumph. . . .

How accurately Octavian had foreseen the consequences is clear from the successive steps that followed. Octavia was very anxious to seize this opportunity to re-establish friendly relations with her husband; and Octavian put no difficulty in her way. But Plutarch, the biographer of An-tony (or his source) in telling the story expresses the opin-ion that Octavian gave his consent for private reasons of his own. . . . Octavia arrived at Athens with supplies of clothes, money, and presents for the troops, and two thousand picked men, whom she can have obtained only from Octavian himself. But Cleopatra was alarmed, and would not rest until Antony had written to Octavia to tell her to remain at Athens, and until he himself had returned to the safety of Alexandria. . . . Octavia went home again disappointed, and all her contributions to the war were useless. . . . But there was no Parthian campaign that year.

Octavia

Octavia had the same power of appealing to the public opinion of her countrymen that her brother possessed—and it may help us to gain a side-light on Octavian, if we note how infallible her touch was. Practically every one in Rome approved of Octavia, and felt her to be a good woman who was being scandalously treated. But by whom was she being so treated? Antony, on the whole, was a popular man, and Octavia, far from complaining of him, devoted herself to his interests with zeal. Public opinion finally decided that Cleopatra was the criminal. Antony was merely her dupe. And this decision was satisfactory to every one—including Octavia.

Plutarch (or his source) has described with skill and psychological insight the means by which Cleopatra put pressure upon Marcus Antonius and reduced him to sentimental subservience: but he had no doubt that Octavia's attitude was absolutely sincere. And it seems to be the truth that no one was capable of such a delicate feat of psychological analysis as to decide just how much of Octavia's conduct was the pose of an injured wife trying to attract the sympathy of public opinion, and how much represented her real feeling. Octavian, a good deal offended at Antony's refusal to see his wife, and not sorry to see him put in the wrong, suggested that Octavia should cease to occupy Antony's house; but to the fervent admiration of Rome, she insisted upon staying there and devoting herself, not only to her own children, but to Fulvia's also. She was at home to all Antony's friends, and continued to form a channel by which their requests could be brought before the favourable notice of Octavian—a calm, stately, unimpassioned woman, who exactly fulfilled the Roman ideal of a good wife. So much did this impress her contemporaries, that criticisms of Antony were universal. How, public opinion asked, could Antony treat so good a wife in so wicked a way? *The ideal of a good wife*

Whether the right hands of Octavian and Octavia knew what their left hands were doing is a question that must remain plunged in obscurity. But whatsoever they may have been doing, they were doing it very well. The connection of Marcus Antonius with Cleopatra was identified, in the minds of most Romans, as the point against which the right feeling of a Roman must necessarily revolt.

VII

The connection of Antony and Cleopatra was to only a slight degree a romance: it was nine-tenths of it a political alliance, designed so that while Antony guaranteed the integrity of Egypt, Egypt should finance the Parthian War and Antony's control of the Roman state. To mobilize public opinion against it was therefore to mobilize public opinion against the political future of Antony. . . . And the strategic weakness of Antony's position was that he would now have to emphasise precisely this side of his policy. He would slip farther and farther into Cleopatra's hands—and she (unintentionally enough) would damage him more and more in the eyes of his own countrymen, till the balance moved decisively in favour of Octavian. *Balance dips against Antony*

This process unmistakably took place. There was never another great Parthian campaign. Marcus Antonius was too important to Cleopatra for her to let him be risked on what was very evidently a most dangerous hazard. But he must regain some part at least of his prestige. The year after Octavia returned from her fruitless mission to Athens, Antony made an Armenian expedition. It was agreed that the defection of the Armenian king should be regarded as the crucial event which had caused the failure of the Parthian campaign, two years before, and that he must now be punished. As a matter of fact the Armenian king had had very little to do with it—but a scape-goat needed to be found, and the Armenian king was conveniently to hand. Armenia therefore was invaded; the king was captured, and sent to Egypt.

The growth of Cleopatra's importance was visible in the scene that concluded the Armenian campaign. Alexandria, not Rome, beheld the triumph of Antony. It was a magnificent spectacle. Its crowning point was reached in a great open-air assembly. On a silver platform two thrones of gold were placed, with, on a lower step in front, thrones for their children. Before a vast concourse of the inhabitants of Alexandria—then the largest, certainly the richest, possibly the best-educated city in the world—Marcus Antonius, dressed as the god Dionysus, and Cleopatra, dressed as the goddess Isis, took their seats. Before this vast assembly Antony proclaimed Cleopatra as queen of Egypt, Cyprus, Libya and Coele-Syria, and her son, Caesarian, the son of Gaius Julius Caesar, as her successor, with the title of King of Kings. Then he proclaimed his elder son by Cleopatra, Alexander Helios, King of Kings and Ruler of Armenia, Media and Parthia, and his other son by Cleopatra, Ptolemy Philadelphos, King of Kings and ruler of Phoenicia, Syria and Cilicia. . . . The proceedings were marred only by the conduct of the dethroned King of Armenia, who refused to bow down and do homage, and maintained his

Distribu-
tion of
the east

protest until he was hurried away to prison—where he still refused to acknowledge these changes.

At Rome, these proceedings gave rise to the most violent repercussions. Antony's friends, perfectly appreciating the view that would be taken of them by the majority of his fellow-countrymen, did their best to hush them up.[4] Antony himself, in communicating with the Roman government, expressed his intention of terminating his connection with the Committee of Three when it lapsed at the end of the second five-year period, and of restoring the control of the state to the ordinary magistrates. The cumulative effect of all these things was to produce the conviction that Antony meant to become an oriental divine monarch, with his capital at Alexandria, and that he meant to restore the old constitution at Rome. But the belief that such was his meaning produced extraordinarily varied results upon different parties. The *optimates* pictured to themselves Antony retiring to the East and leaving them free to live their own lives at Rome. The Caesarians had no doubt that Antony meant to set up an oriental monarchy in Rome itself —with, perhaps, the *optimates* as his local representatives. The optimates had no objection to Cleopatra, as long as she did not interfere with Rome. But the Caesarians developed a violent dislike of Cleopatra, in whom they saw the root and source of the whole trouble. Antony had been one of themselves until he fell into her hands. It was she

Feeling at Rome

[4] Antony's despatch was evidently in the consuls' hands early in 33 B.C., together with his letter of complaints against Octavian. In reply to the first three complaints, that he had appropriated the whole of Sicily, had not returned the ships lent him, and had taken possession of the share of Lepidus, Octavian replied that he would divide all his gains with Antonius when the latter divided Armenia with him. In reply to the fourth complaint, that he had appropriated Italy for his own troops, and left no room for those of Antony, Octavian answered that Antony's soldiers could not possibly need Italy, when their heroic efforts had made them owners of Media and Parthia! This last sarcasm stung! (Plutarch, *Antony*; Dio, L, i, 3.)

who had started all these fantastic ideas. Octavian himself revealed typically Roman prejudices when it came to this point.

The real purposes of Marcus Antonius became obvious before long. The King of Media, having quarrelled with the Parthian King, was anxious to come to an understanding with the powerful Roman; and the result of their negotiations was that Alexander Helios was betrothed to the King's daughter Iotape, and that Antony and the King made an offensive and defensive alliance—each of them to fight the other's battles, Antony against the Parthians and the Mede against Octavian. . . . The long and short of it was that the second Wonder-Child had been as great a failure as the first, and had totally failed to rouse the enthusiasm and effect the unity of Asia; and that, as a consequence, Antony did not propose to wait until he had won a great victory over the Parthians before he returned home to Rome. He was facing the truth, that he never would win a great victory over them. He was going to return home without the success, but with the money of Egypt to back him.

And—naturally—many men began to wonder if he could gain a great victory over Octavian either.

Antony
prepares
to return

VIII

It had gradually become the task of Octavian to oppose the dismemberment of the Roman dominion; and his immediate preoccupation was to unite the public opinion of Italy against the threat of a Hellenistic invasion. The final year of the Committee saw him in office as consul. He laid down the dignity, however, on the first day of his term. He had other matters to think of, and a substitute took his place. There had been difficulty of late in finding men

willing to accept the office of aedile, which involved super-
intendence of the building works and city-planning of
Rome, and consequent heavy expenditure on the part of
the magistrate—out of his own pocket, according to the
Roman custom. Octavian called in Agrippa to help. Instead of Octavian's second consulship, therefore, the year
was marked by a series of magnificent public works put in
hand by Agrippa. He was the right man for the task. The **Agrippa as**
old aqueducts were surveyed and repaired,[5] and a new one, **reformer**
the "Julian," was built, fifteen miles long. Agrippa made
seven hundred watering stations where the general public
could have free access to the water supply, besides one
hundred and five fountains, and a hundred and thirty reser-
voirs. The great drainage system of Rome, which had been
neglected, was flushed out and put into order—the com-
pletion of which work Agrippa celebrated by his famous
journey down the Cloaca Maxima to the Tiber, in a boat.
He improved the arrangements in the circus, opened the
public baths free of charge during his year of office, and
gave away vast quantities of tickets for food, clothes and
other articles. . . . Octavian, with the spoils of his Illyrian
campaigns, built the great portico (named the Octavian,
after his sister) which he intended to be the home of a
public library. All this was Octavian's answer to Antony's
attempt to enlist the sympathies of the *optimates*. He appealed to the *populares:* and it was an effective answer. . . .
More than this, it foreshadowed something much more important than a mere answer to another man's action—it
revealed that Octavian's policy was a distinctively Roman
policy, which involved the reform and reconditioning of

[5] Ninety-two years had passed since the last previous aqueduct had
been built. The work of Agrippa seemed to foreshadow the end of the
Civil Wars and the return of peace. He became the first permanent
head of the Water Supply service, and organized the department on a
systematic basis. (Frontinus, *Aqueducts*, 98.)

the distinctively Roman tradition, and it heralded the later application of this principle upon a much larger scale.

Trium-
virate
ends

On the last day of the year, the thirty-first of December, 33 B. C., the legal term of the Triumvirate ran out, and as it was not renewed the Committee of Three came to an end. Octavian still retained the proconsular power, as every man did, by custom, during the year after his consulship; and he had the *sanctitas*, the special privilege of personal immunity. Antony, on the other hand—who was now at Ephesus watching the progress of events—became a private citizen without any privilege. He entirely ignored these changes. Possibly he did not think they mattered.

The two new consuls were friends of Antony. They knew what he wanted them to do; and they lost no time in bringing up before the senate the question of the position of the members of the Committee. They had communications from Antony, protesting against Octavian.[6] A decree was prepared, declaring Octavian to have no legal authority. This was promptly blocked by a tribune. Octavian had very carefully kept away from the senate, realizing how important it was that he should not seem to be the aggressor. But when the action of the senate had been jammed, and brought to a deadlock, he reappeared and called an informal meeting of senators. This meeting he seriously addressed with a careful defence of his own actions, and an indictment of Antony and of the consuls who subserved Antony's policy. The *optimates*, believing what they believed concerning Antony's intentions, were determined to support him at all costs, and as they could not answer Octavian's arguments, they took refuge in silence.

---

[6] These are the communications referred to by Suetonius, *Divus Augustus*, LXVIII–LXX. Many of the charges are, to a modern eye, mere trifling, though they were doubtless well-calculated for the particular public Antony wanted to affect. As we can see from Plutarch, *Antony*, and Dio, L, 5, Octavian replied in kind.

He adjourned the meeting to another day, when he undertook to prove by documentary evidence the charges he had
brought against Antony. . . . As these documents were **The**
unquestionably the hitherto unpublished despatches of An- **optimates**
tony to the senate respecting the division of the East among **secede**
his children, the consuls determined not to let them influence the opinion of the party. Before the appointed day,
therefore, the consuls had induced a large body of senators,
representing the old party of the *optimates*, to leave Rome
with them for Ephesus, where Antony and Cleopatra were
awaiting them.

The revolt of the *optimates*—and to Antony, of all men!
—was one of the most astonishing features of the situation:
but it was to Octavian's advantage. It helped to convince
the Caesarians that Octavian unmistakably represented the
true Caesarian faith. When Octavian, anxious to support
his case by every testimony possible, took the bold course
of seizing and publishing Antony's will, the belief grew
yet stronger. Marcus Antonius had directed that, no matter where he might die, his body was to be taken to Alexandria and buried beside Cleopatra's. His estate was divided
among his children, and he referred to Caesarion, Cleopatra's son, as the true son of Gaius Julius Caesar.

The evidence of this will was of conclusive effect in convincing public opinion in Rome that Marcus Antonius had
the intention of upsetting Octavian's claim to be the heir
of Julius, of putting forward Caesarion [7] as the true descendant by blood of the Dictator, and of making himself
an oriental monarch, with Alexandria as his capital. Even **Antony's**
old and tried supporters of Antony, such as Asinius Pol- **aims**
lio, were alienated. The Caesarian party became united on

[7] Caesarion could make out a strong case for his claims. Julius had
once projected the use of Egypt as his base from which to exercise
control over Rome. Why might not Caesarion attempt to do what his
father had planned?

the subject, and the union extended to the whole of Italy. All those who inherited the name of Rome turned, with a kind of instinctive unanimity, to the tradition in which they had been bred—and their leader was Octavian. Throughout Italy an oath was taken to support him, and by universal consent the supreme authority which he had possessed for all these years past was informally continued to him.

CHAPTER XI

THE VICTORY OF THE LITTLE PLAN OVER THE GREAT PLAN

I

AN atmosphere of misfortune, misconception and misman-agement hung over the camp of Marcus Antonius. Not only did he do some things wrongly, but even those that he did right became somehow twisted to his detriment. Everything was left-handed and went widdershins. His friends told him flatly that if Cleopatra would only go back to Egypt and stay there, things would be better. He thought so too, at first; but she talked to him, and made it to the interest of some of his advisers to talk as she did. For after all, it was perfectly true that she was as good a business man as most of them; and it was perfectly true that she was footing most of the bill—and she saw to it that Antony had the sort of fun he liked . . . and he let it be as she wished. . . . That was the curse that rested upon Marcus Antonius. He was always letting it be as the woman wished, whether it were Fulvia or Octavia or Cleo-patra. . . . And Cleopatra, having things as she wished, proceeded to destroy all her own hopes and to neutralize all the help she received from other people.

She dared not let Antony out of her sight; sure (not without some reason!) that Octavia would instantly ap-propriate him. She grappled Antony to her with such hoops of steel that he was conscious of the tyranny even while he gave way to it. . . . She it was who induced Antony to send Octavia her divorce notice, and to claim that he

237

had been married to Cleopatra for the past nine years. She did not know how deeply it would alienate Roman opinion. Octavian would never have ventured to seize and publish Antony's will, had he not first been justified in the eyes of public opinion by the divorce of Octavia. . . . So Octavia, in accord with Antony's directions, left his Roman house taking with her all the children save one, Antyllus, who was old enough to be with his father. . . . Admiring eyes followed that model of virtue. It was a black day for Marcus Antonius.

Cleopatra dared not let Antony be too much swayed by his Roman friends. She did her best to come between him and them. The *optimates* were inexpressibly shocked at the political atmosphere of Antony's headquarters. There seemed to be no question of Antony restoring the old Roman constitution and then returning to Egypt. Antony and Cleopatra evidently proposed to interfere in the processes of Roman government as effectively as ever Julius had done. She spoke openly and frankly of the day when she would dispense justice on the Capitol! . . . She was, in fact, a Hellenistic monarch of the most determined type, beside whom Julius and Octavian were models of Roman propriety. The verve and the energy went out of the *optimates* as they realized these things, and they became heavy and disillusioned men, disinclined to do any serious work for such a party or such a leader.

All this might have mattered very little if Cleopatra had at the same time inspired Marcus Antonius to the height of his energies—but that is just what she did not do. Fun, amusement and self-indulgence were not the best means of inspiring Antony. Had he been leading a forlorn hope, without money, clothes or food, he might have been his old splendid self again, as he was at the defeat of Mutina or the victory of Philippi; but he was eating too much and drinking too much, and having a great deal too much of Cleopatra. . . . And this was a point of psychology which Cleopatra was constitutionally incapable of understanding. So she alienated the Caesarians and the *optimates*, drove Antony's friends from him and smothered the flame of genius that flickered in Antony himself. She thought that what she was giving him would more than make up.

But what was she giving him? The word had been sent out throughout the lands included in the circle of Syria, Armenia and the Lake Maeotis (which we know as the Sea of Azov) round to Macedonia. These were Roman dominions, and they had already been drained dry by Sulla, by Lucullus, by Pompeius, by Brutus and Cassius, and by Antony himself. Six kings in person served with Antony, and five others (including the Median King) sent contributions to the auxiliary forces. Finally, Antony had the Roman legions which had been intended for the Parthian War. The total of these forces was about a hundred thousand foot and twelve thousand horse—in fact, pretty much the number of the army which fought the Parthian campaign. Antony had in all some six hundred ships from the Roman dominions—some of them very large, and the advantage of the large ships had been demonstrated by Agrippa in the Sicilian war. . . . These forces Antony had, quite independent of any help from Cleopatra. But the Asiatic contributions were chiefly men and vessels. Of money, there was little. The ships were badly manned, and some of the conscript crews were untrained, and totally unfit for the work. . . . Cleopatra's contribution was two hundred perfectly equipped Egyptian ships—the repute of Alexandrian sailors ranked high—and twenty thousand talents in money, together with supplies for the whole army for the duration of the war. In short, she provided the financial backing without which Antony's vast army could

The army of the east

not operate at all.

Now, all this was vastly different from the victorious army which Sulla—with complete control of the men, the money and the policy of his party—had once led to reconquer Italy. Marcus Antonius had the ungrateful task of bringing an imperfectly equipped and not particularly victorious host all the way from Asia, with all the risks attendant on its defective cohesion, while Cleopatra, who had all the money, had a preponderant influence upon the conduct of the campaign.

Octavian faced the threat of invasion with a somewhat smaller army, but one that had all the prestige of the conquest of Sicily, and all the benefits of two years' active campaigning in Illyria, and with vast reserves of veteran troops whose training would tell if ever they returned to the standards. The fleet was half the size of Antony's. Octavian had about four hundred fighting ships, most of them rather smaller than Antony's, but perfectly manned with highly trained crews, and commanded by Agrippa. His difficulty was money. To equip, supply and pay this army put an intolerable burden upon an Italy which had suffered severely during the civil wars, and was not yet in a state to endure any kind of strain. There was still the possibility that the unity of opinion so recently and so hardly created might be destroyed again by the practical demands of the programme required for the defence of Italy. Octavian was not far off the mark when he represented to the people of Italy that Cleopatra was the enemy. The whole weight of the coming invasion was borne upon the shoulders of Egypt.

Had Octavian been a mere opportunist, the struggle between the Roman and the Hellenistic tradition might easily have been decided by the question of money. But he did not always follow public opinion. He was capable of lead-

The
western
army

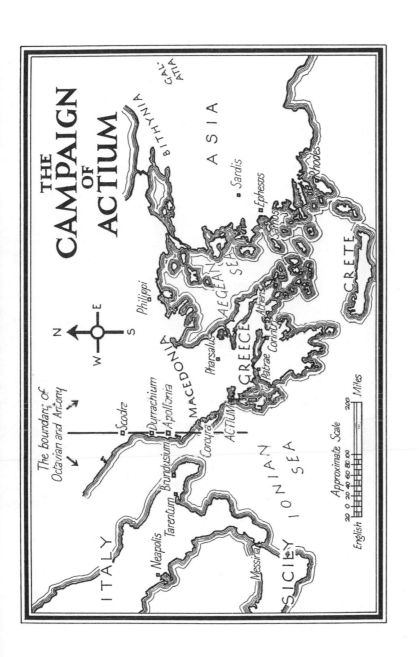

THE
CAMPAIGN
OF
ACTIUM

ing it when a principle was concerned: and now, confronted with so fundamental a principle as this, he had no hesitation in coercing those who also approved the end, but shied at the means.

Contemporary—or nearly contemporary—opinion believed that if Marcus Antonius had struck swiftly, while Octavian was still embarrassed with financial difficulties, he might have been victorious. But he delayed: and Octavian was justified in his use of compulsion, for the very men who had most objected to paying the war taxation **Effects of** calmed down when once it was paid, and unity again pre- **taxation** vailed. The very severity of this taxation had a great effect in stiffening public opinion. It is quite possible that the men of the East went into the war with noble ideals of a grand new world; [1] but it is fairly certain that the men of the West entered into it with a fixed determination to get their money back out of Cleopatra; and a European inspired by the hope of money is as dangerous as an Asiatic inspired by the hope of heaven.

Antony's Grand Army, therefore, was at the point of falling to pieces even before he sailed westward in the au tumn of the year 32 B. C. It was agreed by the Caesarians that the war was a foreign war against the power of Egypt. The name of Antony was by common consent dropped out of the matter, and when, at the temple of Bellona, Octavian, as the representative fetial, the *pater patratus*, performed the ancient customary ritual of declaring war,[2] it was against Egypt and Cleopatra that he declared it. Antony was regarded as merely her agent. Coming to the island of Corcyra, where he had before him open access to the whole Italian peninsula and the seas east and south of it,

[1] W. W. Tarn, *Alexander Helios*, J.R.S. XXII, 135–141.
[2] Not the full ritual, however, which would have involved Octavian in a journey to the frontiers of Egypt.

Marcus Antonius heard that Octavian's ships had been noticed from the neighbouring coast. Interpreting this to mean that the whole fleet of Octavian was at sea, Antony withdrew southward. It was too late in the season to begin a campaign, so he fixed his headquarters at Patrae, at the mouth of the Gulf of Corinth, and sent his army into winter quarters.

II

If things had happened as they had been originally planned, Octavian and Antony would have held the consulship together this spring—the year 31 B. C.—and two Roman consuls would have faced one another in arms at the battle of Actium. If they did not do so, it was purely because the consulship of Antony was cancelled, and M. Valerius Messalla Corvinus was appointed instead. Messalla had once fought side by side with Brutus and Cassius at the battle of Philippi. He had lived to become a close ally of Octavian, and one of the foremost of the Friends of Caesar. . . . The fact indicated a certain shifting of opinion. Antony does not seem to have troubled very much. Victory would wipe out these trifles. But it is probable that his allies, the *optimates*, took a different view, and that many of them wavered when they found themselves opposing a legitimate consul and the legal republic.

With spring and fine weather Antony began to move north again. His army was ordered to concentrate round the Gulf of Ambracia, where his fleet, coasting along the rocky shores of Acarnania, awaited the land forces. From this centre he would command the Ionian Sea, right away southwestward to Sicily. Sulla, when, fifty years before, he had taken the short route from Dyrrachinus to Brundusium, had known before-hand that he would have no se-

rious opposition to face. Antony, realizing that he would
have to face very serious opposition indeed, chose a larger
stage, with more possibilities of action.

Up to a certain point, it would have been to the advantage of both commanders to fight a decisive battle at once,
and get it over. Neither was anxious for a long-drawn-out
war: but neither could afford to give away too many advantages. Octavian is said to have offered Antony a quiet
landing and an adequate camping ground in Italy. But this
was not quite good enough, and Antony answered by
offering to meet Octavian in single combat—a challenge
which squared them up again after that sarcasm at Antony's expense about the conquest of Parthia. On this being
declined (Octavian was no fighting man) Antony proposed
a meeting at Pharsalus. Octavian, however, was not at all
likely to sacrifice the advantage of his sea power: so all these
exchanges ended as mere persiflage.

The eastern fleet still lay at Actium or the Gulf of
Ambracia, and its supporting army was still some distance
away, when the western fleet sailed from Brundusium and
the associated ports. It crossed the Ionian Sea southwest-
wards, and landed an army at the promontory called "The
Ladle," where the Acroceraunian Mountains extend into
the sea, a little south of Apollonia.

Octavian
sails

When the news reached Actium, there was serious concern among the Roman leaders. Cleopatra scoffed; but they
were perfectly right in scenting a vigorous and practical
soldier behind this move. Leaving the army to find its feet
on land, and to begin its march southward, Agrippa pressed
on with his battle fleet. After seizing Corcyra, he went on
to Actium itself, forty miles south of Corcyra. So bad was
the condition of Antony's ships—and their crews—that he
merely drew them up in order of battle and hoped that
the bluff would not be called. It was not. Agrippa, too

thorough a soldier himself to suspect the truth, prudently withdrew and went on southward. After capturing Leucas, the city south of Actium, another forty miles, winding in between the islands, brought him to the mouth of the Gulf of Corinth. Agrippa promptly captured Patrae at the western end of the Gulf, and then Corinth at the eastern end, obtaining complete control of the Gulf and compelling all naval help to seek Antony by the route round the Peloponnesus in the open sea.

Contact at Actium

While Agrippa was engaged in this successful raid, Octavian and the land forces had marched south by the coast road and occupied the position on the northern mandible of the Ambracian Gulf which afterwards became the City of Nicopolis—"Victoria" or "Victory City." Here, on the high ground, he could look down upon the long narrow channel by which the sea gained entrance to the Gulf of Ambracia. Antony had seized and fortified the channel, so that he had free ingress and egress, and he had occupied the southern mandible of the Gulf. Here the ground was very favourable for fighting; but it was not so favourable for waiting, for the water-supply was not good, and the low ground was unhealthy.

Marcus Antonius hesitated a good deal about fighting. The raid of Agrippa to Corinth, and the success of the western army in manoeuvring him into a difficult and damaging position, increased the disintegration among the easterners. The ex-consul Domitius Ahenobarbus, who had never been so fanatical in his zeal as his colleague Sosius, gave up and went over to Octavian. King Amyntas of Lycaonia and King Deiotarus of Galatia both deserted to Octavian, together with Philadelphus of Paphlagonia: and Antony grew angry, suspicious and uncertain of himself.

The rout begins

A sea-fight in the approach to the channel, with the aim of driving off the western fleet, had an unfortunate end for

Antony, since it was changed into an effective victory for the westerners by the sudden appearance of Agrippa, fresh from his successes at Corinth. Antony was now cut off from sea-borne supplies, and felt the pinch. Canidius, the commander of the Roman legions, was perfectly frank about the situation. He gave the plain advice that Cleopatra should be sent back to Egypt, that all idea of a naval victory should be given up, and that Octavian should be drawn into Thrace or Macedonia, as Pompeius Magnus was drawn by Caesar, and should then be crushed by the trustworthy Roman legions. The fleet was not fit for its work.

But Cleopatra would not hear of any plan which allowed Marcus Antonius out of her grasp. She knew—or believed —that he would forget her the moment his back was turned. Her Egyptian ships were in perfect order: they could fight as well as those of Agrippa. They were big ships, too—and Agrippa himself was witness to the advantage possessed by big ships over small ones. Ultimately Cleopatra impressed her own wishes upon the Council of War. She carried the day; and it was resolved to stake the issue upon a sea-fight.

Cleopatra had two strings to her bow. She meant, in all seriousness, to fight on the water; and she meant, if she failed, to run for Egypt. It is possible that with her gift for intrigue she had penetrated to certain truths that the more generous and sentimental Antony was not willing to look at.[3] A sea-fight was her one, single and only chance of escape from the Gulf of Ambracia—and anyhow, the Roman troops, far from being "trustworthy," meant to betray Antony, so they might as well do it in the circumstances most convenient to him. . . . The best of the Egyptian ships were chosen and packed with men. The rest were

Cleo-patra's plan

---

[3] According to the frequent practice of Roman historians, Dio—or his source—gravely attributes the suspicions of Cleopatra to certain omens and signs (Dio, L, 15, 2-3) which we need not take literally.

burned. The valuable property of Antony and Cleopatra was put on board by night, and the masts and sails were stowed in such a way as to be available for use. As it was the invariable custom—if opportunity occurred—to leave masts and sails on shore before a sea-fight, the intention of this order needed explaining. Antony gave an explanation all the more ingenious because it was true. He meant to wait for the mid-day wind, which could be counted upon to blow from the northwest; and then he meant to make a dash to envelop the Roman left, and come down before the wind upon the whole Roman line driving it southward before his big ships. This was why he wanted the sails. . . . The western army, marooned on shore, would then be cut off from help or reinforcement, and would be dealt with by Canidius. It was a clear, coherent and convincing plan, worthy of Marcus Antonius. Perhaps he believed in it himself. But it is improbable that Cleopatra did. She knew two things—that the troops would not fight, and that the great galleys of Antony never could outflank the smaller, lighter and better-manned ships opposed to them. But the excuse was adequate to hide the second plan in the background.

III

The morning of Sept. 2nd, 31 B. C.

This plan was betrayed, and was known to Octavian and Agrippa before the battle opened. Agrippa, therefore, instead of leading the right wing, as he would otherwise have done, came over and took charge of the left, facing Marcus Antonius. Octavian took up an independent position in a small fast ship, whence he could survey the whole scene.

On the morning of the second of September, in the year 31 B. C., the two fleets lay opposite to one another in the mouth of the channel leading into the Gulf of Ambracia. The sun was in the faces of the westerners, and all the morning it continued to be so, as the oarsmen lay on their oars, waiting. Just as the shadow began to pass in front of them, the required wind began to blow, and at that signal the great issue was joined. The big ships of the easterners, led by the huge ten-banker flagship of Antony, moved forward and outward, preparatory to enveloping Agrippa's squadrons: and at the same time Agrippa let drive at them with his smaller and faster ships, grappled them and held them.

The famous battle of Actium was fought entirely between Marcus Antonius and Marcus Agrippa, and as far as it went, and as long as it lasted, it was a fierce struggle. But it did not go far and it did not last long. The right wing of the westerners refrained from rushing in upon their opponents; and those opponents turned, and rowed back into harbour without striking a blow. The centre of the eastern fleet lifted its oars—the Greek sign of surrender.

Antony betrayed

Cleopatra, with the Egyptian fleet, lay in the rear, in reserve—but there never was any battle for her to strike into. The battle was already over in the way she had anticipated; Antony had been betrayed by his own men. . . . The Egyptian fleet at once set up its masts and hoisted sail, and began to make its way towards the open sea. Antony, fighting in the thick of his squadron, saw the move and recognized the signal. He gave the word to cut free and run for the open. All the captains who could do so, obeyed. About forty-five of his ships were soon clear of the battle. The wind that he had designed to help him drive the western fleet on shore now enabled him to run southward with ease. . . . Antony himself could not get his flagship disengaged. It was too tightly held by the enemy. But he transferred himself to a smaller ship, a five-banker, and got away on board. . . . And so, the Egyptians leading, and the ships of Antony following, they sailed away south into the

Ionian Sea before the freshening gale, leaving the western fleet (which had left all its masts and sails on shore) lamenting.

As he drew away from the few sporadic pursuers, Antony went aboard Cleopatra's ship. No one rushed to proffer sympathy: no one's sympathy was worth having. He sat for a long time gazing over the waters. Everything was over, for him. His weapon had broken in his grasp: his instrument had turned against him. The battle of Actium had petered out, and Octavian was receiving the surrender of the eastern fleet. Fifteen of Antony's ships, including the huge flagship, had fallen into his hands, and five thousand of Antony's men had been killed: but three hundred ships surrendered intact. The army on shore—nineteen legions with their auxiliaries—spent seven days in negotiating. . . . Canidius did his best to keep them loyal, but at the end of seven days he saw what was coming and made his escape, and the army, like the fleet, surrendered to Octavian. . . . The battle of Actium was, in fact, one of the leading instances of a decisive result reached with the minimum of bloodshed—a conquest which was a conquest of men's ideas and loyalties rather than of their bodies. As such, it deserves more attention than many great slaughters which decided nothing.

The relief—the blest, the almost unbelievable and overwhelming relief—which came to Italy as a result of that battle, the enthusiastic Horace was immortalizing a few days later in his ninth Epode, written after Maecenas, at Rome, had given him the news. Oh! blest Maecenas!—bring larger cup and better wine! This, indeed, was grander than the day when the sails of Sextus Pompeius sank below the skyline and Sicily was free. Something larger than Sicily—the whole East—was free: something larger than the East, the mind and soul of man, was relieved of what had become

The flight to Egypt

Joy in Rome

an intolerable burden. . . . Bring the golden car of triumph!—not Marius, not Scipio Aemilianus after the fall of
Carthage, was a greater victor! And in all this Horace
merely put into words the great bound of exultation which,
a second time, bore Octavian high above the heads of other
men towards the stars. . . . He had been a very commonplace man in his time, an audacious, but helpless youth, a
sick man carried to Philippi, a fugitive fleeing along the
Straits of Messina: but he began to look divine and immortal at this moment—if not great, at least august. Even the
optimates breathed more freely. Cleopatra, and all she
stood for, would never reign in Rome! . . . Yes—they all
felt like sending for larger cups and better wine!

IV

Octavian for once tore a leaf out of the book of Julius,
when he set out in pursuit of Antony, resolved not to give
up until he had run him to earth.

Before he went, he took measures against the most serious
danger he anticipated at home—the demands of the army.
Antony's men were incorporated into his own forces, and
the time-expired men of both armies were demobilized
forthwith. Those who were still left, being under the control of their officers, and expecting the plunder of Egypt,
remained quiet.

The mor-
row of
Actium

The demobilized men had been dealt with before they
had time to think matters out. As soon as they realized that
they had been discharged without any additional bonus,
they tried to make trouble. Octavian met this with two distinct countermeasures. He placed exceptional—almost dictatorial—powers in the hands of Agrippa and Maecenas,
and he cancelled the arrears of taxes due from the most
hardly pressed section of the community—the freedmen. By

this step he earned the gratitude and support of the freedmen. He could afford the loss, since he anticipated the possession, before long, of the vast Egyptian revenues. . . .
Octavian, in fact, as soon as the battle of Actium was over,
moved away from exclusive dependence upon the army, and
sought support from other sections of the community.

This done, he started immediately for Athens. Here he
made a general settlement which set the country free from
the extraordinary conscription of labour which Antony had
imposed, and restored the normal system of government.
Thence he went on straight to Samos, or the opposite shore
of the Aegean. At this point he was recalled. Agrippa wrote
to tell him that he was needed in Italy. Octavian therefore
toilsomely made his way back—twice in peril from storm
at Naupactus and off the Acroceraunian headland. At
Brundusium he found the demobilized troops, and the senate, together with a great crowd of other people. Evidently
he was not to escape just yet!

Trouble with the army
Another exercise of tact, skill and patience was necessary
to get the dissatisfied elements satisfied without making the
already satisfied more dissatisfied than could be helped. The
lands of some Italian cities which could be accused of being
partisans of Antony were confiscated, and regranted to the
discontented troops—and the dispossessed ones were offered
alternative accommodation at Dyrrachium, Philippi and
similar places. Cases for which no land was available were
offered money—and some had to be asked to accept promises, since Octavian was still spending more than he was
receiving; though this would not last long. His own property, and that of his friends, was put up for sale as a mark
of good faith. Nobody purchased it, and the claimants accepted the promises. Twenty-seven days after his arrival, he
left Brundusium again for the East. To save time and the
passage round Peloponnesus he had his ship pushed across

the Isthmus of Corinth on rollers—and was back in Samos
so quickly that Antony and Cleopatra are said to have heard
simultaneously of his departure and his return.

In the meantime Antony and Cleopatra had divided the
work between themselves. She had returned to Egypt, secured the country, suppressed dangerous critics, and begun
to collect money from the immensely rich temples of Egypt
as well as from more secular sources. Antony had sailed to
Cyrene to negotiate with the Roman army of Pinarius *Situation*
Scarpus, which had been collected for the defence of *in Egypt*
Egypt, and was presumably trustworthy. But Scarpus had
reached very definite conclusions concerning the probabilities of the future, and refused to have any dealings with
him. . . . Antony hastened on to Alexandria. . . . Money
would be useless if the one indispensable article could not
be bought with it.

If the tale of Antony and Cleopatra had really been exclusively a passionate love-romance, the end of their story
would have been very different. But it had all along been a
business partnership in which Antony was to secure Cleopatra's kingdom of Egypt, and Cleopatra was to finance
Antony's control of Rome. When each began to be incapable of fulfilling the bargain, both began to be untrust-
worthy. While the policy of Octavian remained one and
indivisible, they began to waver towards him and towards
one another.

They were not absolutely certain even of what they
meant to do. Cleopatra had sent some ships on rollers across
the isthmus, ready to take to the Red Sea and freedom in
exile. The Arabs burned some of them; and Antony
thought the army at Actium might still be loyal—so she
went no further with the idea. There was even a suggestion of a flight to Spain. When Antony learned from Canidius the real truth about the army at Actium, despair seized

him. They both hoped to stave Octavian off while they
made their preparation for defence: but the very steps they
took defeated their own ends. Antony asked for a quiet retirement in Egypt or Athens. Cleopatra sent Octavian a
sceptre and a golden crown, hoping that he would take the
hint. He did, but not in the way she thought. He saw at
once that she was chiefly interested in the preservation of
her kingdom of Egypt, and that he could part her from
Antony by working upon that motive. Octavian knew that
she and Antony had "brought out" the boys Caesarian and
Antyllus for the express purpose of appealing to the
Caesarian loyalty to the true son of Julius—and that, of
course, necessarily involved the displacement of the
adopted son and legal heir: so he was not in the least de-
ceived into thinking that she would keep faith with him
if he trusted her. . . . It was entirely a question of which
of them could outmanoeuvre the others in a competition of
suggestion and make-believe. . . . In this Octavian had the
advantage because Antony and Cleopatra contradicted and
cancelled one another.

He made no reply at all to Antony, but to Cleopatra he
sent a double message—a public one, that if she would place
herself unreservedly in his hands, he would consider it an
open question what he might do; and a private one in in-
terpretation of this phrase—that he would refuse her nothing if Antony died.

They both sent again—Cleopatra offering large sums of
money, and Antony making a detailed defence of his conduct, and recalling their old friendship. He offered to die
himself, if Cleopatra could be saved. Still Octavian made no
reply to Antony; and the latter sent Antyllus with a present of gold. Octavian took the gold, but sent Antyllus back
without an answer. On both occasions he simply repeated
his first answer to Cleopatra. . . . The effect of this

The triangle

Cleopatra weakens

method—which was a psychological rather than a diplomatic one—was to shatter the mutual confidence of Antony and Cleopatra. It deepened the despondence of Antony, and it strengthened the conviction of Cleopatra that she must try to make terms with Octavian. . . . And Octavian was particularly anxious not to drive her to extremes. According to his information she had collected a vast treasure, which she threatened to destroy at the slightest provocation. He most anxiously wanted that treasure. His future might depend upon his success in getting it.

As soon as he returned from his hasty journey to Brundusium he set out on his march for Egypt. Cornelius Gallus had taken charge of the army of Scarpus and barred the way westward. Octavian himself was closing in from Syria. Little by little all hope of a successful defence of Egypt disappeared. It was believed, rightly or wrongly, that Cleopatra betrayed Pelusium into the hands of Octavian. Antony made ready to defend Alexandria. His efforts and his spirit were paralysed by his growing doubt of her and of every one else. The last blow fell when the fleet at Alexandria surrendered to Octavian—and this, too, was afterwards attributed to Cleopatra. . . . Antony tried to kill himself that night, but only gave himself a mortal wound. He died, later on, in Cleopatra's arms.

This is not the place in which to tell in detail the story that so deeply struck the imagination of contemporaries, and by them was embodied in narratives which posterity did not allow to perish. There is seldom a generation which does not retell the story for its own satisfaction. . . . We have here only to deal with Octavian's share in it. . . . To him, Marcus Antonius was not a hero of romance, but a dangerous reactionary whose survival might be the ruin of the state. If it be said that he cuts a poor figure in the romance, it may be answered that he never wished to cut

Octavian in Alexandria

any figure in it at all. He was a statesman, not a character in romance.

A day or two later, he met Cleopatra.

v

The meeting of Octavian and Cleopatra was—if the historians are to be believed—a very remarkable one. She was thirty-nine years of age, and the mother of four children, but she still hoped that the charm which had conquered Julius and Antony might act no less effectively upon Octavian. At any rate, it was worth trying. . . . But Octavian, though conscious of her charm, was unmoved by it. After all, he was no sex-starved lad. He was himself married to a very beautiful and very clever woman, who was capable of giving him anything that a woman can give to a man; and he was not likely to be swayed, much against his
Octavian and Cleopatra own interests, by a charmer several years older than himself, whom he knew to be actuated by hopes and aims entirely opposed to his own. . . . And she went the wrong way about it. She was so accustomed to deal with men whose emotions were more powerful than their intelligence, that she did not know how to influence one who was far more accessible to reason than to any appeal to his feelings. She wept—it was a mistake; she read him extracts from the letters of Julius—but they only reminded him that Caesarion had been put forward as the true son of Julius, to the detriment of his own claims as legal heir. . . . He merely assured her that she need fear nothing, and that all would be better than she expected. But she realized that she had failed. . . . Some time later she learnt that she was to go to Rome. She asked and obtained permission to visit the tomb of Antony. There she died by her own hand—but how is not known. There was a legend, contemporaneous

with the event,[4] that she died by the bite of an asp—but even those who tell the story admit that the real truth was never known.

Octavian was mildly grieved, and full of pity at her end.[5] She had been a remarkable personality—beautiful, though perhaps not more so than many others—clever and charming to a wonderful degree, and strong far beyond most women. He would very willingly have saved her. . . . But it is very unlikely that he ever felt the slightest compunction at being the cause of the deaths of Antony and Cleopatra. They had been obstacles to the peace and happiness of the world.

Octavian's attitude

So now Octavian, gazing upon the dead queen of Egypt, could reflect that he had accomplished the third of his great works. He had avenged the murder of Julius, reconquered Sicily, and now he had completed the special aim and hope of Julius—the acquisition of Egypt. After that, the settlement of Rome was all that would remain for him to achieve.

He abolished the Ptolemaic monarchy, and annexed Egypt to the Roman dominion. Its government was vested in himself, personally; it was far too important to be entrusted to any other person or power. Julius had foreseen, long ago, that the possession of Egypt would be the cornerstone of the new political power that was arising, and this implied its personal possession by the man who embodied the new system. Its vast wealth would be the necessary support of his authority.

Caesarion, the son of Cleopatra and Julius, had attempted to escape to Ethiopia. He was caught and executed. He was the last King of Egypt; but his death was much more due to the fact that Antony had set him up as a pretender with

---

[4] It was known to Horace, *Odes*, I, 37; and to Virgil, *Aeneid*, VIII, 697.

[5] Plutarch, *Antony*, Dio, LI, 14(6).

prior claims to the heritage of Caesar. As a son by blood, he would easily outweigh the son by adoption. Antyllus, the eldest son of Antony and Fulvia, was also slain. He had been the destined successor to Antony, and while he lived he, too, would be a dangerous centre of conspiracy and counter-revolution. . . . A certain number of determined, subordinate enemies were also caught and executed: some were let off with heavy fines. But beyond this Octavian had no particular enmity to gratify. The twins Alexander Helios and Cleopatra Selene he took into his own guardianship. . . . Antony and Cleopatra themselves were buried together in the same tomb, which Octavian completed for them. . . . And that is the end of their strange story.

The end of Antony and Cleopatra

In one essential respect, Octavian's hopes were perfectly realized. He *did* obtain the vast wealth of Egypt. Cleopatra had emptied the royal treasury and stripped the chief temples in her ardour, and now all this accumulation fell, without further trouble or charge of sacrilege, into Octavian's possession. Together with the fines imposed upon individual offenders, this vast treasure paid the debts Octavian had incurred and the promises for which he had made himself responsible, and left a balance which became the foundation of the power of the new government.

Octavian and Alexander

Octavian spent the best part of a year in Egypt. During this time he had the irrigation system renovated. He himself visited one shrine for which he had a peculiar reverence—the tomb of Alexander. He laid an offering of flowers upon the resting place of the man who had first dreamed of the Unity of the Civilized World. . . . On being asked whether he wished to see the other Kings of Egypt, he replied: "I wanted to see a king, not dead people." . . . Alexander, the apostle of world-unity, was the only king a Roman could reverence.

Early in the year 29 B. C. he was in Syria on his way home. The news of his presence on the Euphrates reached Virgil just as the poet was completing the Georgics,[6] a subject to which we will presently recur. Some of the strange good-fortune which seems inseparable from men who achieve great success now attached itself to Octavian. He reached Syria just when the first great wave of Parthian energy had expended itself; and without effort or expense he was able to achieve results which had been beyond all the armies and strategy of Antony. The kings of the East wanted peace for their own purposes; they bowed down without hesitation to the great conqueror (as he seemed to them) who had so completely crushed and disposed of the hero Marcus Antonius. . . . As in so many other cases, no one examined too closely into the facts. Men did homage to the outward appearance of things. Octavian merely had to assume the appropriate poses; and he was quite clever enough to understand the fact and the reasons behind it.

VI

He had fought a stiff and an up-hill fight, in which only realities had counted, and they scantily and disappointingly. But now, as if he had rolled the ship of his fate to a divide of waters, and henceforward could launch it down-hill, he began to enjoy to the full all the advantages of the habits, the conventions and the inertia of mankind; fancies and fictions, as well as facts, began to propel the weight for him; all the forces that had once been against him were now for him. After Actium the senate had granted him a triumph, and two triumphal arches—one at Brundusium and one in the Forum—his birthday, and the anniversary of his victory were appointed days of public thanksgiving; the front seat

The change

[6] *Georgics*, IV, 560–562.

on public occasions was bestowed upon him, and the right to be met on his entry into the city by the senate and people with their wives and children, headed by the Vestal Virgins.[7] When the news of Antony's death arrived, another shower of compliments began: another triumph, this time over the Egyptians, was voted. It would be natural enough if Agrippa and Maecenas, on general principles, gently encouraged this profusion—but for the most part it was a spontaneous product of the circumstances. Nearly all these honours were in the strict sense honorary: they conveyed, in their totality, a general sense that Octavian was the first citizen of the republic, but they conveyed no political power. It was purely an honour that he should always have a libation poured to his name at banquets, or that his name should be publicly prayed for, or that the casting vote for acquittal, which was automatically given when a tie took place among the jurors in court, should be given in his name. But one such honour, dropped almost casually among the rest, was more than a mere compliment. It was the gift of the tribunician power for life. Octavian was created, in his own person, a permanent tribune, with all the peculiar powers which tradition and legislation had attached to the office. This was destined to be more than a compliment. Finally, to his own satisfaction, the senate solemnly closed the Temple of Janus, as a sign that the state was at peace. There were, in actual fact, a few small struggles in progress: but nothing that a Roman would dignify by the serious name of War.

The precise import of the tribunician power is a question

Prestige

---

[7] There was perhaps some misunderstanding about this. When he left Brundusium, Octavian had half jocularly forgiven the people of Rome for not coming to meet him (as well as the senate and the army). This bit of sarcasm was evidently taken seriously by some one—hence the suggestion mentioned above. When Octavian heard of it, he at once disclaimed any wish for such a privilege. Dio, LI, 5(1); 19(2); 20(5).

to which we will return presently. But the closing of the
Temple of Janus marked the achievement of the aim which
the Roman people expected Octavian to fulfil. It was a solemn declaration of his success. More than anything else,
they had asked from him the supreme boon of peace—a
cessation of strife—a termination of the endless wars and
dissensions—a grand reconciliation—a social stabilization.
For this they had supported him; they had followed him,
rather than Marcus Antonius, because they thought him
more likely to give them peace. Now he could turn to them
and say:

"It is done! What you have asked of me I have now
given you."

For this reason the closing of the Temple of Janus was
the great event of his life—the public endorsement of his
position as the representative of the will of the Roman
people.

VII

The return of Octavian to Rome was one of the most
splendid celebrations the city had ever seen. No one pre
cisely had designed such magnificence; it had evolved out
of years of war, dissatisfaction, hope deferred, painful ten-
sion now suddenly relaxed into peace and reconciliation.
Horace, looking on, could run over in his mind the names
of the gods and their splendour, until he arrived at the all-
mighty Jove; and over the names of the Roman heroes, until at last he came to the Julians; and then he could without
a sense of unfitness consign the greatest of the heroes—this
Octavian—to the greatest of the gods—that Jove—whose
vicegerent on earth he was.[8] As this hero entered the city,

[8] *Odes*, I, 12. There is no reason to doubt that Horace simply expressed the enthusiasm of the day, and the prevailing sense of public
opinion—in which most of us, if we had been alive then, would have
shared.

The return to Rome

the other consul, his colleague, himself welcomed him with the formal sacrifices on behalf of the senate and people of Rome, while all citizens stood round in participation.

Everything that any one could wish for was there. First came the eulogies—the public thanks for distinguished services, and the distribution of honours, the chief of these being the presentation of a blue banner to Marcus Vipsanius Agrippa, in remembrance of Actium. Next came the distribution of a bonus to the troops, and then presents to the civil population and the children. Octavian did not stop at this. The impoverished cities of Italy, according to old precedent, had voted the hero crowns of gold. He declined them. It was unnecessary for his creditors to spoil the festivities by thinking about their money. He paid them in full. And—just Heaven!—his debtors did not need to keep away from the feast: he cancelled all the sums owing to him, in honour of the time! A festive occasion, indeed, to be marked by such cheerful events! What wonder that Italy lauded the hero and celebrated his triumph? Men are always happy to think that their ideals have been realised: but to present them with solid cash brings home to them the reality of achievement as nothing else does. . . . So much money came into Italy with Octavian, that prices rose and interest fell.[9]

The three Triumphs

Then followed three separate triumphs on three successive days of unparalleled magnificence. On the first day was his triumph over the Pannonians and Dalmatians; on the

---

[9] The treasury of the Ptolemies seems to have become a gigantic reservoir of capital—now set free, to the destruction of the social classes which had lived upon it. The agriculturist was at first unaffected by the change. In due time, however, the drain began to exercise its effect, and Egypt sank to the level it was in during the century just prior to the Arab invasion: but this time was still a long way off. If Mr. Milne is right ("The Ruin of Egypt by Roman Mismanagement" in JRS, vol. XVII [1927], p. 1), the success of the Roman empire was based upon the ruin of Egypt.

second, the triumph for Actium, with the naval trophies; on the third, the triumph for Egypt, which far surpassed the others. Cleopatra, indeed, was dead, but a wax figure of her, with asp complete, occupied her place; and there were Alexander Helios and Cleopatra Selene, the two would-be Wonder-Children, who had not, after all, turned out to be the King and the Queen of the Golden Age; and all the wonders of Egypt that could be made available for a procession—the black men and the elephants, the ivory, the apes and the peacocks, the marvels of the mysterious tropics. . . . One innovation was made in the traditional order of the procession. The hero, in his four-horse car, rode in front of the senators instead of behind them. No one seems to have thought it more than he deserved. . . . The unity of the Roman dominion had been vindicated. Peace had come; the temple of Janus was closed; and men asked nothing better than that the hero should continue, with his strong arm, to enforce this Peace.

CHAPTER XII

THE KING OF THE GOLDEN AGE

I

THE story of Octavian has sped so fast, and each event has been so intimately linked to the event before and after, that this is the first moment at which we can easily pause **Retrospect** and survey the man himself. . . . He is an older man than when he set out from Apollonia to claim his heritage; fifteen years have emphasised certain main features of his character. The man who returned to Italy after the death of Antony and Cleopatra was now clearly distinguishable from other men by definite characteristics no longer to be questioned as possibly accidental, or conceivably due to the circumstances of the moment. The young Octavian who dealt with Cicero may have been a bewildered youth swept hither and thither by forces beyond his control, and led by men more experienced than himself. But the man who returned after Actium was very clearly and certainly not a youth nor at all bewildered: and he showed a preternatural skill in shooting the rapids of diplomacy and in guiding his ship through the contending whirlpools of Roman politics. . . . And he was not alone. After him trooped a number of men—the "Friends of Caesar"—hardly less famous than himself, as necessary to him as hands and feet, and not very clearly to be thought of apart from him. . . . Rome had given up expecting him to be a great general, or an imposing hero, another Marcus Antonius or Julius Caesar. It had **Portrait of a man** begun to divine the truth that there was nothing heroic or romantic about him, and that although he seemed a man apart, a miracle-worker and a master-man, this was not in virtue of any of the familiar labels generally recognized by the man in the street, but because of some qualities so peculiar as to have no name among the people—a bleak persistence, a cold justice, a rather elusive humour, an unimpassioned desire to remove the troubles of the world, and above all, an infallible judgment in guessing the exact sort of argument that would carry conviction to any particular man. . . . So, like some force set spinning in space, he had gradually sucked into his vortex a greater and a greater spread of mankind, until now they were all following him. He had become indispensable. He was the power which guided and gave coherence to all the once warring elements of Rome. If his fellow-citizens seemed to overflow with compliments and praises and honours, it was because all recognized that he stood between them and the forces they hated. The *populares* saw that he held the *optimates* in check. The *optimates* saw that he kept the *populares* at bay. Both were perfectly right. To do so was his mission in life.

II

Even though some urgency and stress disappeared from Octavian's life with the conquest of Egypt, his work was far from done. A vast prospect stretched before him, upon which he could enter at his leisure—and it was characteristic of him that he did those things best which he could do in cool blood, without haste and with ample thought. Perhaps this was the secret why he had never been a great soldier.

The whole Roman world wanted, not revolution, but reform. Nothing is easier than to overthrow institutions; nothing is harder than the subtle process of readjustment and reharmonizing, the refitting of the square pegs and the round holes, which is the essence of Reform. Octavian had

The task ahead

been, for some years past, slowly divesting himself of the character of a party-leader. By prudent steps he made himself more and more a representative of Roman civilization. He had carefully refrained from taking up the attitude of one triumvir overthrowing another triumvir. He had not fought Antony until the Committee of Three had dissolved. He had as far as possible emphasised his position as a leader of the Roman tradition against the Hellenistic tradition of Cleopatra and the Ptolemies. It was on this programme that he had appealed to his fellow-citizens—and by holding to it he had brought back to his side many of the men who, under a mistaken impression of the truth, had deserted him to go over to Antony. After Actium his mildness completed the reconciliation. Many men went over to him with relief, who had only clung to Antony because they felt that honour compelled them.

It was time that certain things should be modified. After the battle of Actium he took steps to dissolve and disperse those revolutionary armies which for twenty years had been dictating policy to their commanders. He did not, indeed abolish the army and throw power back into the hands of the optimates and their private bands of gladiators. He might not have lasted long after so tempting an opportunity. The army remained—a permanent standing army, so numerous and so highly trained that no private force could possibly dispute with it. But it no longer acted as an irresponsible dictator. It took the place given it in the new scheme of things. . . . The place given it . . . by whom?

The question, who it was that was organizing this new scheme, and the question of the origin and necessity of the new scheme, are inter-connected. It used at one time to be the fashion to write as if all that Octavian had to do were to Restore the Republic—as if the republic were a sum of

Authority

money or a wooden scaffolding, or anything else similarly impersonal and objective. But the "republic" was an agreement, a temper of mind, an attitude, a psychological state—the republic was within men; it was not in Octavian's power to restore this state by any exertion of his own. The *optimates* and the *populares* would soon have been at one another's throats again if his control had been relaxed; and they had put him where he was simply and solely to prevent any more civil war. After his return to Italy and his triumph, he explored the state of public opinion on these matters. He himself was quite willing to restore as much of the old system as people would agree to work, or could work.[1] How much was that? The result of his enquiries convinced him that the "old system" was understood in far too many different senses to be a satisfactory basis of agreement. What was wanted was a power in the state which could supersede the uncertain and fluctuating rule of mutual agreement by an authoritative declaration of the sense in which the system was to be taken. Naturally, it ceased to be the old system when this element of authority crept in. Indeed, the moment this element was introduced it involved one change after another until the total result was very considerable. But it never was intended to be a change in principle. It was meant merely to enable the old principles to function.

The old consti-tution

If Octavian were to become this seat of authority, this permanent umpire or referee, he would need not merely to divest himself of his character as a party leader, but to make men forget it. He did what few other men have ever succeeded in doing: he actually changed his name, and very nearly his identity. A kind of gulf cuts off the man Octavian from the imposing phoenix who rose from his ashes as *Augustus.* . . . Munatius Plancus was the person who

[1] Suetonius, *Divus Augustus*, XXVIII, 1–2.

Augustus
16th Jan.
27 B. C.

thought of the name. The idea spread, and was approved. It conveyed just the meaning people wanted—the meaning it still, to this very day, retains in the English usage: something majestic, mature, summer-like, of good augury, conveying a hint of peace and repose, as well as of power. . . . On the sixteenth of January in the year 27 B. C., on the motion of Plancus,[2] the senate solemnly bestowed upon Octavian this new name as an additional cognomen. It soon almost displaced the old, and became his especial name: and as *Augustus* we may accordingly know him. . . . As Augustus he stepped easily into that position which Virgil had once predicted for the son of Marcus Antonius and Octavia, and which he now as confidently bestowed upon Augustus—that of King of the Golden Age.

III

King in, of course, only a highly symbolical and metaphorical sense. In his abhorrence of monarchy and his detestation of the name of King, the Roman had not in the least altered, and Augustus himself had grown up in a world so wholly anti-monarchical that we need feel no surprise if he himself was tinged with the same prejudice. But in many other things a great change had come to pass among the Roman people. After the fall of Carthage, a craze for money and urban life had raged among them as if it were some destructive pestilence brought back from the ruins of the great commercial city. This was now rapidly passing away. The Roman was returning with zeal to the agricultural tastes of the earlier age. He was tired, not only of war, but of the life of great cities, with its tyranny over the freedom of the individual. He was hun-

A
new
age

---

[2] Suetonius, *Divus Augustus*, VII (2) with the quotation from Ennius there given.

gering again for the quiet rural life, the life of the single separate person. He was tired of politics. Nowhere can we see this state of mind more completely or more vividly portrayed than in the pages of Horace. It is hardly possible to open a volume of his works without finding his touch upon this theme. This new tone of thought penetrated to every level of the Roman people. Maecenas—himself a refined Sybarite—listened with enchantment to the little bird that sang so sweetly of the rustic paradise into which, we may be sure, Maecenas did not himself adventure. And the whole change, in all its details, called for a change in the system of government. When Augustus turned to study the possibilities of a new system, he had to consider all the changes in public feeling that were taking place, and in which he shared. What he might plan to do would necessarily be conditioned by the public demand.

His starting point was the particular feature of the case which had been spontaneously evolved by the process of change—his own position. The stability of the new world would depend upon the stability of the new directing authority—at present, himself. If this authority at any time collapsed, the work would be undone. It was necessary therefore to fix the new authority and make it permanent. A new authority This, which at first sounds a very simple thing to do, was, as a matter of fact, one of extraordinary difficulty. He had to find out what he wanted to fix, and then to discover means of fixing it. Neither was self-evident. What the new authority really consisted of it is not easy even now to say. Whether the policy he adopted was the best, we know no better than he did. We can only record the simple fact that he did try to discover the nature of the new authority, and the methods which would enable the state to perpetuate it.

The constitutional reforms of Augustus are of especial

interest therefore because they formed one of the boldest experiments ever carried out in deliberate political construction. We see a statesman endeavouring to establish a social system demanded of him by his people. We see him noting the ideals that are to be fulfilled, and adapting or creating means to embody these ideals. If, sometimes, they seem to lead us far afield from conventional politics, that is because Augustus grasped the truth that conventional politics were not enough. Something much more—in fact a whole Golden Age was demanded.

The power Augustus possessed, of constructing his new system unhindered by any opposition, was due to the general confidence he had come to possess; and this, in turn, **The** sprang from the certainty felt first of all by his own victori- **source** ous party that he had in the past given them what they **of con-** wanted, and would continue to do so. And the contentment **fidence** in him felt by the army enabled him to take those steps which contented the other parties in the state. Neither he nor any other statesmen contented every one or pleased every one. There were conspiracies and murder-plots directed against him throughout his life. He had to face hatred, restless malice and blank impatience—but in most cases these things came from people incapable of rational thought. Taking it on the whole, few men have been more completely accepted than he was.

IV

The social system which Augustus was called upon to establish was the consummation of a great change which had its origin in events which had begun a century—or even two centuries—earlier. We have already noted in the course of this story the way in which the Caesarian armies expropriated large parts of the soil of Italy for distribution to discharged veterans. This process, which had been foreshadowed by the Gracchi, and begun by Marius and Sulla,[3] was carried to its highest pitch by the Caesarian armies. The peculiarity of the process was the spontaneous nature of the movement. Julius had stamped the idea so effectually into the minds of his followers that they carried it on after his death. Augustus needed to restrain rather than to stimulate them. The passion for land—especially the passion for a small estate—is something that has dwindled and diminished in the modern world until it possibly strikes the present-day observer as strange. But it has been a very common and normal human passion in the past, and no men ever held it more intensely than the Caesarian legionaries. The Caesarian revolution was essentially an agrarian revolution.

The small estates

The vast results of this change need emphasizing, because it has been the custom to think of Caesar's revolution as purely political in its nature. But the political part was secondary and merely legalized and made permanent the agrarian change. The solid-based and unshakeable supremacy of Augustus and his successors rested upon the support of the small landholders who were the material of their armies. Their power changed and shifted as the small holdings changed. The large estates had not been destroyed, and there was a perpetual tendency for the small ones to coalesce and fall into the hands of the owners of large estates. But as long as the agrarian revolution of the Caesars lasted, so long the Italian military small-holders were the support of the principate and the main part of the Roman armies. When Italy had again fallen into the possession of great proprietors, the military small-holders of the Rhine and Danube became the dominant power of the Roman world. . . . And when the small estate, based upon a town

The military small-holders

[3] *Twelve Centuries of Rome,* pp. 226–280.

tenement, faded altogether away, the legionary soldier faded with it, and Rome faded, too.

Virgil, the real inventor of the Golden Age, was, even more than Horace, the specific glorifier of the small country estate. The Georgics are not so much an attempt to see life as it really was, as an attempt to idealize agriculture and to make it an inspiring, almost a religious, mode of life. The praise of Italy which Virgil sang [4] may have been only the zeal of a true patriot: but he let no mistake remain as to the purpose he wished the Georgics to fulfil.[5] He desired to lead men to live a happy life and to feel rightly about it. In this he helped Augustus to lay the foundations of the new era. He was not its product—he was much more its creator. The garden at Tarentum [6] which he depicted in the last of the Georgics is an expression of what Virgil and the public opinion of his age considered to be the noblest work of man. The picture showed not so much what the age had attained, as what he thought it ought to attain.

Ideal-
ization

This imaginative element, this persistent attempt to idealize the material change and to glorify it by the poet's art, was something very close to the heart of Augustus, which he took seriously. He created very few things: he always utilized and adapted what was to hand. He could not have compelled the art of Horace and Virgil, but he eagerly accepted their help, and gave them scope to do their best. By their aid he conquered the good opinion not only of his contemporaries, but of ages to come.

v

We do not need, after all, to go very far to discover some of the principles underlying the Golden Age. Horace him-

[4] *Georgics*, II, 475–542.
[5] *Georgics*, II, 136–176.
[6] *Georgics*, IV, 116–148.

self was fond of contemplating them. It is by him that we are reminded that every man is governed by his ruling passion—one of those broad, simple truths that are true at all times and in all places.[7] The magnetism which drew Horace and Augustus together was the same sympathy which enabled Augustus to plumb the demand of the age and satisfy it, to trace the motives and wishes of men, and to deal with them as they deserved. A certain fondness for reality was the ruling passion of Augustus. Just as he liked Raetian wine and white grapes and an apple to lick—it would have been a lemon, had he lived nowadays—so he liked life with a perceptibly acid quality. The statesman who complained that an applicant presented his petition like a man presenting a bun to an elephant was the same man who was accessible to the sort of humour with which Horace dedicated the second book of his Epistles, when he remarked that Augustus was far too busy doing good to the world to be able to read a dedication, so he would just leave it at that. . . . It is not in every age that it has been perfectly safe to write as Horace did in the first satire of his second book. . . . If Augustus was amused, or even tolerant, we can fix certain main lines of his character with assurance. He liked a tang to things: he did not want everything sickly sweet. The sense that he had knocked against reality pleased him—perhaps it pleased his sense of caution and prudence. . . . As a highly nervous type, who could not remain awake in the dark without company,[8] he may only have felt safe when he knew, by the feel of things, that he had hold of them.

Horace has stated with candour and good sense his idea of the relation that subsists between a man of his own kind and the great and powerful. Horace had no sympathy with

[7] *Odes*, I, i.
[8] Suetonius, *Divus Augustus*, LXXVIII.

the morose stoicism which declined to make any advance towards the great, or share anything with them. A man (he thought)who was content with inferior things on the ground that he wanted nothing, had no claim to think himself better than a man who paid court to the great because **Co-op-** he wanted superior things. To please the great is not the **eration** most important aim in life, but neither is it despicable, if it has a good reason. . . . Augustus met this spirit half way. He too agreed that it is the business of the great man to find out those that can help him, and to provide them with opportunity to do so. This principle (not by any means entirely novel, but already traditional among some, at least, of the Roman governing class) received a remarkable embodiment in actual life when the poet put it into immortal words, and the great leader put it into immortal practice, and a whole era of great men, interlinked and interlocked, stepped forward simultaneously upon the world's stage, in a kind of spontaneous agreement to exhibit the principle at work. . . . The testimony of later ages has certainly been that it must be a magnificent principle, if it is to be judged by its fruits—but that there seems a curious difficulty in copying it.

The Golden Age was not a golden frame for a number of ordinary men, but was much rather a name for a number of very extraordinary men whose co-operation, and even whose co-existence, seems almost accidental. Augustus was the first, the original of the group; he brought with him Agrippa the soldier and engineer, and Maecenas the diplomat and connoisseur; and Maecenas brought Horace and **The** Virgil, the philosopher and the prophet, as well as Pro- **Augustans** pertius. But these, who were Caesarians, were not all the tale. Messalla Corvinus, who had begun by being an anti-Caesarian, finally linked his fortunes with those of Augus-

tus, bringing his poet Tibullus with him: while Titus Livius
the historian, being himself a man of means and position,
stood upon his own feet independently, as a Friend of
Caesar, although an anti-Caesarian in political theory.

Among these Agrippa was (as we have already noticed)
a man with exceptional talent for constructive engineering.
He was the architect and engineer by whose inventiveness
the age was chiefly marked. He was destined to do other
remarkable works besides building the two aqueducts during his aedileship and reforming the drainage system of
Rome. While Augustus was thinking out the first steps of
political reorganization, and Virgil was revolving the idea
of the Aeneid, Agrippa executed a number of works which
made an indelible impression upon the Roman tradition. He
built the first baths which had ever been known in Rome
—a city in which baths and bathing were later on destined
to assume exceptional importance. Close by them he built
a temple to the gods of the Julian house—the Pantheon.
Baths and temple have long been swept away in the fires
and disasters and changes of Rome: but his Thermae had
a wonderful progeny which became indissolubly linked
with the name and fame of Rome. And his Pantheon was
rebuilt by Hadrian with the huge dome of solid concrete   **Agrippa**
which is to this very day one of the wonders of the world.   **as builder**

There was something profoundly appropriate in the
celebration of Agrippa's name by the concrete dome of
Hadrian's Pantheon, even though Agrippa did not himself
build it: for Agrippa was in all probability the man by
whom the idea of building in concrete was first founded.
The style of architecture which afterwards became typical
of Rome sprang full-fledged into being in these days, and
never was much improved upon, though it was afterwards
used upon a vaster and more impressive scale: and Agrippa

stands at this beginning as, if not its inventor, certainly the
man who first made it fashionable. It consisted of building
in concrete and facing the concrete with more decorative
materials—especially marble. It is an invention which, after
a long interval, the modern world has seized and adapted.

Agrippa was not the only builder. Another soldier,
T. Statilius Taurus, one of the trustworthy die-hard Caesarians, round about the time when Agrippa built the first
baths, built the first stone amphitheatre. This, too, had an
amazing progeny: and perhaps, for some of us, the amphitheatre is the most typically Roman of all buildings. The
work of Statilius, like that of Agrippa, has been swept
away: but the tremendous Colosseum was its offspring.
Asinius Pollio founded another building which was the first
of its kind in Rome—and his will probably appeal to modern taste as a more desirable model for imitation than either
Pantheon or Amphitheatre: he built the first public library.
Augustus, when he erected the rich and magnificent Porticus Octavial in honour of his sister, instituted a second
public library on an even greater scale, with Gaius Melissus
as librarian. Part of the design of his stately house on the
Palatine hill—the Palatium or "Palace" which has given its
name to all magnificent dwelling houses ever since—was a
temple to Apollo in recognition of the god's assistance at
Actium. Above it blazed a quadriga driven by the sun-god,
while within it and in its precincts were many marvels, including a great candelabrum made like a tree, and the Sibylline books. Round it ran a portico or cloister, linking it to
twin libraries, one for Latin books and one for Greek,
with their staffs of keepers and copyists, over which first
Pompeius Macer, and then Gaius Julius Hyginus presided.
These libraries were by no means neglected institutions.
That of Asinius Pollio seems to have been swept away a
century and a half later to make room for the Forum of

The libraries

Trajan,[9] with its enlarged and improved library, which was in turn taken over and preserved by Diocletian. The library in the Porticus Octaviae [10] lasted until 80 A. D., when it was destroyed by fire. The library on the Palatine was approaching its four hundredth year of existence when, on the night of the eighteenth and nineteenth of March, A. D. 363, fire destroyed the temple and library together. So the collection of Pollio, after its two removals, may after all have outlived the others. *The libraries endure*

Agrippa does not seem to have entertained any passion for books. His share in things of the mind was, nevertheless, a very notable one. Julius had planned a vast survey of the Roman dominions, so that its governors might have some notion of what they were dealing with. After his death, Agrippa took over the material and designed a great map of the Roman world, which was engraved on marble and was made accessible to the public in the Court of Octavia. Agrippa wrote a commentary on the map; and on this map and its commentary is based a good deal of the information transmitted to us by later geographers, such as Ptolemy and Strabo. *The great map*

All this invention and design was a great deal more than mere display and advertisement; and at the same time it was a great deal more than mere abstract interest in the arts

---

[9] The Atrium Libertatis, in which it lay, is frequently said to have been on the Aventine; but this depends upon the assumption that the Atrium Libertatis was the same as the Templum Libertatis.

[10] Besides the magnificent Porticus Octaviae, with the treasures of art it contained, and its libraries and walks, Augustus built the Forum Augusti, a very much admired public resort, with walls a hundred feet high; and the mausoleum, in which were buried all his family and successors up to Nerva. The Forum was designed in memory of the victory of Philippi and the vengeance for Julius, and was dedicated in 2 B. C. The Mausoleum was a remarkable circular building with a huge earthen tumulus upon its roof, planted with trees, and surmounted by a statue of Augustus. It stood in the midst of a small park. The restorations and minor works of Augustus were numberless.

and sciences. "Abstract" and "disinterested" are words hardly ever applicable to Augustus. He was always regardful of the practical application of these things. He thoroughly grasped the maxim that intellectual activity is part of the vitality of the state, and he encouraged it because Rome lived better and more ardently with such pursuits to absorb her attention. And besides, all this imposing splendour of art disciplines men, and awes them into respect for the power which has created it. The special note of the Golden Age is not any given example of art or science (for there is hardly a single one of its works which cannot be excelled by some work of another age) [11] but the general appreciation of intellectual values. And this appreciation was rooted in the belief that in these values was enshrined a conserving power which at once inspired and justified and rationalized the social system over which Augustus ruled.

VI

The
Augustan
attitude

The new attitude that these men sought to introduce we may see in Horace.[12] It began with a call to repentance for what they felt to be a dreadful past which had produced an evil present and was destined, if not checked, to produce a still more dreadful future. Horace even surmises that there must be some awful reason in the distant past—some crime like the murder of Remus by Romulus, for example —which needs to be expiated before Rome could have peace from civil strife. . . . Men must be deeply impressed by the evil of their days when they go back to such explanations for a clue to its cause. . . . Horace sketches the morality of his age, and asks whether the men who made

[11] E. g., the Aeneid is excelled by the *Iliad* and *Odyssey*; the *Eclogues* by the pastorals of Theocritus; Livy is not superior to Herodotus or Thucydides; and so round the compass. The only exception seems to be Horace, who is supreme in his own line.

[12] *Odes*, III, 6; II, 1; Epodes, VII.

the greatness of Rome sprang from such parents. The new attitude, of which Horace was the mild and genial prophet, and which Augustus helped to make fashionable where his influence penetrated, had some affinity with that of Ecclesiastes.[13] Not to worry, nor to attribute importance to trifles; to have faith in good sense, and to hold ourselves quiet; to follow our own genius and to enjoy what we really like best—and to accept the consequences, concerning which we most of us have shrewder ideas than we are willing to admit—this was the new attitude; perhaps a little puzzling at first, until we have grasped its implications. The philosophy of the Golden Mean was the natural basis for the Golden Age.[14] To avoid extremes and take the middle road was the whole theory on which Augustus had worked.

The general idea [15] is that we should set limits to our passions, our desires and even our wishes, and should not be carried away by the peculiar impatience and restlessness which is so common among men. The uselessness—even the danger—of excessive wealth is that it does not satisfy the passion that inspires it: and it certainly alienates, and ultimately destroys, the social sympathies. The fear of poverty is a worse thing than poverty itself. The Golden Mean is the ideal we need to study. . . . Horace returns to this theme again and again.[16] The weak point about great wealth is that it does not procure us the greatest and most indispensable of all gifts—security and salvation. The ideal human life is really that of the Scythian barbarians, a rough, healthy, moral life which does produce the essential virtues. The ideal property is a small estate—say a river, a wood and a cornfield.[17] Peace and balance of mind are the necessary

Moderation

13 *Epistles*, I, 6.
14 *Odes*, II, 10.
15 *Satires*, I, 1.
16 *Odes*, III, 24.
17 *Odes*, III, 16.

conditions without which we cannot enjoy property at all.[18] And tolerance of other people's faults, and sympathy with them, is the first step to such a balance.[19]

Professed philosophers are apt to talk as if the moral virtues were remote, and even chilly affairs, to be cultivated purely as ornaments to the soul of man. Horace, like the earlier Hebrew prophets, takes a more practical view. He sees that the essence of the moral virtues is that they make men much happier, and, in the strict sense—the sense in which he understands it—more prosperous. That little estate, which was always floating before Horace's mental eye, is a good thing not merely because it is calculated to make him a better man, but because it certainly makes him a jollier one. In that famous satire which contains the story of the Town Mouse and the Country Mouse, Horace contemplates the horrors of the town [20] and the blessings of the country—the boredom of the manifold trifles that distract a man in town, and the profound luxury of quiet days in the country, his work, his rest, his pleasant suppers and congenial conversation. . . . A good deal of this may have been simple reaction from the excess of earlier days, when Crassus and Lucullus were in their heyday, and money and ostentation were everything.[21] Such excess was by no means extinct. One of the satires contains a detailed description of a dinner of this kind, while another is a dissertation upon the art of gastronomy as it was practised in Horace's age. . . . The art of Horace makes his simple recital of these things somewhat blasting. . . . But, however much reaction may have intensified Horace's feelings on such subjects, there can be no doubt of their depth and

The rural paradise

[18] *Epistles*, I, 1, 2.
[19] *Satires*, I, 3.
[20] *Satires*, I, 6. Horace, of course, lived in Italy. He might have written a little differently if he had lived in a harder climate.
[21] *Satires*, I, 2; I, 8 (the feast of Nasidienus); I, 4.

sincerity, and of the extent to which he reflected a similar Horace's
depth and sincerity in other men. Horace perhaps did not genuine
extensively explore the vast country to which he opened a
gate: but that gate he did open, and to it he has led numberless readers, both in his own day and in later ages, who
were drawn thither by his gospel of peace, contemplation
and moderation. Such an art was the natural prologue to
the Golden Age.

VII

Augustus had not, by natural temperament, any sympathy at all with the romantic. His own literary style was
terse, clear, sober, unornamented. In this, too, he was in
harmony with his age, and accepted the verdict of the preponderant opinion.[22] The age that saw the fall of Cicero
and the triumph of Caesar saw also the fall of the Ciceronic
period and the triumph of the style of which the author of
the *Gallic War* was a supreme exponent. This style—a
statesman's style, an administrator's style—rapidly became
universal. The prose of Augustus was far from being fea-
tureless. It had its peculiarities and its marked characteristics in choice of words, some of which Suetonius has preserved for us. He had the good sense to understand his own
limitations. As a method of study, he attempted to write an
epic—but it was a failure, and his critical sense told him as
much. His taste was for history and for the detail of crafts-
manship; and probably he was most thoroughly at home in Titus
following the development of the great Roman history of Livius
Titus Livius,[23] and (when allowed) in helping, as only he
could help, in the verification of historical data. Livy gives

[22] See Professor Tenney Frank in *Roman Life and Literature*, pp. 165–
167, quoting Dionysius of Halicarnassus.
[23] Titus Livius was writing this book between 29 B.C. and shortly after
9 B.C., at which date it stopped.

one interesting glimpse of Augustus,[24] when he describes the statements in his authorities concerning the *spolia opima* of Aulus Cornelius Cossus. We see Augustus busy with the restoration of temples; himself entering and examining the ancient and dilapidated temple of Jupiter Feretrius, and there noting the inscriptions on the old trophies that had in ages past been dedicated to the god. His recollection of what he had seen there was sufficiently vivid to enable him to correct the literary sources followed by Livy, and to certify that Cossus filled the office of consul (not of military tribune) in the year in which he took the "royal spoils." . . . And, in fact, the religious interests of Augustus were so interwoven with his interest in the history, archaeology and tradition of Rome—implying by tradition the code of manners and conduct handed down through the ages—that it is quite impossible to think of them separately. It is likely enough that the interesting details about the Fetial ritual, which Livy gives us, may have come from Augustus, who had acted as Pater Patratus, and was fully qualified to explain it. Not many men were.

Liberty   The idea that the supremacy of Augustus involved any restriction in the liberty of the writer and thinker is groundless. Livy—an anti-Caesarian in principle—was careful to preserve his own independence, and was not too eager to accept the guidance of Augustus. The repute of his work certainly did not suffer on this account—though its accuracy probably did. It was the distinctive note of Livy that he put forward a definite theory of the political development of Rome. His history is no mere string of facts, but the tale of a coherent evolution.[25] In spite of his op-

[24] IV, 20.

[25] Livy is the historian of the Golden Age, and one of the high peaks of its literary splendour. But he was far from being the only important historical writer. Dionysius of Halicarnassus, who wrote in Greek, and therefore does not count as an Augustan, was a writer of considerable

position to the prevailing party in Rome, his history was accepted as the standard and orthodox history of his country.[26]

The triumph of anti-Caesarianism in Livy moved Augustus to certain thoughts. He wanted something that Livy did not give—something more deeply interwoven with all those old immemorial traditions that he loved. There are signs that he suggested to Horace (directly or indirectly) the idea of a poem which should supply an epic or mythic prologue to Livy. Horace excused himself on the ground that he was totally unqualified to write such a work—and his own judgment of himself was probably correct.[27] Virgil undertook the task: and the fruit was the Aeneid. Augustus suggested the idea, and Virgil worked it out. But the idea was not intended as a mere exercise in virtuosity. The Aeneid was not a mere string of adventures, but the unrolling of a definite thought concerning the predestination of Rome and of certain families in it. The Aeneid, like the tale of King Arthur, was an instrument of lofty patriotic propaganda: and it went deep—so deep that from being a species of fairy tale, it solidified into a great religious poem

Idea of the Aeneid

---

importance. We ought not to forget Dellius, the freedman of Marcus Antonius, and the historian on whom, probably, Plutarch's life of Antony is based—with all its consequences—including Shakespeare's *Antony and Cleopatra*. His works are lost, together with those of Fenestella, a Latin writer who supplied Plutarch with some interesting pages: and there was Asinius Pollio, a true Augustan of high merit, who preserved "The die is cast," and who did not fear to criticise the style of Livy or the impartiality of Julius. The works of Varro, the supreme Roman antiquarian, are also lost.

[26] Before many years are over, Livy is pretty certain to be re-edited and reconsidered by a man trained in the modern school of social science. When this happens, our conceptions of Livy are likely to be revolutionized, and we shall realize for the first time that he bequeathed to us an amount of information which earlier generations were not in a position to utilize, or even to understand. The recovery of the lost books of Livy would be the greatest gift from the Augustan age that Fortune could give to the modern world.

[27] *Satires*, II, i; *Epistles*, II, i.

which provided Rome with a theory and a principle.

For Marcus Antònius, Virgil had created the Fourth
Eclogue; for Augustus, he created a vast epic, going back
to the fall of Troy, and tracing the adventures of Aeneas
on his way westward to seek a new home; his settlement,
and the prophecies accompanying it, foretelling the mighty
city that was to be built and ruled by his progeny—the men
of the Julian house. . . . It gave Augustus a peculiar prestige which he had not possessed before. The tellers of
stories are often the first to be excited or frightened by the
products of their own fancy; and it is possible that Augustus grew greater and greater in the poet's vision as the poem
proceeded. Augustus certainly grew greater in other men's
eyes. Even now it is extremely difficult to think ourselves
out of the magic circle that Virgil drew for us. It is almost
impossible really to convince ourselves that the man Gaius
Octavius sprang from a small middle-class family of Velitrae, not for a moment to be taken seriously among the
great houses of Rome: our minds—once we have read Virgil—insist upon believing that Augustus was the predestined
hero, the golden child, the scion of a divine line. All this
was at once a stimulus and a protection in the Roman
world. It helped to produce a noble faith in the mission of
Rome, and a conviction of the divine authority of government. And it is highly beneficial to mankind that it should
believe in the divine authority of government. It is a great
evil that (as Horace said) we should fancy that a grove is
nothing but logs. Not Horace, however, but Virgil wove
the spell of holiness that gilded the Roman name and the
Roman destiny, and transformed the Roman authority
from a coarse and worldly domination to a supremacy intended by the divine powers and directed by their benefi-
cent will. This character ever afterwards marked the Roman dominion. It adduced, as its claim to rule, a divine

**Effect
of the
Aeneid**

origin and guidance; it showed this guidance as resulting from the obedience and submission with which the remote forefathers had borne themselves towards the sources of all power. It based itself, not upon the right of conquest or any superiority of force, but upon a moral right which entitled it to the direction of the world.

A moral right

We may doubt very much whether Virgil would ever have thought of the Aeneid, had not Augustus suggested the idea, and provided in his own person a model for the pious Aeneas. It was Augustus who foresaw the results and reactions, the effect of the idea as it spread. . . . But it was always Augustus—inducing other men to do what he could not do himself: laying the road for them, cutting the path, suggesting the objective, and in all things, for every purpose, acting through the persons of his Friends.

VIII

There was one feature of the Augustan age which we have come to look upon as an essential part of its greatness. Augustus and his circle agreed in admiring and seeking for a perfect and exquisite workmanship, both in the written word and in the fine arts; and some of the work done to please them still startles us with its passionate striving after the faultless. Augustus always liked to contemplate the thing well done. His love of the perfect was wholly disinterested, for it was not forced upon him by any such necessity as that which makes it compulsory upon a mechanician. What he sought was a spiritual or artistic perfection, which he loved for its own intrinsic desirability. It supplied the place of those great acts of faith which comfort some men. He knew nothing of the conceptions which complete our moral satisfaction by their promise of a perfection realized hereafter, or in some dimension not known to us here. He

Cult of the perfect

was never able to sit down, sure that God was in his heaven, and all was right with the world. But as it is necessary for our spiritual health that we should be able to look upon something without fault or flaw, he sought it in these things. A perfect thing, however trifling, is after all a promise that something larger can also be perfect—even to the whole itself.

IX

To the Roman—and even more to the unfortunate provincial—who had experienced something of the long-drawn-out civil strife which for a century had been wasting the time, the wealth, the courage and the hopes of the Roman world, the supremacy of Augustus did indeed seem a golden age. To know that peace was secure under his strong guardianship—to see the works of peace that everywhere arose around him—to realize the current of new thought and new art, that everywhere was setting in—this was to enter, if not the Golden Age, at any rate a new world. Some deadly drain had been stopped, and once more the **The Augustan world** natural vitality of mankind began to accumulate, and its level to rise. . . . The rise in the level was one of the things that struck the attention of men. There never seemed to have been a statesman so profoundly wise as Augustus: there never seemed to have been an art so great as that of the poets who wrote under his protection, the architects who built under his orders, or the governors who ruled the world in his name. For the first time, in fact, mankind was reaping the benefit of a unified civilization governed by a single law and a single group of men. Hitherto they had paid the price and received none of the reward. Now—suddenly—together with the Augustan peace, the reward began to flow in upon them in a full and abundant stream.

No wonder they sometimes said things that sound extravagant to us!

The standard so established remained a permanent conquest for mankind. Even during those times when they have receded furthest from it, men have remembered the Augustus age, and have judged themselves by its criterion. Many a century was to pass before the world again saw four such poets as Horace, Virgil, Propertius and Tibullus alive together; but the new world which had once contained them was a far better and richer place than the old world which had not, and it had a far greater hope in front of it.

A permanent conquest

CHAPTER XIII

THE GHOST OF MARCUS ANTONIUS

I

ALL this being so, we can see what the things were, which Augustus needed to fix into some sort of permanency. By what means could he be invested with a permanent power to keep the peace throughout the Roman world, and to **The problem** protect the persons and property of its citizens, in accordance with the great traditions he represented?

We have seen the process by which the position of Augustus evolved. For the first ten years of his career he had been a member of the Committee of Three appointed for the reorganization of the state. For a year after the Committee lapsed, he continued to hold the same powers by common consent. He then became consul, and for a number of years in succession held this supreme dignity of the Roman state, as well as his old powers and the large and strange assortment of complimentary privileges which had been bestowed upon him by the enthusiasm of his contemporaries. He needed to reduce all this to order, and make his official position and his actual power square with one another, so that they became a coherent, intelligible whole with which other men, his successors, could be invested when their due time came. For if all that he had done was merely temporary, it had all been useless; it had been worth doing only if it were a permanent gain to Rome.

Augustus not a monarch Those of us who still have a fancy that Augustus was a Roman emperor must try to forget the idea. The meaning and the connotation which the word "emperor" have for us were totally foreign to him. The word "imperator," which was part of his title, had associations wholly different. He would have paused in surprise, and perhaps in some ironic amusement, before a picture, not only of an Austrian emperor or a Russian tsar, but even of one of his own successors a few hundred years later. The thought had hardly occurred to him. Antony was the man to whom it had occurred. The ghost of Antony haunted the new era from its beginning.

Augustus was led to seek for a new arrangement by the serious objections to which his provisional status was open. For any one to hold an exceptional, an emergency office like the triumvirate, after it had lapsed, by a mere informal consensus, the immediate occasion for which had passed away—this was obviously to stand on a false foundation, liable to crumble dangerously if any reliance were placed upon it. For one man to hold the consulship year after year was entirely contrary to the tradition of the Roman constitution, which, from time to time, had even enacted laws to prevent it. Augustus did not wish to violate the spirit of the constitution in this way. Moreover, there were obvious objections to turning the old collegiate office of consul into a new, semi-dictatorial office. Finally the consulship was essentially an aristocratic dignity which the army might respect, but did not love. Hence Augustus was anxious to find some new basis for his power, if the ingenuity of politicians and jurisconsults could find one; and he was open to suggestions.

He rejected many, perhaps most, of the suggestions made to him from time to time. He would not be a dictator; he declined the censorship, which would have given him the right to determine the status of any citizen. It was only after a considerable time, and much reflection, that he came

Restoration of the republic, 28–27 B.C.

to any definite conclusion. The year 27 B. C. is famous because it was in that year that the first systematic legislation was passed with the object of rationalizing his position. Those who took part in the transaction had perfectly
clear notions of what they were doing. He handed his
powers back to the sovereign republic; and the sovereign
republic in the plenitude of its authority invested him
with such new powers as it thought good. As to any aboli-
tion of the republic—no one as much as thought of such a
thing. What was abolished was the old closed oligarchy
which had ruled Rome so long—not the republic.

For the new status of Augustus was preceded by a census
which he himself, as consul, superintended. The citizen roll
was reviewed, with startling results which even to this day
cause the earnest student to wrestle with his thoughts. The
citizen population had nearly doubled itself since the last
census forty-two years before. From what source did the
new citizens come? Most of them, probably, owed their
existence to bold grants of citizenship made by Julius or by
Marcus Antonius. This expansion of the citizen body had
been expedient, and even imperative, at the time. But Augustus, having gathered a little experience, and seen something of the world, thought that it had gone far enough. In
closing the register he initiated a new policy, of granting
citizenship on easier terms, indeed, than had once been the
case, but still with rather more circumspection, and more
careful regard for the quality of the new citizen, than
Julius had shown.

The expansion of the citizen body had been accompanied
by a corresponding expansion of the senate, which now
numbered nearly twice its old membership. During the days
of party strife and civil war, many persons had obtained
admission who, when reviewed in cold blood, did not excite the enthusiasm of an investigator. It was the definite

AUGUSTUS

as an elderly man

LIVIA

wife of Augustus

JULIA

daughter of Augustus

AGRIPPA

as an elderly man

(From coins in the British Museum)

policy of Augustus to check the influx and to reduce the number of senators. His aim was, as with the citizen-body, to obtain a better quality in the entrants. The oligarchs, the *optimates*, recognizing in this the policy they had always themselves maintained, were only too happy to support him. What was practically a working compromise between the Caesarian and the anti-Caesarian policies was therefore established. The old narrow basis of both citizenship and senatorial rank was surrendered by the surviving oligarchs and a new and more liberal basis was agreed upon, which should provide the Roman world with a more ample governing class, without at the same time laying it open to indiscriminate entry. In the past, Rome had ruled Italy. She had tried to rule the world, but had failed. She now merged herself in Italy; and the task which had been impossible for Rome became possible for Italy. Review of the senate, 29 B. C.

The compromise so reached enabled Augustus to secure agreement on points which otherwise might have been bitterly contested. The senate, satisfied that his principles and intentions were such as it could approve of, willingly made concessions on other points, and met him half way in the matter of his own personal position.

He therefore laid down the powers he had acquired as a member of the Committee of Three, and they were extinguished. He was then invested for ten years with the command in chief of the Roman army, which was no longer to be entirely a conscripted citizen levy, but principally a volunteer professional army, deriving its organization and tradition direct from the Caesarian army: and he was to possess full proconsular authority in all the provinces in which that army was supposed to be stationed. By this means he was given both the legal authority and the practical power to impose order upon the Roman world. Changes of 27 B. C.

He would hardly have obtained this authority unless he

had distinctly shown, by his policy after Actium, that he intended to restrain the army and to put it under a sharper discipline. The army itself was no longer in a position to object, and it no longer had any serious motive to object. Every one, therefore, was satisfied, and the Caesarian army, the embodiment of the rank and file of Roman citizens, became the permanent guarantee of peace and the enforcer of law. It was stationed, henceforth, in the newer or frontier provinces, where it could gain experience and training against the unruly tribes of the borders.

This military power, however, gave him direct authority only in the provinces where the army was stationed. In order to possess power elsewhere he still needed to be consul each year, and to be the supreme magistrate. For four years he tried this plan; then by the light of the experience he had gained he reorganized his position on a new basis.

The new plan was to cast aside the consulship altogether, and restore it to its old possessors, the senatorial oligarchy, as an annual magistracy, according to the old and correct usage. Instead, Augustus turned to the tribunician power which he had been given years before—the authority of that ancient and famous office which from the earliest times had been the protection of the common people. The power possessed by these annual popular officers was now permanently employed by Augustus as the basis of his civil authority. He became the Grand Tribune of the Roman people, perpetually authorized to intervene in their interest. In order to fill up the gap left—for the tribuneship lacked some of the high prerogatives of the consulship—his military powers were defined afresh, so that he became legally equal to an ordinary consul, although he was not one. Hence he had become a Grand Tribune—something of the ideal that Gaius Gracchus had tried to realize—and this Grand Tribune held approximately the same military au-

Further changes, 23 B. C.

thority that Marius had once held: and this composite authority was the substance of the power Augustus held for the rest of his life.

The restoration of the consulship to its old condition pleased the oligarchy. The revival of the tribuneship pleased the man in the street, who saw in it his own safety and protection, backed by the invincible power of the legions. The new authority was permanent, and lasted until, centuries afterwards, time and changes transformed it into another shape.

Permanent settlement

II

The transference of the army to the frontier provinces by Augustus was possibly a necessary step: but the practical result, whether intended or unintended, was to part those old rivals, the senate and the people, far from one another. The senate remained at Rome with its consuls. The mass of citizen electors was dispersed to all parts of the empire. The old Assembly naturally withered and died. It was no longer the centre of legislation and the stage on which the political drama was played. Its place, as representing the people, was taken by the army, headed by the grand tribune who was also its commander.

Those who most regret the passing of the old Roman constitutional practice are least able to point to any method by which it could have been avoided. As a result of the century-long struggle between the senate and the Assembly, the senate had preserved its form and lost its power; and the Assembly had preserved its power and lost its form. They had to be parted as "incompatibles"—but it was not Augustus who overthrew the republic, nor did he ever wish to abolish it. To the best of his own knowledge he had very dexterously patched it up to the contentment of all parties.

III

The succession

And now came the problem that trips up all statesmen and destroys all systems: the problem of the transference of authority from one holder to another, his successor. . . . Granting that Augustus had succeeded in creating and establishing an authority that could hold the Roman factions apart, and the Roman world together—how was he to provide for a successor to follow him? If he could not so provide, then he had done only half the work he had purported to do: he had stemmed the civil war for his own life-time only, and after his death it would break out again —as in fact it nearly did.

There were two possible ways in which he could attack the problem. For one, he could make it hereditary: or for another, he could pick a successor, as Julius had, from the persons most suitable in character and ability—he could "co-opt" his successor. The advantage of the hereditary method was that he would have full control over the education and training of his successor, and that the succession being automatically determined, from the start, would not be subject to rivalry, competition, intrigue or party-strife. The advantage of co-option was that he could pick from a much larger field of candidates—but its disadvantage was that it laid the chieftainship open to competition: and competition would be only another name for civil war. . . . This problem Augustus never solved. Instead, he provided that either solution should be possible when the necessity arose. He spent the rest of his life in securing this possibility.

Alternatives

The truth was, that he did not know which course would be best, nor which he preferred. He could not bring himself to a definite decision when he himself felt the question to be so open. Most men like to think of their children as their successors. It adds to their own distinction and to the distinction of the family. But Augustus never had a son. His marriage with Livia—the love-match which lasted his whole life long without serious dissension—was barren. A child was indeed born—but it was still-born. He was deeply disappointed: but there was no help for it.[1] His only child was Julia, the daughter of Scribonia—and if Scribonia did not sometimes reflect over the dramatic revenge this fact had taken on her behalf, she was an unusual woman. Scribonia had been bundled out of wedlock with little ceremony or consideration. But she held the master-card— she was Julia's mother! Nothing could alter that fact.

Julia sole heiress

Augustus had a paternal instinct, without which he would not have been the man he was. He had quite a house-hold of children around him, although only Julia was his own. There were the two sons of Livia by her former marriage, Tiberius Claudius Nero and Nero Claudius Drusus. Then there were Antonia "major" and Antonia "minor," the two daughters of his sister Octavia and Marcus An-

---

[1] The possibility of an heir for Augustus is so important a considera-tion, and the failure to provide one had such far-reaching results, that we are justified in considering whether there was indeed "no help for it." That Augustus was not in fault is suggested by the promptitude with which Scribonia produced Julia. The natural inference would be that Livia was barren: but then she was the mother of Tiberius and Drusus, so no such deduction will do. There is a tradition, duly re-corded by Suetonius (*Divus Augustus*, LXXI) which bears upon the subject. After saying that Augustus had easily refuted certain other moral accusations, he adds: "Circa libidines haesit, postea quoque, ut ferunt, ad vitiandas virgines promptior, quae sibi undique etiam ab uxore conquirerentur." Was this true? If so, a good deal is explained. But it is much more likely to be part of the torrent of slander which was always at work in Roman society. The remark comes so suddenly, is so short, is introduced so significantly by "ut ferunt," and is so entirely unsup-ported, that it is difficult to accept. The only reason for considering it at all is that Augustus had no child after Julia. The allegation was made, that Drusus was the son of Augustus; but if he had been, the probability is overwhelmingly strong that Augustus would have acknowledged him.

tonius: the two who had so disappointingly proved not to be the Kings of the Golden Age. Finally, there was Iullus Antonius, Mark Antony's son by Fulvia, besides Alexander Helios and Cleopatra Selene, the twin children of Cleo-

The family of Augustus

patra. The history of Alexander has not survived, but we know that Cleopatra Selene was in due course married to King Juba of Numidia and Mauretania, and lived more or less happily ever after, without complaints. Her own parents could hardly have done very much better for her. . . . Altogether, they formed a large household—most of them Antony's children. Augustus took a great liking to Iullus, and treated him as a son. The fact remained that Julia was his only child.

This, perhaps, is a suitable place at which to diverge for a moment to glance at the picture of the domestic life of Augustus which Suetonius draws. It is an interesting one. That the side of the new age which Horace and Virgil so insisted upon—the return to simplicity and tradition—was no mere figment of the poetic imagination, we can see clearly enough. Augustus very distinctly had two soul-sides —one to face the world with (and he could be very magnificent when he thought fit) and one for his family. He disliked large and labour-absorbing houses. His own houses were simple, and were decorated, not with works of fine art, but with woods and avenues, and with objects of interest like the fossil bones of extinct monsters which he found at Capri and set up in his garden. Suetonius speaks as if he had actually seen some of the domestic furniture of Augustus, still preserved when he wrote, and had been surprised at its plainness. Even the houses in Rome in which he actually lived were never very ornate. The glory of the

Augustus at home

Apolline temple, on the Palatine, with its attached libraries and museums, and its magnificent works of art, was quite unrelated to his private residence where, for forty years,

Augustus slept, winter and summer, in the same old room, on a low and simply furnished bed, without any marble about his halls or any mosaic pavements under foot. He had a small room at the top of the house, jocularly known as "Syracuse" from its lofty impregnability, or as his Little Study, and there he would work when he wished to be uninterrupted. Here, no doubt, he wrote out those careful speeches and public pronouncements which he took pains should be prepared beforehand, and not forced out of him extempore—he was a man who did not do his best when in a hurry—and the poems which he did not allow to survive, as well as other works, such as the tragedy of *Ajax*, who "fell upon his 'sponge' " and so came to a premature end. Here he sat in his home-made clothes, worked up by his own household—and (so it was said) woven on the loom by his own daughter and grand-daughters, whom he wished to keep up the old Roman arts of spinning and weaving. . . . But here, too, he kept ready to hand suitable clothing for important occasions, lest he should be surprised by unexpected visitors.

He ate and drank very little, and his private tastes were **Personal habits** for the second-quality bread, coarser than any modern wholemeal, the soft cheese and green figs which were much more likely to be on the table of Horace than on that of Maecenas. . . . But he had a reason. He seems to have suffered from that nervous type of digestion which is instantly upset by anything too rich, or too much in quantity, or even by too much thought or excitement. For this reason he usually ate just when the mood took him, and often did not touch food at all at the ceremonious dinners he gave, spending his time in looking after his guests. He was a good and amusing host, not at all too imposing for the ordinary sensual man or the simple fellow. He went to bed late, and hated getting up early. He slept badly—never more than seven hours, and that by fits and starts. He could not endure lying awake by himself. . . . As a result, he was apt to drop off to sleep at unofficial and unexpected moments—which sometimes gave rise to misunderstandings.

In spite of this simplicity—or because of it—he was extremely particular about his daughter and grand-daughters. They were brought up in the old Roman fashion, somewhat in seclusion: and Suetonius records one occasion on which Augustus severely rebuked a young man of good repute and status for venturing to call upon Julia. But this was not entirely nor exclusively in the interests of their moral training. None of the simplicity of Augustus's habits and household was to be understood as an admission of the humble level of his family. So far from this being the case, he was a somewhat exclusive person who drew social lines with great sharpness, and approved of the system of social classes and levels. He never admitted freedmen to his table, save in two exceptional cases which prove the rule. Hence we have to take Augustus as an example of a man who felt pride in his social rank—which he himself, with Virgil's help, had created—and who preserved it with exactitude, but who did not include personal luxury or ostentation among its characteristics.

Exclusiveness

There was (as all this shows) very little of the sensual in either the life or the personality of Augustus. It was part of his policy to encourage the old traditional virtues, including the virtues of domesticity and marital faithfulness—and he encouraged them in others most probably because he liked them himself. If he ever had a mistress, the world has never heard of her. He has been accused of intrigue with married women—but that was before his marriage, and his biographer admits that it was for a political purpose.[2]

[2] The only definite allegation is that Augustus took one lady out of the room, and brought her back later on with her hair loose and her

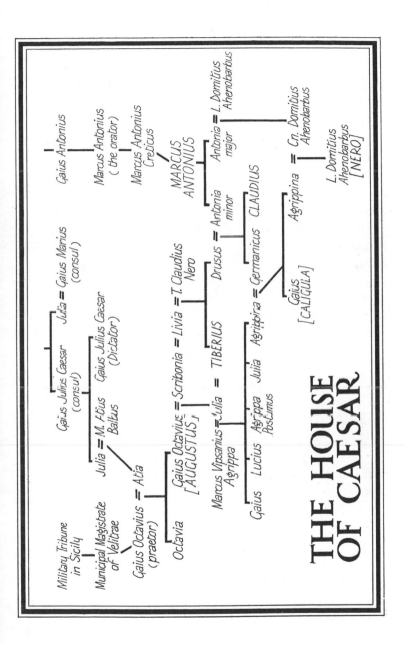

THE HOUSE
OF CAESAR

The one serious and positive charge against his moral character is a general one: and we may take it that in these matters a general charge is a sure sign that there are no specific cases to quote.[3] We may search in vain through the records of his life for any specific evidence against him. He had not the physical robustness nor the exuberance of temperament necessary to emulate the exploits of Marcus Antonius, even if he had wished to do so—and he never did· wish.

Moral
character

It was in such an atmosphere as this that Julia grew up —feeling her own importance and that of her family, restrained from luxury or from very much freedom, and having before her continually the example of a father who was delicate, and even a little ascetic in his private tastes, and interested in poetry and history. She is not likely to have realized much of the side of her father which has been his chief claim to fame—his skill as a political strategist. Part of his skill had been to conceal his skill.

IV

The first plan which Augustus formed was to marry Julia to Octavia's son by her first marriage, the young Mar-

---

ears very red: but it is questionable whether even the severest divorce judge would consider the lady's ears conclusive evidence of a breach of the seventh commandment. But all the details in *Divus Augustus*, LXIX, are admittedly taken from the statements of Marcus Antonius, which are merely a ribald bit of political pamphleteering without the slightest serious value. We have already seen the incident of the Second Philippic and Antony's reply. Similar accusations are still made; and probably it is only the lightness with which Augustus escaped that calls for any comment.

[3] The cases against Julius (Suetonius, *Divus Julius*, L–LII) are perfectly definite, and were always well known. Classical writers invariably give a plain story, when there is a plain story to give. . . . On the other hand, the case of Cicero may be quoted as an instance of a contemporary who by general consent had a clean bill in respect of sensuality. Whatsoever faults Cicero may have had, they were not of that type— and Augustus seems to have been of a similar temperament.

Julia and
Marcellus

cellus. It was a very natural and obvious plan. The young
people were cousins, yet were not too closely related, for
Augustus and Octavia were brother and sister only through
their father. The plan pleased Octavia and conduced to the
contentment of the domestic circle: but whether it was politically expedient is one of those historical conundrums
which are quite unanswerable. Julia was fourteen years of
age. Marcellus was a little older—a youth of good family
and ancestry, but entirely an unknown quantity. Yet Augustus adopted him, as he himself had once been adopted
by Julius. As Augustus was no fool, we may reasonably
conclude that he saw characteristics of promise in Marcellus. We shall never know, for two years after his wedding
Marcellus died.

The death of Marcellus was a profound grief to Octavia,
and it raises questions of some interest, which we have no
means of answering. Julia, suddenly free from the restrain-
ing regime which we have just noted, and launched upon
the great sea of life, was evidently too much for her youthful husband. By general testimony we may take it that she
was a very beautiful woman—at any rate, a beautiful girl—
and her portrait, if we can accept it as reasonably accurate,

Julia's
tempera-
ment

shows her to have been of the active, vital, clever but essentially rather brainless type common to all ages. Once
the leash was taken off, she went away with a bound. Augustus could still, in some things, restrain her with a firm
hand. But some things he could not restrain; and it is obvious that Julia found these particular pleasures very in-
toxicating. She sympathized with her father's sense of the
importance of the family, and took very little heed of the
Simple Life or the Rustic Paradise of Horace. She clearly
did not belong to the Golden Age.

Augustus had only too obviously set free a force which
was not going to come back into his control too sub-

missively. A number of things needed his consideration at almost the same time. He was by now convinced that his tenure of the consulship ought to terminate, and be replaced by the tribunician power, with all the changes involved, which we have already noticed. A serious illness had warned him that events might not wait on the birth and growth of a grandson, and that he might find it necessary to co-opt a successor rather than count upon an heir of his own blood. Nothing was more natural than that when he made his own exchange from consulship to tribuneship, he should obtain from the senate at the same time the investiture of Marcus Agrippa with some of his own powers. If, **Agrippa** then, Augustus should die (as at one time had seemed very likely during that year of trouble and thought) Agrippa, already possessed of the best part of his authority, could carry on. So little was there anything expressly hereditary about the position of Augustus at this time, that Agrippa expected as a matter of course this solution of the problem, and Augustus had no very determined bent to any other. But the death of young Marcellus opened up a totally new prospect. The marriage of Julia and Agrippa would ensure that while a very powerful and capable successor should be ready to take charge of the state, yet an heir of his own blood might subsequently hold the reins in the person of one of Julia's sons. . . . Agrippa, who, up to this point, had shown little sympathy with the idea of an hereditary dignity, would be automatically enlisted on the side of that solution. It is evident that Augustus was much struck with this plan, for he took a good deal of trouble to realize it.

The same year that saw Augustus become the Grand Tribune, therefore saw him inspire the senate to confer upon Agrippa the proconsular prerogatives which he himself possessed; and immediately after the death of Marcellus, Agrippa was persuaded to divorce his own wife and to take charge of Julia.

It was an admirable and a most ingenious plan. Agrippa was a faithful friend: his faith would be rewarded and strengthened by the advance of dignity, and Rome would receive a splendid successor to Augustus, who had already earned the admiration and respect of the Roman world. Julia, for her share of the advantages, would receive a (presumably) very satisfactory husband—or so Augustus was resolved to think. The plan pleased him so well, that perhaps he looked a little less closely at this last question than he should have done.

V

But what, we may ask, was the private character of Agrippa? This is a question difficult to answer. We know enough of him to be able to draw a very distinct sketch of a man of strongly marked character: but the details hardly go far enough to justify us in making positive deductions respecting his qualities as a husband. But while we cannot be positive, we can, starting from what we really do know of him, suggest some considerations that deserve reflection.

Agrippa belonged to a marked Roman plebeian type— and we can fill in some of the missing details by referring to other specimens of the type. He was a man who carried determined will far past the limits which we normally consider decorous today. Possibly some of the men of the seventeenth and eighteenth century, puritans, sea-dogs and adventurers, may have approximated to it; but that strong unbending will and driving force would seem a little mad to most of us now. . . . It was associated with (and indeed partly created by) an entire freedom from some of the inhibitions which weigh on the modern man. Like some of the British flogging captains of the eighteenth century, or the mates of some of the old Boston clippers, Agrippa was capable of letting himself go without restraint: and he owed his success to this power. Certain ideas of chivalry, commonplace to the modern, ahd no part in Agrippa's world —nor were they in any way to be expected. To marry Julia to a man of this type will probably strike most of us as a rather questionable expedient. . . . We may grant that Julia hardly expected that chivalry to which we have just referred. All the same, she was a delicate and malleable subject, only too ready to take the pattern stamped upon her by a rude hand. And although we are not entitled to say positively that Agrippa was a very rude hand indeed, there is every reason for surmising that such may have been the case.

Julia, of course, herself brought something to add to the result. She was evidently a person whose passions went very high without being very profound, and who went off very quickly and easily for very little reason. Marcellus seems to have found her a great deal too much for his stamina; for he died, and passed from the scene, after having waked Julia to a very decided womanhood. This being so, a very difficult problem had confronted Augustus, which we must not under-rate. He could not let Julia run about the world with all her new-found stores of energy. To have allowed it would have been asking for trouble. His idea was to put her into the hands of some one who could be trusted to hold her tight, keep her in order, and satisfy her. In thinking that Agrippa was such a man he may have judged rightly; but it is possible that he did not realise that Julia would get a good deal bruised and distorted in the process. It is quite certain in any case that the process of bruising and distorting Julia would not be an externally visible one. Neither Agrippa, nor Julia, nor Augustus, nor any one else, had any notion of what was taking place be-

Reasons for the match

fore their very eyes. Psychology was not a science in the Golden Age, and its foundations had not yet been laid by the great artists of poetry and drama who were in due time to ask the questions that needed answer, and who were to excite mankind into demanding the answer.

Julia, then, a very bright sort of butterfly, went into her new state of wifehood to Agrippa full of undeveloped potentialities; and when Agrippa died, he left her with those potentialities fully developed—and a terrible dragon's-brood they were. Cadmus never sowed dragon's teeth in Colchis more deadly than those which Agrippa sowed in the soul of Julia. He had taught her a habit of letting herself go without restraint which she had used first of all to kill her husband, and which she was not likely to drop merely because of the quite irrelevant circumstance that he was dead. People who had been trained by the iron will and decisive hand of Agrippa did not forget their training. His work endured.

Death of
Agrippa,
12 B. C.

Augustus needed to look about a second time. He had perhaps not perfectly apprehended on the first occasion the sort of explosive with which he was dealing. Still less did he understand what he was handling now. He looked about, however, for a man as strong and as faithful as Agrippa —and he chose Tiberius.

He was right in this judgment of Tiberius, who was indeed a strong and faithful man, in whom reliance could be placed. But we have only to consider the facts in the light of our modern knowledge to guess that the problems involved were not going to be solved merely by putting the butterfly under another sledge-hammer. For one thing, Tiberius was very unlike Agrippa: as a soldier he operated much more through persuasion and conviction than by brute force; as an aristocrat, he had never found it necessary to employ the methods of the centurion. And even if

he had been another Agrippa, he could not by main force
have knocked the fixed pattern of Julia's mind back into
some other arrangement that would suit himself. A mind
and temperament—even a woman's—once fixed, is fixed
permanently; it cannot, by any external agency, be tossed
back into the furnace and hammered into a new shape.
What may conceivably be done to it we may consider elsewhere; but in any case this was far beyond the horizon of
the Augustan age, and far beyond the understanding and
power even of an educated and enlightened man such as
Tiberius. So, as far as all these actors were concerned, the
destiny was fixed and became irrevocable. We who live
now might—perhaps—have done better. Those who will follow us might do better still: but as far as Augustus and his
friends were concerned the destiny became definitely
fixed.

*Tiberius
and Julia*

VI

The marriage of Tiberius and Julia lasted five years.
Tiberius was a peculiar, moody man, who perfectly recognized that it might be his duty to succeed Augustus and
carry on his work. Augustus must do as he liked. In the
meantime Tiberius was prepared to act as protector to
Julia's children and to guard their interests. He was satisfied, apparently, that Augustus preferred to dwell in a
fool's paradise. If so, it was no business of his. Julia was
now twenty-eight. She had done her duty by bearing two
heirs to the empire, and if Augustus was not disposed to
look too censoriously on what she might do now, then
Tiberius also did not care. At any rate, he did not care for
five years. At the end of that time he threw up all his
offices and retired into exile on the island of Rhodes. Augustus protested, but Tiberius was firm. He refused all ex-

*Tiberius
withdraws*

planations. Augustus therefore himself took in hand the task of training and protecting his grandsons Lucius and Gaius, the sons of Julia and Agrippa, who were to be his heirs and successors.

It is very difficult to understand why the children of Agrippa should be so strangely unsatisfactory; but it is certain that they were a faulty and flawed breed. Augustus himself slowly realized that his grandsons were hardly worthy of the great heritage they were to receive. There seemed to be misfortune in the very air during these years. Agrippa, who had been the second self of Augustus, died in the year 12 B. C.: Octavia in the year following. Drusus, Livia's younger son, the high favourite of Augustus, lost his life during the invasion of Germany in 9 B. C.: a year later, Horace and Maecenas died. It seemed the crowning touch that Tiberius should forsake him in 6 B. C. But the real crowning touch was not yet come. Tiberius had been four years in Rhodes when certain communications were made to Augustus, the nature of which is still obscure. But from the consequences which followed it is possible to guess the accusations made. They concerned Julia.

Scandal
of Julia Julia had involved herself in an expanding circle of scandal the very magnitude of which had been her protection. No one had cared to take the responsibility of divulging to Augustus the rumours, the suspicions, the gossip and the allegations which were circulating—the more so since no private person was in a position to investigate them, and separate the facts from the fiction. As soon as they came before the cold eye of Augustus, the truth was ascertained. A whole list of Julia's lovers was supplied to her father, and they numbered among them the names of some of the oldest and proudest families among the *optimates*. And the chief and principal name among them was Iullus Antonius.

The identity of Iullus was a shock to Augustus, and

touched him where he was weakest. The daughter of
Scribonia and the son of Antony! The ghost of Marcus
Antonius was walking, with all the charm and fascination
that Antony had possessed in life; and it was addressing itself, with all the old unerring skill of Antony in these matters, to the strategic point, the chink in the armour, the
Achilles' heel: to Julia, the heiress. In possession of Julia,
Iullus would be in possession of the future of Augustus's
work. . . . And it was only too clear that he had got her.
A skilful mingling of fascination and blackmail had closed
his grip over Julia. . . . She had been married in turn to
a commonplace boy; then to a despotic man of middle age, **Iullus**
a friend of her father's; and finally to a moody and peculiar **Antonius**
man whose mind was far from her. And now, at the age
of thirty-seven, she fell irrevocably for a man who was a
charming companion, able to dazzle her and sweep her
away with arts as bright as her own, and who had tied
her up with deeds in common which she dared not confess,
and sayings and schemes which she could not retract or
deny. Man-traps are an ill thing for butterflies to fall into;
and the teeth of this tremendous engine had closed upon
Julia past escape or remedy.

According to tradition, Livia was the person who told
Augustus; and it is probably true. She was the only person who had either the opportunity or the authority to
make Augustus listen; she, with her social contacts, was of
all persons the likeliest to hear every breath of scandal and
rumour that thrilled the social world of Rome; she had her
son Tiberius to guard and justify—and it is not impossible
that she kept her counsel until Scribonia's daughter was too
hopelessly involved to extricate herself. She had only to induce Augustus to exercise his power of enquiry, before
which all men and all things must give way, and she could
then wash her hands of the consequences.

The facts suppressed

It is Augustus's own fault if we do not really know what was revealed. He let it be supposed that his action was that of a shocked father horrified at the misdeeds of his daughter: but it is asking too much of our credulity to expect us to believe such a version. Augustus was not bound by any moral code that would have caused him to make quite as much fuss as he did over a merely moral lapse. The wrath, the indignation, the irreconcilable resentment, the terror that he obviously felt, point to something much more tangible than a shock to his moral delicacy. If that had been all, he would have punished his wicked daughter, forgiven her, and hushed the scandal up. But he did not take this course. He did what statesman have done many times before and since when they were in fear of deadly peril. He caused Julia to be arrested, and sent into such secure exile on the islands of the Italian coast that she was never seen again by the social world of Rome. She became, like the Man in the Iron Mask, a state-prisoner, a legend, a subject discreetly whispered by the wise. The child born to her in captivity was not allowed to live. Iullus Antonius, the son of Marcus Antonius and of Fulvia, was commanded to take his own life; others of the conspiracy were imprisoned or banished.

Julia arrested

The whole conduct of Augustus over this matter was so strange, so unlike his usual temper, that it is obvious that the full truth was never revealed, though the scandal could not be altogether hidden. He was normally a mild and good-tempered man, not by any means given to unreasoning vindictiveness; but he never relented or softened or changed his mind, nor heeded the appeals made to him on Julia's behalf. He was as unbending as this only when he was afraid. Some tradition always lingered among Roman historians of how dangerous Augustus could be when he was afraid.

VII

The ghost lingered. There had been something prophetic in Horace's suggestion that the spirit of Remus still followed the fate of Rome; certainly the spirit of Marcus Antonius followed Augustus. One after another, the two elder sons of Agrippa and Julia died. As the third was hopelessly insane, he was out of the question as a successor. This terminated all hope that Augustus could be followed by a successor of his own blood in the male line. Co-option was the only resort. Tiberius was recalled from Rhodes, and adopted by Augustus as his successor.

The line of Augustus was not entirely wiped out. It lived on in the persons of two girls, Agrippina and Julia, *The* the surviving daughters of Agrippa and the Butterfly. *ghost* Among the children of the Augustan circle was a youth of whom great hopes were entertained: Germanicus, the son of Drusus and grandson of Livia. Augustus formed the plan—the last and final plan—of marrying the young man to Agrippina. After all, he was the nephew of Tiberius—the son of Tiberius's much-loved brother. Everything seemed in favour of this arrangement. The children of Germanicus and Agrippina would be descendants alike of Augustus, Livia and Agrippa—a thought warming to the heart of the old grandparents.

But the strange thing was that Germanicus was also the grandson of Marcus Antonius. Do what he would, Augustus could not keep the ghost out of the succession! And he never did keep it out. With a sure and certain hand, the dead Antony took possession of the primacy from which he had been excluded while he was alive. Of the three successors of Tiberius, ending with Nero, whom we know as the "Caesarian house," only two had the blood of Augustus in them, but all three had the blood of Marcus Antonius. And far more than his actual blood, they possessed

Supremacy of Antony

his spirit. The mad Caligula and the fantastic Nero were in the fashion of Mark Antony, and entertained his opinions and repeated his temperament. It was against this wild Antonian spirit that the Roman world revolted when Nero died; and it was the Augustan spirit that Vespasian brought back when he calmed the strife and ushered in yet another age.

VIII

Men have often wondered over the remarkable change that seemed to turn the world of Augustus and Virgil into the world of Nero and Seneca. It was this return of the spirit of Marcus Antonius. There was war in heaven—a clash of ideas and obediences that did not cease until Trojan's day. But the fever, the fret, the discomfort and the smoke of these times did not destroy the work of Augustus. This endured through all the time of trouble, became the foundation of the long period of peace under the emperors of the second century, and formed the basis of the future.

From the day of the beginning of his reign as Augustus, he reigned forty-one years. If we count from the day he came to Italy to look for the heritage of Caesar, he stood before the public fifty-seven years. He had won that heritage, established himself as the rightful heir and successor of Julius, avenged his murder, put down all rivals and competitors, and created a secure and lasting peace throughout the Roman world. He had reformed the constitution of

The work of Augustus

Rome so that his pacifying and ordering power should be permanent—he had improved the administration and caused it to be conducted, more than ever it had been conducted before, for the benefit of the common people. He had ex-

tended the frontier of Rome to the Danube, linked it up
with the Rhine frontier, penetrated to the Elbe, recovered
the standards which the Parthians had taken from Crassus,
and made the world as safe for mankind at large as the work
of the soldier and the statesman can make it. Horace and
Virgil had written for him, and—although he knew nothing
of this—there was already a young carpenter in Palestine
who was destined to give his reign an even greater immortality, and to make it a still more conspicuous landmark
in history. Augustus had fought his way to the front; he
was the survivor of a generation of extraordinary men, and
his own greatness shone before his contemporaries with a
splendour that laid all serious disputes to rest. He was
seventy-five years old when he died. He had outlived all
his contemporaries, all the wonderful men who had made
the Golden Age. He had been the youngest of them, and he
lived to be the oldest: he, with his delicacy, his chest protector, his diet and his regimen—he had lived longer and
done more than any of them. Only one thing had been
forbidden him by Providence—he was not allowed to control the future.

It was agreed afterwards that the omens and portents
had foretold what was coming. He had intended to see He goes
Tiberius off on the latter's impending journey to Illyricum, home
but being much detained by business, he finally exclaimed
that he would stay no longer in Rome, even if every one
else did. Men reminded one another significantly of the
phrase afterwards, as foretelling his death. He went by road
to Astura, and took ship for Campania, according to custom, as he found it less fatiguing than travelling by land.
But in doing so he caught some kind of chill or dysentry.

The details of his last journey were preserved, as if they
had been especially memorable. As he coasted south by
Puteoli, an Alexandrian ship, newly arrived, lay there. The

passengers and crew, assuming their white ceremonial garments, and burning incense, heaped upon his head good wishes and fervent praises, declaring that it was through him that they lived, sailed the seas, and enjoyed their freedom and fortune. Much pleased at this, he distributed forty golden aurei to each of the members of his entourage, on condition that they used the money exclusively to buy Alexandrian goods. He stayed four days in his villa on Capri, watching the gymnastic exercises of the local schoolboys, and giving them a party at which he was himself present. There was great fun, and a little harmless horseplay. He was quite cheerful, though still suffering from intermittent attacks of dysentery. He amused himself by inventing Greek verses and then asking the Greek companion of Tiberius, the famous Thrasyllus, from what author they were quotations. Thrasyllus was a great deal too acute to be taken in, and tactfully replied that they were very good, whosoever their author might be—which amused Augustus afresh. Finally, he saw Tiberius off at Beneventum—but it was his last action. He had to go to bed at Nola, and Tiberius was hastily recalled from his journey.

A little
leisure

The old man—he was old, who had been so young when he began—faded by degrees. On the nineteenth of August—his own month: his lucky month—he felt himself going. He asked if there were any disorders on account of his condition: and then (having evidently been assured that all was quiet) he called for a mirror and had his hair arranged, and himself made seemly. His friends were admitted to see him for the last time. He asked them if he had rightly played his part in the comedy of life, and quoted a Greek verse to the effect that if he had done well, he asked their applause at his exit. . . . Then they left him. Some time later he kissed Livia, with the words: "Livia! Live with remembrance of our life together—and goodbye": and so

quietly died. He had always wished for such a death, and
had admired those who achieved it.

. . . and
goodbye
Aug. 19th
A. D. 14

What he left behind, the contents of his will, the details
of his funeral and of the memorials erected to him, can be
read in the pages of Suetonius. The chief thing he left was
a tradition. Peace, reconciliation, and government in the interests of the governed throughout the regional divisions
of a world that was one unified state—these were the
principles he embodied and left to posterity. They still remain the principles which mankind would most like to see
realized—if it dared to hope that they could be.

SOURCES

APPIAN: Text and Translation. Horace White (Loeb, 1912–1933).

CICERO: *Letters*, Text, Tyrrell and Purser.

    Letters to Friends, Text and Translation, W. G. Williams (Loeb   ) English Translation, Wm. Melmoth.

    Letters to Atticus, Text and Translation, E. O. Winstedt (Loeb   ) English Translation, Wm. Heberden.

    De Re Publica, Text and Translation, C. W. Keyes (Loeb   ).

    Philippics, Text and Translation, W. A. Ker (Loeb   ).

DION CASSIUS: *History*, Text and Translation, E. Cary (Loeb   ).

FRONTINUS: *Stratagems and Aqueducts*, Text and Translation, C. E. Bennett, C. Herschel, M. B. McElwain (Loeb, 1925).

HORACE: Text, *Works of Horace*, with Commentary by E. C. Wickham. (Oxford, 3 vols.)

    Works, Translated into English Prose by James Lonsdale and Samuel Lee (Globe edition, 1881).

PLUTARCH: Text and Translation, Bernadotte Perrin (Loeb, 1912). (Lives of *Caesar*, *Antony*, *Cicero* and *Brutus*.)

SUETONIUS: *Lives*, Text and Translation, J. C. Rolfe (Loeb, 1935).

VIRGIL: Text and notes, J. Conington. (1888). Translated into English Prose by James Lonsdale and Samuel Lee (1882).

CORPUS INSCRIPTIONUM LATINARUM. Vol. I.

GUIDES

JRS = Journal of Roman Studies.

Anderson (J. G. C.) Review of Dr. Rice Holmes's *Architect of the Roman Empire* (JRS, vol. xvii, 1927, p. 223).

Bevan (E.) *A History of Egypt under the Ptolemaic Dynasty* (1927).

Bury (J. B.) *A History of the Roman Empire to Marcus Aurelius.*

Clark, A. C. *Cicero* (in Encyclopaedia Britannica, 13th Ed. Vol. VI).

Clinton (F.) *Epitome of Chronology.*

Fowler (W. Warde) *Social Life in Rome in the Age of Cicero* (1908).

Frank (Tenney): *Roman Imperialism.*
"   "   *Life and Literature in the Roman Republic* (1930).
"   "   "Dominium in Solo Provinciali" and "Ager Publicus" (JRS, Vol. xvii, 1927, p. 141).
"   "   "On Augustus and the Aerarium" (JRS, vol. xxiii, p. 143).

Grueber (H. A.) *Coins of the Roman Republic in the British Museum.* 3 vols. (1910).

Heitland (W. E.) *The Roman Republic*, 3 vols. (1909).
"   "   *Agricola* (1921).

Holmes (T. Rice) *The Architect of the Roman Empire*, 2 vols. (1928–1931).

Lanciani (R.) *Ancient and Modern Rome* (

McFayden (D.) *History of the title Imperator under the Roman Empire* (1927).

313

Mattingly (H.) *The Imperial Civil Service of Rome* (1910).
"   " *Coins of the Roman Empire in the British Museum.* (Vol I)
Meiklejohn (K. W.) "Alexander Helios and Caesarion" (JRS, vol. xxiv, 1934, p. 191).
Middleton (Conyers) *Life of Marcus Tullius Cicero.*
Milne (J. Grafton) "The Ruin of Egypt by Roman Mismanagement" (JRS, vol. xvii, 1927, p. 1).
Pelham (H. F.) *Essays* (1911).
"   " and Jones (Sir H. S.) *Rome* (in Encyclopaedia Britannica, 13th ed., vol. xxiii).
Sergeant (Philip W.) *Cleopatra of Egypt* (1909).
Strachan-Davidson (J. L.) *Cicero* (1929).
Syme (Ronald) "Some Notes on the Legions under Augustus" (JRS, vol. xxiii, p. 14).
Tarn (W. W.) "The Battle of Actium" (JRS, vol. xxi, 1931, p. 173).
"   " "Alexander Helios and the Golden Age" (JRS, vol. xxii, 1932, p. 135).

INDEX

315

OTHER COOPER SQUARE PRESS TITLES OF INTEREST

HANNIBAL
G. P. Baker
366 pp., 3 b/w illustrations, 5 maps
0-8154-1005-0
$16.95

HISTORY OF THE CONQUEST OF MEXICO &
HISTORY OF THE CONQUEST OF PERU
William H. Prescott
1330 pp., 2 maps
0-8154-1004-2
$29.95

AGINCOURT
Christopher Hibbert
176 pp., 33 b/w illustrations, 3 b/w maps
0-8154-1053-0
$16.95

THE DREAM AND THE TOMB
A History of the Crusades
Robert Payne
456 pp., 37 b/w illustrations
0-8154-1092-1
$19.95

THE LIFE AND TIMES OF AKHNATON
Pharaoh of Egypt
Arthur Weigall
320 pp., 33 b/w illustrations
0-8154-1092-1
$17.95

T. E. LAWRENCE
A Biography
Michael Yardley
308 pp., 71 b/w photos, 5 b/w maps
0-8154-1054-9
$17.95

GENGHIS KHAN
R. P. Lister
256 pp., 1 b/w illustration
0-8154-1052-2
$16.95

WOLFE AT QUEBEC
The Man Who Won the French and Indian War
Christopher Hibbert
208 pp., 1 b/w illustration, 4 b/w maps
0-8154-1016-6
$15.95

MAN AGAINST NATURE
Firsthand Accounts of Adventure and Exploration
Edited by Charles Neider
512 pp.
0-8154-1040-9
$18.95

Available at bookstores; or call 1-800-462-6420

Cooper Square Press

150 Fifth Avenue
Suite 911
New York, NY 10011